ALEXANDER PUSHKIN

Alexander Pushkin

A Critical Study

A.D.P. Briggs

CROOM HELM
London & Canberra

BARNES & NOBLE BOOKS
Totowa, New Jersey

© 1983 A.D.P. Briggs
Croom Helm Ltd, Provident House, Burrell Row,
Beckenham, Kent BR3 1AT

British Library Cataloguing in Publication Data

Briggs, A.D.P.
  Alexander Pushkin.
  1. Pushkin, A.S. – Criticism and interpretation
  I. Title
  891.71'3   PG 3350.Z8
  ISBN 0-7099-0688-9

First published in the USA 1983 by
BARNES & NOBLE BOOKS
81 ADAMS DRIVE,
TOTOWA, NEW JERSEY, 07512

Library of Congress Cataloging in Publication Data

Briggs, A.D.P.
  Alexander Pushkin: a critical study.

  Bibliography: p.
  Includes index.
  1. Pushkin, Aleksandr Sergeevich, 1799-1837 –
Criticism and interpretation.   I. Title.
PG3356.B74   1982   891.71'3   82-16242
ISBN 0-389-20340-8

Printed and bound in Great Britain by
Biddles Ltd, Guildford and King's Lynn

CONTENTS

To Pamela, Fiona, Antonia and Julian.

PREFACE

The first aim of this study is to explain Pushkin's literary and linguistic achievement. An attempt will also be made to capture something even more elusive, that curious quality of the spirit emanating from this poet's work which has had such a positive effect on the Russian nation and ought to be known to a wider audience. Pushkin's life story has been excluded (except for a brief Biographical Survey), as have events of contemporary historical significance, apart from a few incidental references. Unevenness of treatment is intentional, emphasis being placed upon three categories of his work: the acknowledged masterpieces, a number of undervalued pieces which deserve a closer scrutiny, and their opposite, works which appear not to merit all the praise that they have attracted. Much attention is given to the lyric poems; a detailed look at one of the shorter poems is succeeded by a survey of many. Although half of Pushkin's work was in prose this is treated briefly, more in accordance with its modest literary achievement than its quantity. The reader will need little specialist knowledge, though a few technicalities are unavoidable here and there in determining what lies behind certain special effects.

Parts of this text have been published before. In particular, Chapters 5 and 7 draw on earlier articles dealing with *The Bronze Horseman* and *Boris Godunov*. Thanks are due to the editors of *Forum for Modern Language Studies*, *The New Zealand Slavonic Journal* and *Canadian-American Slavic Studies* for permission to re-use materials indicated in the notes.

I am much indebted to my patient family, to my typist Mrs Barbara Case, and to the many excellent students who have passed through the Department of Russian Studies at Bristol University and seem to have shared my enthusiasm for the fine poet who is the subject of this study.

A.D.P.B.

BIOGRAPHICAL SURVEY

1799	26 May: Aleksandr Sergeyevich Pushkin born in Moscow.
1800-11	Entrusted to nursemaids, French tutors and governesses, Pushkin grew up without parental affection. A lazy child, but an avid, precocious reader. Learned Russian from household serfs and especially his nanny, Arina Rodionovna.
1811-17	Studied at the new lycée of Tsarskoye Selo, near St Petersburg.
1817-20	Occupied an undemanding government post in St Petersburg. Dissipated life style. Tenuous connexions with revolutionary-minded young people. Some poems, unpublishable because of their liberal sentiments, circulated in manuscript form.
1820	26 March: completed *Ruslan and Lyudmila* after two years' work.
	6 May: exiled to Yekaterinoslav in the south.
	21 September: transferred to Kishinev, the capital of Bessarabia.
1820-1	*The Captive of the Caucasus.*
1821	*The Robber Brothers.*
1822	*The Fountain of Bakhchisaray.*
1823	9 May: began *Yevgeniy Onegin.*
	July: transferred to Odessa. The last year of his four-year 'southern exile'.
1824	August: returned north to his parents' estate at Mikhaylovskoye. Two further years of exile.
	The Gipsies.
1825	*Count Nulin.*
	Boris Godunov.
1826	8 September: freed from exile and summoned to Moscow by Nicholas I, who became his personal censor. Returned to dissipated life style.
1828	*Poltava.*
1829	May-September: four-month visit to Transcaucasia, including action with the Russian army at war with the Turks.
1830	September-November: stranded at his new estate of Bol-

dino by an outbreak of cholera.
The Little House in Kolomna.
The 'Little Tragedies'.
The Tales of Belkin.

1831	18 February: married to Natalya Goncharova.
	5 October: completed *Yevgeniy Onegin* after more than eight years' writing.
1833	Travelled east to the Urals, engaged in historical research. October-November: the second 'Boldino autumn'.
	Andzhelo.
	The Bronze Horseman.
	The Queen of Spades.
1833-5	*The Captain's Daughter.*
1833-6	An unhappy period in St Petersburg: humiliation in court circles, jealousy of his wife's admirers, mounting debts. Little creative work.
1837	Goaded by scandalous rumours into a duel with Georges D'Anthès, an adopted son of the Dutch ambassador. The duel took place on 27 January; Pushkin was wounded in the stomach and died two days later.

1 THE PROBLEM OF PUSHKIN

The Doubts Surrounding Pushkin's Reputation

The extraordinary achievement of Alexander Pushkin, Russia's foremost poet (some would say leading writer), still requires a good deal of explanation. His position in Russian history is without parallel in any other country and he is celebrated for three quite different reasons. Pushkin created a body of poetry enduring in its appeal and still unsurpassed in quality. At the same time he reconstituted the very language of the educated Russian people. By changing the course of the literature and the language he passed on to his successors not only a fund of artistic potential but also the means of its practical realisation. The results are known to the world, ironically better than his own works, in those of Tolstoy, Dostoyevsky, Turgenev, Gogol, Chekhov and many other famous Russian writers. As if these two bequests were not enough he left a third one, more mysterious and hard to define, but as real to the Russians as their climate and culture. This is a kind of unreligious spiritual fortification. To outsiders it may seem ludicrous that such a claim should be made even for the national poet of a country, but in the case of Russia and Alexander Pushkin the idea is no exaggeration. Pushkin has done more than divert the child, amuse the adolescent and appeal to the cultivated adult population of his country. He has accompanied Russian citizens into the darkest recesses of personal anguish, including persecution, the prison-house and permanent exile, and sustained their spirits against all the odds. The magnitude of this literary, linguistic and spiritual achievement is difficult for foreigners either to accept or understand.

Not that there is any shortage of commentaries on Pushkin and his works. In his native country hundreds of millions of words have been devoted to this writer and he has been interpreted from every conceivable critical angle. For various reasons, however, there is still no single work which, if translated, would give anything like the universal explanation of this phenomenon which is required. Even abroad a corpus of interpretative literature has grown up around the poet in this century and taken on substantial proportions. Anyone who doubts this should consult a recent article by Patrick and April Wreath, two American bibliographers.[1] They conceived the idea of dispelling the prevalent impression that Pushkin is an unjustly neglected literary figure by listing

17

the translations of his works, together with the articles and books written about him in English over the previous half-century. The articles, books and reviews come to about four hundred items. Plenty has been written, yet much remains obscure.

One reason for the lingering obscurity is that it is so easy, when fascinated by Pushkin and taken with the idea of explaining him to others, to slide off the main subject into an interesting side-issue. The danger of this was once neatly expressed by Donald Davie: 'We continue to learn everything about Pushkin the poet except his poetry.'[2] The same critic has referred more than once to the unhappy need for non-Russian speakers, and even for those with a good smattering of Russian, to take Pushkin's achievement on trust. 'And it is a bad thing', he argues, 'for any field of study to have at its centre . . . such a large patch of the unverified and unverifiable.'[3] The worst part of this bad thing is that as the years go by and Pushkin remains inadequately explained, those who began by taking him on trust are going to have their doubts. Davie himself seems to have proceeded from impatience to near-despair when he writes, 'Pushkin's notorious and unhappy pre-eminence as the least translatable of poets is not going to disappear in a hurry . . .' He then commits himself to the sort of barbed challenge to which the only response is refutation by means of a long and detailed argument. In a reference to Pushkin's apparently lofty reputation, which communicates itself so imperfectly to other nations, he asks the most pointed question of all. 'Is it all, perhaps, a confidence trick? The suspicion is unworthy but unavoidable.'[4] Even with due allowance for a touch of devil's advocacy this cry is not to be ignored. Perhaps Donald Davie is voicing the disappointment of countless other readers? They will only be satisfied if we can set down in clear, comprehensible language what it is that excites the Russians so much when they read their favourite writer and commit great tracts of his verses to memory.

Since Davie's challenge was issued, a decade and a half ago now, a great deal more has been written about Pushkin, including two books in English, Walter Vickery's *Alexander Pushkin* in 1970[5] and John Bayley's *Pushkin: a Comparative Commentary* in 1971.[6] Both are very helpful and contain valuable insights: they will be referred to frequently in the following pages. If they have faults, the former — because of its format — is often sidetracked into biographical detail and plot summaries, while the latter sometimes bedazzles the reader by its enormous range of reference, taking in allusions to two or three hundred other literary figures as far away in time and space as Suetonius, Joyce, Robbe-Grillet and Bishop Percy. Both books dwell, moreover, on anything but that inner core of the poet's work where his spirit is most intimately sensed — the lyric poems. Twenty or thirty lyrics are discussed, some of them only in passing references, out of the many hundreds available. Vickery and Bayley have done much to dispel the doubts surrounding Pushkin's reputation but it remains possible to take the work further without serious duplication of what they have written.

Entertainment, Illusion and Paradox

One mistake that has often been made in approaching Pushkin is to proceed with undue deference and solemnity. Soviet criticism is particularly guilty in this regard. Modern Russian Pushkinists have been diligent, devoted and well informed scholars. Their researches and writings have added much to our total knowledge of the poet. As a British scholar has suggested recently, however,

> It is sad that they are generally marked also by a characteristic Soviet heaviness and a most un-Pushkinian solemnity which informs and instructs but seldom inspires. Pushkin . . . is a classic who has become an institution, surrounded by ritual expressions of homage and respect . . .[7]

The danger here is that such an attitude will place this poet in the ranks of those classics whom everyone wants to have read but nobody wants to read. Pushkin is, in fact, widely read and remembered, at home and abroad, for pure pleasure. The first duty of any critic is to begin and end his commentary with a clear statement that reading Pushkin is an intensely enjoyable experience. When this point is established with certainty we can look for some of the reasons behind it.

In the first place, Pushkin is a great humorist; a spirit of play characterises almost all his work. Secondly, he is a marvellous musician; his manipulation of the expressive sounds of the Russian language provides us with a concert hall full of acoustic pleasures. (This outstanding quality is entirely abandoned in translation but it is readily accessible to anyone patient enough to acquire even a little knowledge of the language.) Thirdly, his sense of merely being alive and drinking down the many delights that our bodily senses can provide should establish an immediate spiritual kinship between the poet and any reader. He succeeds at the task undertaken by all poets — that of capturing the essence of a sensual experience and depositing it, brilliantly recognisable and retrievable, in a memory bank open to us all. Quite often, as it happens, it is a question not merely of sensual but sexual experience, one of the most intense of the bodily pleasures which Pushkin, as an expert in the field, transmits to the page with excitement and delight enough to arouse the interest of the most languid of observers.

Entertainment, lovely music, sensual pleasure — this is by no means the whole of Pushkin but it is where to begin enjoying his art. To do so is to act like Pushkin himself, by putting the delights in their proper place, at the fountainhead of human experience, and only then proceeding to work out the practical details by which they are to be expressed. Those three preoccupations alone and unsupported would indicate nothing more than a poet of superficial, if beguiling, skills and hedonistic interests. Such a man might induce a sense of gratification in his readers but would not be able to supply them with much strength of spirit. There is more to Alexander Pushkin than this. Far from being as simple and superficial as he might appear to the idle ear — and he was the first to encourage an attitude of levity — Pushkin is a complex, subtle and paradoxical poet. Far from being an empty-headed entertainer, he is capable of serious and stirring ideas. He will invite us, as we read him, to reappraise our attitudes and standards, and to think more deeply about the condition of humanity and our surrounding universe. He will speak to us about morality and conscience, destiny and free will, power and violence, on a human and an elemental scale. He will enhance our appreciation of design and artistry. He will look into the problems of imposing order on chaos and of searching through the many-sided complexity of human experience with a view to determining, or at least predicting, future events. He will consider the ways in which human relationships are established and leave us to draw our own conclusions about the need and the methods for improving them. He will deepen and enrich our capacity to live, to enjoy living and to anticipate our deaths with a philosophical spirit. Most of his ideas will be affirmative and dynamic but, in the last analysis, he will communicate an awareness of actual sadness and impending tragedy which seems to be at variance with the overall tone of his work.

This rather serious statement of Pushkin's greater significance has to be deposited at an early stage lest his apparent flippancy delude anyone into dismissing him as a bit of literary thistledown. It contains an obvious paradox. Is there not a contradiction between the light-heartedness upon which we have already insisted and the dour seriousness to which we are also laying claim? The two may, in fact, co-exist and in Pushkin sometimes they do. A proper appreciation of Pushkin depends upon an ability to enjoy, but simultaneously to see through, a series of illusions. It is common for him to present an idea, an attitude or an expression with a disarmingly winsome but offhand manner while actually hoping for us to look beyond this in order to achieve a deeper awareness of a different truth, or at least to appreciate the complexity or difficulty which actually lies behind what seems simple or unimportant. This sounds, and is, a complicated idea which will be explained and exemplified later. But we cannot proceed further without facing the fact that paradox is something to live with when evaluating Pushkin's achievement. Not only is he both flippant and serious-minded, he is also at one and the same time insouciant and laborious, Romantic and Classical, spontaneous and strictly disciplined, amateur and professional, dismissive of literature as a serious pursuit and yet deeply reverential towards his trade and his fellow practitioners.

Almost embarrassed by his own wonderful skills, he dismisses them and everything to do with them continually, pretending that nothing matters, that he is an idle chatterer, that he has no real message, that he cannot wait to finish the next line and then put down the pen and get on with real life. This is all a smoke screen to keep us, and perhaps even Pushkin himself, from the deepest truth of all — that this poet was, from his earliest days of consciousness through to his death in a disastrous duel, an alienated and unhappy spirit incapable of establishing a deep and permanent relationship with any person. (The only exceptions were one or two school friends from whom he was in any case physically separated for most of his adult years.) Throughout his life a single sur-rogate stood for mother, father, wife and friend, and this was literature. To have admitted that openly would have been to acknowledge failure and a life sentence of imprisonment within the restrictions of vicarious rather than real relationships. It was clearly preferable to create an air of easy dismissiveness so that the reading public, contemporary and sub-sequent, should be persuaded that although the acclaim was welcome, its recipient did not depend on it. This was, in any case, the aristocrat's way of doing things — no well-born person should be seen to have toiled like a labourer.

This explanation, oversimplified though it may be, helps to span the abyss between Pushkin's seeming flippancy and actual seriousness. The remaining inconsistencies will be resolved in due course. For the moment it is enough to retain an awareness that illusion and paradox need to be assimilated if we are to embrace all that Pushkin stood for in his poetry and prose.

Pushkinolatry

Another serious obstacle stands between the reader and the poet: Pushkinolatry. This phrase originates in Prince Mirsky's references to 'Pushkin
idolatry' as early as 1926,[8] but the shorter version was coined by John
Bayley in 1971.[9] Although neither author defines the concept it clearly
denotes an unduly reverential attitude towards Pushkin's work as a
whole, a refusal even to think that he might have made mistakes and
thus an inability to offset his true masterpieces from his run-of-the-mill,
mediocre, or even, on occasions, decidedly weak pieces. Pushkinolatry
comes in two forms. Some Pushkinolaters, among them well-intended
native Russians who have absorbed Pushkin with their mother's milk,
simply recite or appraise his every line with a gush of enthusiasm which
shows little understanding of what is actually written.

On one gramophone record issued several years ago in the USA an
émigré Russian lady applied her rich contralto voice with grand sonority
to half a dozen of Pushkin's lyrics. All was well with a poem like *Prorok*
(*The Prophet*) which uses deliberately archaic expressions in an apoca-
lyptic statement of the God-given powers of the prophet and, by inference, also of the poet. But it was a serious mistake to read the prologue
to *Ruslan and Lyudmila* in precisely the same way. Certainly this little
poem has its moments of grandeur when thirty handsome knights emerge from the waters and join company with other exotic figures from
Russian folklore, and some exuberance of expression is appropriate
when reading these lines. On the other hand there is no justification
for investing the lines which end the prologue with any kind of magnificence, solemnity, sonority or reverence. Their meaning is simply this:

> And I have been there and drunk mead. I have seen the green oak-
> tree by the sea and sat under it, and the learned cat has told me his
> tales. One of them I remember: this is the tale which I shall now
> relate to the world.

The first of these lines consists entirely of monosyllables: 'I tam ya byl
i med ya pil.' That is a very rare thing in Russian verse and it is a clear
pointer to the utter simplicity of what is being said. Everyone knows, in
addition, that clarity and simplicity are the signs by which Pushkin is
instantly recognised. Nevertheless on this recording these lines are read
with such impassioned sincerity, such exclamatory effusiveness, that
their unassuming loveliness turns into something ludicrous. This results
from undiscriminating Pushkinolatry.

The second form of this affliction is a more serious matter since it causes people to step over from a mere lack of discrimination into positive misjudgement. Worse still, it seems to have affected not only good Pushkin-loving Russians going about their ordinary affairs but even experts in literary matters and, among them, some of the most reliable and respectable. We shall see in due course that claims have been made with regard to certain works by Pushkin which are difficult to substantiate and in some cases outrageously untrue. Various critics have maintained, for example, that the fairytale narrative *Tsar Saltan* is Pushkin's finest work, that the slender *Tales of Belkin* amount to a heavyweight production, and that the characterisation in *The Captain's Daughter* is largely successful. Here are three judgements which need to be contradicted. More surprisingly still, *The Stone Guest*, a minor playlet, one of the 'Little Tragedies', has been regularly and emphatically accorded a status near the very top of the hierarchy of Pushkin's works which demonstrably it does not deserve. These cases will be argued through at a later stage. For the time being it is sufficient to record the warning that Pushkinolatry, along with the practice of endorsing received opinion do seem to have combined sometimes to distort the overall evaluation of Pushkin's achievement — apparently to his advantage, by suggesting that he never fell below an exceedingly high level of attainment, but actually to his detriment.

One purpose of this book is — without denying Pushkin's consistency as a writer — to distinguish between outstanding success, relatively modest achievement and even some degree of failure, and also to isolate certain works which ought to be accepted by everyone as overriding masterpieces. It is as well to state in advance that this latter category will exclude *Tsar Saltan*, *The Tales of Belkin*, *The Captain's Daughter* and *The Stone Guest*. It will certainly include *Yevgeniy Onegin*, *The Bronze Horseman*, *Count Nulin*, *The Queen of Spades* and a rather large number of the shorter poems.

The Problem of the Lyric Poetry

Pushkin's lyric poetry needs to be dealt with in first place. It contains the essence of his literary achievement and yet, ironically, it has been downgraded in most critical studies, perhaps because of the more tangible merits of works such as *Yevgeniy Onegin*, the narrative poems and the prose. One of the most daunting tasks in the entire range of Russian literary criticism consists in evaluating and explaining Pushkin's lyric poetry. The subject is both extensive and elusive. The term 'lyric poetry' itself need not detain us. Prince Dmitri Mirsky used it in relation to Pushkin simply to include 'every kind of poetry that is neither narrative nor dramatic',[10] and this negative definition will serve our present purposes. That leaves us with about eight hundred poems to be considered and they vary so much in theme and form, attitude and manner, success and significance that it is difficult to embrace the whole range. Their many qualities are no less diffuse, being both difficult to determine and sometimes even contradictory, to the extent that individual poems may appear to be personalised yet universal, archaic yet modern, trivial yet indicative of valuable hidden truths, independent in achievement yet tied into a greater system of meanings. This quality of complexity and ambiguity accounts for what Roman Jakobson described as 'the eternal variability of the myth about Pushkin'[11] whereby the same body of poetry may be construed alternatively − to give only one example − as the embodiment of humility and of revolution.

At the beginning of the same essay Jakobson makes the telling point that, despite the obvious magnitude and importance of the subject, 'Pushkin's lyric poetry remains the least studied of all the literary genres that he practised.'[12] This is borne out by even a cursory awareness of what has been written about the poet in English. The several hundred Pushkin items catalogued by the Wreaths include a sadly small proportion of works devoted to the lyric poems and the amount of space allotted to this subject within longer works is not much more impressive. Mirsky, Lavrin,[13] Bayley − all of them permit the lyrics to speak for themselves only in passing and their small voice is soon drowned by the creations of apparently greater substance. There is a clear tendency on the part of critics, viewed *en masse*, to allow themselves to be seduced into the equally rich but firmer ground outside the *lirika*. It is not hard to see why. John Fennell states part of the difficulty as follows:

It has long been an accepted practice . . . to call Pushkin the greatest of Russian poets, and to lavish extravagant, if hackneyed, eulogy on his poetry. Few critics can talk of Pushkin's art or describe his greatness without using phrases such as 'classical restraint', 'universality of spirit', 'harmony between style and content', 'humanity of outlook' and so on. Now all these tags may be applicable to some or all of Pushkin's poetry; but at the same time they are often singularly unhelpful to the reader − especially the non-Russian reader − who is trying to understand the essence of Pushkin's greatness as a poet.

But can this greatness be explained in a satisfactory way? Must the commonplaces of literary criticism be used?[14]

The tags are still in service. Many others, such as the epithets 'Mozartian', 'protean', 'succinct and laconic', 'mercurial' etc. have been added to the total. If they are so often applied unimaginatively to Pushkin's all-round achievement what hope is there for any explanation of Pushkin's successes in the field of lyric poetry? Fennell, himself an accomplished writer on Pushkin, goes on to describe as 'thankless and hopeless' the task of communicating anything so subjective as one's own feelings on the poetry of a given poet. This, however, is precisely what must be done, in as unsentimental a way as possible and by as many poetry-lovers as may be found, if we are ever to arrive at a comprehensive, and readily comprehensible, assessment of the qualities of Pushkin's shorter poems which continue to give such pleasure to those millions of people who read, listen to, learn and recite them.

The determination of these qualities would be greatly facilitated if there existed a single poem, or a small group of poems, in which they could be seen epitomised. Part of the trouble is the changeability of Pushkin's genius. How can one begin to compare a poem like *Prorok* (*The Prophet*) with 'Ya vas lyubil . . .' ('I loved you . . .'); *Besy* (*The Devils*) with, say, *Arion* or *Kinzhal* (*The Dagger*); *K A.P. Kern* (*To A.P. Kern*) or *Talisman* (*The Talisman*) with *Anchar* (*The Upas Tree*)? There is no easy formula which can be universally applied and little in the way of common factors which might help towards definition. Is there no short poem by Pushkin which truly bears an individual stamp, which typifies a manner and a whole series of preoccupations unique to this poet and against which other lyrics might be measured?

It scarcely needs stating that the one utterly definitive poem does not exist. However, a careful search through the hundreds of possible candidates has thrown up a single serious contender. One poem of forty-seven lines may be shown to incorporate, either in an obvious form or by clear and immediate reference, so many qualities, ideas and mannerisms which are recognisably Pushkinian that it might be proposed seriously as a near-epitome of his poetic art in the lyrical field. It is worth while devoting a whole chapter to this poem, 'Zima. Chto delat' nam v derevne? Ya vstrechayu . . .' ('Winter. What are we to do out in the country? I greet . . .') by way of an introduction to the poet. The small particulars which may be observed at work in it are of a significance which extends beyond their immediate impact on the conscious mind. One of Pushkin's most meticulous commentators, Vladimir

Nabokov, claims at the outset of his encyclopaedic companion to *Yevgeniy Onegin* that 'In art as in science there is no delight without the detail.'[15] A detailed examination of this single poem (to be followed up by an extensive survey of the whole range of Pushkin's lyric poetry), cannot fail to reilluminate the particular skills of this poet and thus convey us further towards a fuller understanding of his widely acknowledged but still ill-defined genius.

2 AN APPROACH TO PUSHKIN THROUGH ONE POEM

A Poem of Early Winter

The events described in 'Zima. Chto delat' nam v derevne? Ya vstrechayu . . .' actually happened to Alexander Pushkin. He tells of his
experiences when staying with friends in the country at the onset of
winter, on November 2nd 1829 to be precise. His story recounts some
of the pleasures and day-to-day occupations of country life during that
season — and some of the drawbacks. It then proceeds to the enlivening
effect on a dull household created by the unexpected arrival of guests
— including two beautiful young sisters. Here is the poem set out in
full with a line-by-line English translation. Some clues to the ideas and
effects which are hidden away within the simple story may be apparent
merely from the layout of the poem on the page and the numbering of
its lines.

November 2nd

1 Зима. Что делать нам в деревне? Я встречаю
Слугу, несущего мне утром чашку чаю,
Вопросами: тепло ль? утихла ли метель?
Пороша есть иль нет? и можно ли постель
5 Покинуть для седла, иль лучше до обеда
Возиться с старыми журналами соседа?
Пороша. Мы встаем, и тотчас на коня,
И рысью по полю при первом свете дня;
Арапники в руках, собаки вслед за нами;
10 Глядим на бледный снег прилежными глазами;
Кружимся, рыскаем и поздней уж порой,
Двух зайцев протравив, являемся домой.
Куда как весело! Вот вечер: вьюга воет;
Свеча темно горит; стесняясь, сердце ноет;
15 По капле, медленно глотаю скуки яд.
Читать хочу; глаза над буквами скользят,
А мысли далеко... Я книгу закрываю;
Беру перо, сижу; насильно вырываю
20 У музы дремлющей несвязные слова.
Ко звуку звук нейдет... Теряю все права

Над рифмой, над моей прислужницею странной:
Стих вяло тянется, холодный и туманный.
Усталый, с лирою я прекращаю спор,
Иду в гостиную; там слышу разговор
25 О близких выборах, о сахарном заводе;
Хозяйка хмурится в подобие погоде,
Стальными спицами проворно шевеля,
Иль про червонного гадает короля.
Тоска! Так день за днем идет в уединеньи!
30 Но если под вечер в печальное селенье,
Когда за шашками сижу я в уголке,
Приедет издали в кибитке иль возке
Нежданая семья: старушка, две девицы
(Две белокурые, две стройные сестрицы), —
35 Как оживляется глухая сторона!
Как жизнь, о боже мой, становится полна!
Сначала косвенно-внимательные взоры,
Потом слов несколько, потом и разговоры,
А там и дружный смех, и песни вечерком,
40 И вальсы резвые, и шопот за столом,
И взоры томные, и ветреные речи,
На узкой лестнице замедленные встречи;
И дева в сумерки выходит на крыльцо:
Открыты шея, грудь, и вьюга ей в лицо!
45 Но бури севера не вредны русской розе.
Как жарко поцалуй пылает на морозе!
Как дева русская свежа в пыли снегов!

1 Winter. What are we to do out in the country? I greet
The servant bringing me in a morning cup of tea
With questions. Is it warm? Has the snowstorm died down?
Is there fresh snow or not? Is it better to quit the bed
5 For the saddle, or spend until dinner-time
Going through old journals borrowed from a neighbour?
There is fresh snow. We get up. Straight on to our horses
And off we go trotting over the fields at first light of day,
Our crops in our hands, the dogs following on behind;
10 We watch the pale snow with eyes peeled,
Round we go a-roaming and then, when it is late,
Twice having missed the hare, — here we are back home again.

What fun it is! Now evening is here, the blizzard howls,
The candle gutters, my aching heart shrinks,
15 Drop by drop, slowly I swallow the poisoned drink of
                                                   boredom.
I try reading; my eyes slide over the letters
And my thoughts are far away . . . I shut the book,
Take up my pen and sit there, violently wrenching
Disjointed words from my nodding muse.
20 The sounds won't come together . . . I lose all control
Over rhyme, that strange handmaiden of mine.
The verses drag out their sluggish way, cold and misty.
Wearying, I stop arguing with my lyre
And go into the drawing-room. There I come upon a
                                                   conversation
25 About the impending election and the sugar refinery.
My hostess scowls, at one with the weather,
Knitting away expertly with her steel needles
— Or does some fortune-telling with the King of Hearts.
Oh aching boredom! This is how day follows day out in the
                                                   wilds!
30 But if as evening falls on the sad village
As I sit playing draughts in a quiet corner
A carriage or a sleigh should drive up after a long journey,
Much to our surprise, with a family group — an old lady and
                                                   two young maids
(Two sisters, two shapely blondes) —
35 Then how the godforsaken place takes on a new life
And life itself brims over with good things!
We start with angled glances, lingering,
Then a word or two, a conversation or two,
Friendly laughter, some songs on the evening air,
40 Then whirling waltzes, whisperings at table,
Languor in the eyes, a gentle bantering,
Protracted meetings on the narrow stairs.
Then one of the girls comes out on to the twilit porch,
Her neck, her bosom open, the snowstorm in her face!
45 But storms from the north cannot harm the Russian rose.
Oh how a searing kiss burns through the frost!
How cool and pure my Russian maid is with her dusting of
                                                   snow!

How to Execute the Alexandrine

This poem has Pushkin's special mark on it from the first few lines. To begin with, his choice and exploitation of metre present immediate interest. Down the page, in apparently dutiful couplets, are ranked a set of familiar-looking lines. They are, of course, Alexandrines. (Technically speaking that means iambic hexameters, each divided into two hemistichs by a caesura, grouped in couplets and alternating feminine (two-syllable) rhymes with masculine (one-syllable) ones. Readers of French classical drama and much of French poetry will be familiar with the form.) It appears, then, that Russian verse is parading a metre of long and noble pedigree. The appearance is, in fact, so persuasive that the compiler of a recent Russian poetical dictionary, A. Kvyatkovsky, has chosen the opening of this very poem as a good example of the *Aleksandriyskiy Stikh* (Alexandrine Verse).[1] Under that heading Kvyatkovsky presents a brief definition and history of the metre. He emphasises its use in eighteenth-century narrative poems, tragedies and triumphal lyrics by those most conscientious of early Russian versifiers Tredyakovsky, Lomonsov, Kheraskov and Sumarokov. Two examples follow. The first is the opening of a poem by Vyazemsky in which he discusses the Alexandrine itself and concludes that it is admirably suited to the ponderous, muscular, elephantine Russian language. This is all so light-hearted that we are clearly meant to take the opening six lines of Pushkin's 'Zima . . .' to be a sound and serious exemplar. Nothing could be further from the truth.

In the first place, Pushkin's subject is Russian country life with all its tedium and non-achievement. The use of this aristocrat among metres for such prosaic musings can be nothing other than ironical. Secondly, in case anyone should doubt this, the actual deployment of the hexameters at the very head of the poem demonstrates that the poet is anything but doggedly serious in his purpose. The two formulations 'What are we to do out in the country?' (Chto delat' nam v derevne?) and 'I greet my servant . . .' (Ya vstrechayu slugu . . .) can only be read as complete entities without the slightest breath of a pause. Yet to do so is to undermine and debase this noble old form by ignoring both the obligatory caesura and the desirability of end-stopping. It is true technically that the caesura after the third foot is, according to the strict letter of poetic law, observed in every line of this poem; that is to say no line fails in its official duty to finish a word at the caesura point in mid-line. In many lines, however, the sense goes sweeping across the tiny gulf thus created and any true sense of a division into hemistichs is lost. At no place in the poem is this more clearly noticeable than in the very first line, where the disparity between theoretical observance of the caesura and the total disregard for it in practice, all of this followed up immediately by a muscular enjambement, amounts to nothing less than a literary joke.

Nor is this the only bit of amusement at the head of the poem. The actual content of the second line, so unspectacular in itself — 'the servant bringing me in a morning cup of tea' — is devastatingly inappropriate material for employment in Alexandrine couplets. This patrician form which has spent all its long decades in the depiction of noble deeds and elevated ideas is now reduced, at the beginning of a poem, to dealing with servants and, worse still, cups of tea. Line two also flops over into line three with another inescapable enjambement, by which time the well-born Alexandrine has been sunnily ridiculed out of all recognition and almost out of existence. This is an excellent example of Pushkin's attitude to inherited literary canons, an attitude nicely summed up by a modern Russian writer as follows: 'Pushkin did not develop and extend tradition, he teased it, lapsing at every end and turn into parody'.[2]

Two points here relate specifically to Pushkin, his 'democratisation' of poetry and his parodic playing with forms. Both are typical of his particular manner and have been widely referred to by many critics in general terms. Both are central to an appreciation of the spirit of Pushkin's work as a whole. He believed in poetry as both natural and entertaining. Nothing should be excluded from poetry, not even the most ordinary of day-to-day objects and expressions. More important still, it was unnecessary to approach poetry, as reader or writer, with an attitude of solemn deference. Levity, or at least a confident expectation of enjoyment, must be encouraged. There is, however, a further convolution of meaning to his choice of metre. Whenever Pushkin indulges in gentle parody of a literary form, which he does with some frequency in order to ensure his own and his readers' continuing sense of entertainment, he performs with such skill that, firstly, one hardly notices the mischievous attack being mounted and, secondly, he normally provides a brilliant demonstration of the full resources of the particular form with which he is toying. Much of Pushkin's work hovers tantalisingly between virtuosic fulfilment of the chosen literary possibilities and a genial mockery of them. In 'Zima . . .' the mockery comes first, unmistakably, but the serious exploitation of the chosen form will follow with the usual impressiveness. There is, it transpires, a perfectly good reason for the choice of the iambic hexameter, apart from the potential for ridicule which it bears. In English verse this line has never made a serious mark. Pope rejects it as unacceptably long, padded out and tedious:

> A needless Alexandrine ends the song,
> That, like a wounded snake, drags its slow length along.[3]

But a large part of Pushkin's purpose in this poem will be actually to depict tedium. How appropriate it will be to use a long, potentially boring line of verse. Two or three lines in 'Zima . . .' could only have been written in hexameters; anything shorter would have destroyed the languid flow necessary for the depiction of utter boredom. This is, in fact, precisely what happens in another winter poem (of 1826), *Zimnyaya Doroga* (*Winter Road*), in which the poet tells of the tedium of a long journey and looks forward to being reunited with his beloved Nina. The poem contains some striking sound effects and certainly imitates the drumming monotony of the noise from the carriage wheels. What it fails to convey is the feeling of sheer boredom; this is scarcely possible because of the unfortunate choice of trochaic tetrameter, a line which, as well as being relatively short, possesses enough irrepressible energy, even urgency, to militate against the depiction of tedium. A line like

> Dremlya smolknul moy yamshchik
> My nodding driver has fallen silent

appeals exclusively to the intellect and neglects the emotions. It should be compared with those lines in 'Zima . . .' which have a similar aim but come nearer to achieving it. Perhaps the best three examples are:

line 15 Po kaple, medlenno, glotayu skuki yad.
Drop by drop, slowly I swallow the poisoned drink of
boredom.

line 22 Stikh vyalo tyanetsya, kholodnyy i tumannyy.
The verses drag out their sluggish way, cold and misty.

line 29 Toska! Tak den' za dnem idet v uyedinenii.
Oh aching boredom! This is how day follows day out in the
wilds.

Each of these lines must be read at a fearfully slow pace, with long pauses in the appropriate places, so that they seem to drag out their length interminably like the dull hours and days of which they speak. By coincidence, *stikh vyalo tyanetsya* (line 22) is a very good translation of Pope's 'drags its slow length along'; the difference is that Alexander Pope was at pains to demonstrate the pitfalls awaiting the user of this line whereas Alexander Pushkin is using it for an entirely appropriate purpose.

Not for the first time in his career Pushkin sees to it that he has the best of both worlds. He proves himself able to exploit the natural characteristics of his chosen metre in a proper manner and yet also, at any given moment, to turn it inside out and make it perform tricks which seem to be right out of character. His attitude to the Alexandrine, as to any other metrical form, is one of total (and amused) self-confidence. Elsewhere he wrote,

> A stikh aleksandriyskoy? . . .
> . . . Izvivistyy, provornyy, dlinnyy, sklizkoy
> I s zhalom dazhe — tochnaya zmiya;
> Mne kazhetsya, chto s nim upravlyus' ya.

> And what of the Alexandrine? . . .
> . . . Sinuous, nimble, long, slippery
> And even equipped with a sting, just like a serpent.
> I think I shall be able to cope with it.

Sinuous, nimble, long and slippery — these are revealing adjectives which come to his mind when this poet considers the line. Pope's wounded snake has now become a serpent with a sting and Vyazemsky's elephant has left the scene altogether. Pushkin's confident attitude, nicely understated in the final line of this quotation, determines the career of this line throughout the poem. More could be said about Pushkin's use and neglect of the caesura and enjambement but this seems unnecessary. There is no need to go into further metrical detail; one may state with assurance that in 'Zima . . .' Pushkin demonstrates his unique capacity in versification for the exact attunement of ends and means — which is another characteristic of his work as a whole.

A Parade of Poetic Skills

Let us turn to look briefly at some of the other devices with which this poem is liberally strewn and which attest the most sophisticated of poetic skills. Line 18, for example, tells of the poet's decision to wrest verses from his unwilling muse by a violent effort of concentration. The first three words convey this process to perfection, three exact, scientifically precise, iambic words 'Beru pero, sizhu . . .' containing all the teeth-gritting determination in the world and as much poetic inspiration as a computer-written jingle. The words are cleverly chosen. Lines 25 and 34, on the other hand, demonstrate slightly different uses of syntactical parallelism:

25   O blizkikh vyborakh, o sakharnom zavode
      About the impending election and the sugar refinery

34   (Dve belokuryye, dve stroynyye sestritsy)
      (Two sisters, two shapely blondes)

but there is a world of difference between the effects produced. The former has the unenviable poetic task of representing the dullest drawing-room conversation conceivable; it carries out this function in the only possible way, the least imaginative available, through the use of exact parallelism of form, O + adjective + noun, always ensuring, of course, that the actual words chosen are themselves mindbendingly devoid of interest. (They speak of the forthcoming election and the sugar refinery, which like the cup of tea would hardly have found their way so easily into Russian verse before Pushkin.) Line 34 is quite different, despite its similarly neat division into two halves. By the simple process of withholding the noun from his first hemistich Pushkin creates a sense of mounting curiosity and excitement exactly in accord with the idea of the two enticing sisters under description.

However, most interesting of all, in formal terms, is Pushkin's use of alliteration in this poem. This device is used in several places but the two most striking examples are in lines 8 and 13:

8   I rys'yu po polyu pri pervom svete dnya

13   Kuda kak veselo! Vot vecher, v'yuga voyet

Alliteration will sound differently to every reader — some can take more than others — but it is usually clear when the poet has overstepped the mark. The differences between these two examples are rather striking. To put it simply the former is a delightful use of the device and the latter is much less successful. In fact the matter goes deeper. In all seriousness a case could be made that line 8 is one of the happiest ever penned by this poet whereas line 13 possesses an abecedarian clumsiness that seems unbelievable in such an accomplished versifier. How are we to account for such a discrepancy? In the latter instance have we caught Pushkin out in the simplest of errors – overdoing his effects? This may be so, but before jumping to any such conclusion it behoves us to look closely at the two examples concerned.

Line 8 imparts a lot of information in a small compass, it represents dynamism without employing a single verb, it appeals to the ear and the mind's eye at the same time and it slips gently through from mere pleasing alliteration to the most unassertive use of onomatopoeia one could wish to encounter. This is based on that gentle and unlikely consonant the letter p, here employed repeatedly not only to provide a pleasing echo of the earlier words *porosha* (twice used) and *postel'/pokinut'* but also to represent the muffled padding clip-clop of horses over powdery snow. It would be hard to imagine a more succinct or successful representation in words of such an activity. From the jerky ups-and-downs of the first half-line, which include the light bridling of the enclitic form pó polyu, through to the smooth running of the second this line is immaculately conceived. It is surely one that lingers in the memory by dint of its double appeal to the ear and the mind's eye.

By contrast, everything seems to have gone wrong with the unlucky line 13. Things are being overdone. There are seven words in the line; the first two begin with 'k' and all the other five with 'v', a sound to be picked up yet again in 'svecha' at the start of line 14. Because of its vocalisation the letter 'v' carries much greater impact when used repetitively than the 'p' of line 8. The words *veselo* and *vecher* sound closely similar; even more intimately related are *Vot* and *voyet*, with their lugubrious and obtrusive stressed 'o', drawing much attention to themselves. The line contains both an exclamation mark and a strong verb yet these energetic devices fail to animate the ideas with anything like the infectious and charming enthusiasm of the early-morning hunting scene of only five lines earlier. Pushkin may on occasions fail to inspire through insipidity in a poem of minor significance but his sureness of instinct, vast literary experience and constant application to the art of poetry render bad taste or elementary mistakes a virtual impossibility. Restraint is his hallmark; excess was his direst enemy never to be allowed near the gates of his work. The only possible explanation of the apparently unsuccessful use of alliteration – onomatopoeia in line thirteen is that it is deliberate, or, to say the least, amply justified. Pushkin is known to have

revised the poem carefully, rearranging in particular the exciting pro-
gression towards eroticism at the end until it satisfied every need sensed
by his keen critical eye.[5] It is scarcely conceivable that he would have
overlooked bad technique elsewhere unless he considered it to have a
purpose.

The purpose of the over-emphatic alliteration in line 13, apart from
its obvious function of actually describing the snowstorm, is to mark a
change from good times to bad. The hunting has been an enlivening
experience — now it dawns on the poet that the deadening dullness of
empty country life is about to descend once more. Things have gone
well and the poetry has flowed normally and to good effect. Everything
now changes. The entertainment is over, the weather has turned bad. If
a touch of less competent versifying is allowed into the poem it comes
at the very point where everything else is less than perfect. Within a few
lines the poet will tell us of his experiences in the doldrums of poetic
inspiration — here is the first foretaste of those unprofitable moments.

That particular line marks, in a rather obvious way, a change from
one mood to another. In point of fact there are about half a dozen
clearly differentiated moods in this poem, in particular the tranquil
contemplation of the day ahead, the hunting scene with its movement,
colour and excitement, the dog-days of unrelievable boredom, the
renewal of excitement when visitors arrive and the crescendo of erotic
interest with which the poem ends. It is another distinguishing feature
of Pushkin's work that he is attracted to the depiction of different
moods in quick succession and has a particular facility for easy modulation from one to the next. This skill is to be seen in full flower in *The
Bronze Horseman*. It is more clearly apparent *between* rather than
within the lyric poems, though 'Zima . . .' gives us multiple examples
of this kind of poetic engineering. On each occasion except the one
under discussion the change is so delicately brought about that one
scarcely notices that affairs have begun to move in another direction.
The heavy-handed treatment of the modulation in line 13 contributes
a blunt shock of awareness entirely appropriate to the suddenness with
which the stranded poet realises how temporary delight has changed
into near-despair.

The last line of the poem is important. It shows the poet carried
away into a state of exclamatory ecstasy brought on by near proximity
to a pretty girl in a setting close to nature and the promise of even
headier pleasures to come. His artistic spirit, however, remains in control. Certain properties in this last line have caught the eye of several
critics,[6] but its most important characteristic, a very simple one, has

not received sufficient emphasis. It is this: line 47 has no partner — there is no rhymed fulfilment of the expectations aroused by the word *snegov*. The effect of the omission is striking. It projects the unsatisfied imagination forward in eager calculation of what must be about to follow. It does so, moreover, in a secret, joking manner. The poet seems to say he is leaving it to the reader to draw his own conclusions about what happens next and, in any case, he's damned if he will carry on writing verses when things have become so exciting. There are, as it happens, other iambic hexameter poems of Pushkin's which possess a similarly inchoate ending, though none of them uses this device to such telling effect. Here the omission looks anything but accidental; it is deliberate, tantalising and full of flavour.

No doubt much more could be winkled out of the formal crevices of this poem which possesses greater intricacy than a quick reading would at first suggest. However, enough is enough. An examination of those formal properties which stand out in the poem is sufficient to demonstrate two things; firstly that they are used meaningfully by a real master of the fundamental arts of poetry and, secondly, that at least some of them are used here by Pushkin in a distinctive and even inimitable manner. This is part of the case that 'Zima . . .' may be taken not only as a good poem but as one which epitomises this poet in particular.

Country Life and its Distractions

If the formal characteristics of this poem may be taken as typical of Pushkin's method, it is no less true that the content reflects a number of familiar Pushkinian preoccupations and attitudes. The naturalistic, detailed depiction of country life, thoughts about the distractions available for bored people, the consolation provided by literature, the processes of poetic inspiration, the transcendent excitement of erotic adventures, the deep integration of the poem into actual events in the poet's life and its lightly mocking general tone — all of these salient characteristics of 'Zima . . .', here presented in encapsulated form, are to be found widely dispersed and embellished throughout the whole body of Pushkin's lyric and other poetry. It may safely be said, in fact, that they account for most of it and that few other poems encompass such a broad range of the poet's main ideas. There is value to be gained from a closer look at each of these preoccupations.

In Pushkin's treatment of his rural theme there is enough individuality to mark the poem as typically his and to evoke many reminders of similar scenes elsewhere in his work. The properties of the first dozen lines of 'Zima . . .' stand out clearly: succinctness, speed and dynamism. There are no wasted words: on the contrary, Pushkin's carefully revised deposition of minor details creates a suggestiveness capable of establishing a broader picture than would seem possible in such a short space. The energy generated early on by questions directed first at the reader and then at the servant, far from being wasted or dissipated, proceeds by inertia right through this first section, animating every line and so dictating the choice of words that the adjective, that yeoman standby of lesser poets and other situations, is virtually debarred from service. In the first eighteen lines of the poem there are only three adjectives, *starymi* (line 6), *blednyy* and *prilezhnymi* (line 10), whereas in mid-poem, when tedium has become thoroughly established, Pushkin will slow down the action by employing his adjectives at a rate of more than one per line: (there are eight in the seven lines 19-25). At his most breathlessly dynamic, Pushkin will even do without verbs, as in lines 8 and 9, which are nevertheless easily the most vigorous ones in the whole poem. At the end of this section his choice of the words '*yavlyayemsya domoy*' cannily puts all the emphasis on *being* back home, *getting* there, rather than the progressive process of merely returning. Thus the reader is whisked through the whole sequence of events speedily and easily, all the more susceptible to the excitement of the day and therefore also to a greater bump of disappointment when that is all over. In these dozen lines we see demonstrations of some of those qualities which critics take to be at the centre of Pushkin's artistry. To take one example, Richard Freeborn, writing about *Yevgeniy Onegin*, refers in the course of three or four pages, to 'richness and intricacy', 'vigour and concreteness', 'sense of factuality', 'careful, detailed observation', 'lucidity and simple directness', 'commonsense discipline of a viewpoint', and 'verisimilitude . . . achieved by an act of miniaturisation'.[7] All of these very qualities, writ large in the novel, are to be seen clearly, though scaled down to an impressionistic sketchiness, (miniaturised *again*) at the opening of 'Zima . . .'.

It is mainly in *Yevgeniy Onegin*, *Count Nulin* and other long poems and stories that Pushkin's depiction of country life comes into its own. Rather surprisingly, he wrote few rural lyrics inspired by the natural scene alone. Thus the poem 'Zima . . .' epitomises at its beginning Pushkinian qualities extending beyond the narrow territory of his *lirika*. For this reason Slonimsky refers to the poem, shrewdly and accurately, as 'seemingly a page taken from a long story'.[8] This observation is a further pointer towards the wide-ranging and allusive character of the poem, a principal part of the present argument.

The central section, from line 13 to line 29, also raises preoccupations which call out to be related to other writings by the same author. Their main burden concerns the staleness of humdrum country life once the few possibilities for excitement have been exhausted. Under those conditions what do people do? Pushkin tells us, again descending to small details of specification which epitomise broader considerations. They talk, they indulge in minor drawing-room distractions and they turn to the written word. The devastating drabness of the conversation is represented here by the latest news about the local election and the sugar refinery. Knitting and fortune-telling are the sublimest heights attained by the depressed and gloomy hostess whose three-line vignette is so eloquent; the scowl, the clacking needles, the fortune-telling tell us all we need to know about her temperament, situation, occupations and intellect — she is closely related to Natalya Pavlovna, the neglected rural hostess of the earlier narrative *Count Nulin*. From all the trivial particularities, so neatly arranged by the poet, the reader is able to construct for himself an extended awareness of this old-fashioned and unimaginative rural existence. Once again Pushkin's minutely specific shorthand communicates more than seems possible.

Much the most interesting references in the central section of the poem are, however, to literature. Again, hints and suggestions are the medium of expression but a great deal is to be made of them. In the first place, there is the rather obvious fact that this writer turns automatically to the written word when excitement is at a low ebb. Early on in the poem the only alternative to a day's hunting is a morning in bed leafing through borrowed back-number journals. (It was apparently under these circumstances and in one such journal that Pushkin read of the legend of the Upas Tree (Antiaris Toxicaris) which inspired what is deservedly one of his most famous poems, *Anchar*.)[9] Now the poet attacks the cruel problem of boredom more directly. His casual attempts at reading fail because he cannot concentrate. His coercive attempts to produce poetry fail equally because the mood is not on him, and here we are treated, *en passant*, to several revealing comments on the subject of the poet's trade as seen by this man. He refers to rhyme as a 'strange handmaiden' over whom, at normal times, he exercises total control. This is no tyrant muse who tears him apart, no elusive inspirational force after whom he is constantly chasing, no beguiling, heady seductress who bends him to her will. Pushkin's attitude to literature is one of absolute confidence in his own abilities. The gentle arrogance which we know so well from Pushkin's sweeping career through so many genres is here encapsulated in a couple of words. So, too, is his idea of what poetry should be when it is flowing normally. The concept is overturned into a negative expression of what happens when inspiration is missing:

22   The verses drag out their sluggish way, cold and misty

From this statement the essence of true poetry is easily derived. It should be springy, supple, warm, precise and clear — all adjectives which we readily apply to Pushkin's poetry as a whole. A further clue, the vital one, has been deposited a couple of lines earlier on. Faced with the problem of expressing the absence of inspiration the poet must have considered what particular branch of his trade to mention in a synecdochic reference. He does not say that the *ideas* will not present themselves, that *themes* are proving elusive, that *words* withhold cooperation, nor that *images* fail to arise in his mind. He refers quite specifically to *sounds*, which will not come together: 'Ko zvuku zvuk neydet.' Most certainly this should be taken as a deliberate rather than an arbitrary reference. Pushkin's highest quality is that of creating spontaneous verbal music in patterns more beguiling and agreeable than any other Russian poet. Such an assertion risks debasement of his art by inviting comparison with minor poets in other languages of whom something similar is true — Swinburne in English, Ruben Darío in Spanish, the minor Symbolists in French poetry, whose actual equivalent in Russian poetry might be said to be Zhukovsky or perhaps Balmont. The risk is unavoidable and the possible delusion must be dispelled elsewhere and at greater length. It has to be stated plainly that Pushkin is a musical poet *par excellence*. Despite the differences between him and, let us say, Verlaine, over the matter of precision versus vagueness in poetry, the two poets are at one in their belief that the vital preoccupation of poetry must be 'De la musique avant toute chose'.

Thus, in a line or two we encounter a casual but uniquely concise and accurate Pushkinian *art poétique*, verifiable time after time throughout the great body of his poems, long and short. By this means, 'Zima . . .' casts many a side glance into two different kinds of lyric for which Pushkin is well known, those in which he theorises about poetic inspiration and methods (for example, *Osen'* (*Autumn*) (1833), *Poet* (*The Poet*) (1827 and 1830), *Razgovor knigoprodavtsa s poetom* (*A conversation between bookseller and poet*) (1824)) and those in which it may be said that the *zvukopis'* (total sound picture) is the prime, though never the sole, *raison d'être* and achievement of the poem (such

as 'Khrani menya, moy talisman . . .' ('Keep me, my talisman . . .')
(1825) and *Besy* (*The Devils*) (1830)).

A Sexual Encounter

It is now clear that the opening and middle sections of 'Zima . . .' contain many particulars in both form and content which are strongly typical of Pushkin's work as a whole. What of the concluding section, lines 30-47? Here we come upon a quite different theme, but again it is one which is close to the poet's heart, widely expressed in other poems and indispensable in any piece claimed as typifying Pushkin: namely, the commanding excitement of a sexual encounter. Pushkin's most profound and enduring fondness was for literature, though his affection for a handful of personal friends was also an important part of his adolescent and adult life. Capable of overriding both of these at a moment's notice, because of its inexorable intensity, was his physical attraction to the fair sex. His long and varied amatory experience gave rise to two different, though associated, tendencies in his poetry, bawdy verse and love poetry. This poem recalls them both, at something of a distance, it is true, but nevertheless unmistakably. The last eighteen lines form a long, delicious crescendo of excitement, from the first hints that the tedium is to be relieved by visitors, then the realisation that these include two beautiful young women, then the clear possibility that a sexual encounter is on the cards, then the heady stimulation of secret love play amid the company and finally the promise of fulfilment when the poet and his lover are at last alone, kissing each other out in the snowstorm. By the end of the poem all the emphasis has been transferred from sights and sounds indoors to physical contact away from other people. The poem breaks off in an exclamatory half-couplet — there is no need to tell us any more.

If, by any chance, anyone should doubt that this is a sexual encounter in the fullest sense then reference should be made to the very next poem written by Pushkin, *Zimneye Utro*, describing the 'Winter Morning' on the day after the events recounted in 'Zima . . .'. In the first stanza of this poem Pushkin actually addresses himself to his new love who is still in bed with him asleep, with her head on the next pillow. He refers to her eyes as having been 'closed in voluptuous pleasure'. Thus we must accept the strong hints of 'Zima . . .' for what they obviously are, a description of an actual and mutually enjoyable seduction. The restraint with which these wonderful moments are put into poetry and the perfect timing with which Pushkin switches off his poem are both natural and exemplary. It is also as well to accept this passing reminder that, although each individual lyric stands up independently, an even richer sense of enjoyment is obtainable by the reader if he knows a number of other poems and something of the circumstances of Pushkin's life.

The Spirit of Play

Finally, it is useful to review the overall tone of this poem, which is jocular throughout and sometimes gently mocking. At his lowest ebb, although there is no doubting the actuality of his excruciating boredom, the poet expresses his exasperation in terms of wry humour. When times are good he attempts either a good-natured communication of his own pleasures or an amused sense of temporary superiority as (at the end of the poem) he contemplates his own present pleasure and impending gratification, fully aware of the reader's 'lucky devil!' attitude. Comprehension of this amused stance, so frequently assumed by Pushkin elsewhere, is another important step towards a rounded appreciation of his art. Richard Freeborn, again speaking of *Yevgeniy Onegin*, observes that, 'Playfulness, flippancy, wit, youthful in their freshness though not always lighthearted in their manner, contribute to the stylistic tone and make it uniquely Pushkinian.'[10] The Soviet critic D.D. Blagoy reminds us of a comment made by the nineteenth-century critic Nadezhdin:

> Pushkin's muse is a mischievous young girl, who does not care tuppence for the world. Her element is to mock at everything, good and bad ... not out of spite or scorn but simply out of the desire to poke fun.[11]

Even allowing for some overstatement in the latter quotation these remarks point to an important truth: Pushkin enjoyed literature and wanted everyone else to enjoy it. Much of his work is written in a spirit of play and this quality, like so many others, is clearly represented in 'Zima . . .'.

It seems demonstrable, therefore, that this poem, in its themes, ideas and attitudes, not only amounts to a satisfying and integrated piece which ranges widely without putting unity at risk, but also serves as a useful indicator to preoccupations and perceptions running right through the poet's work. Of course it is true that not all of Pushkin is here in this poem. The depiction of urban life, the recurrent involvement with politics, the expressions of affection for close friends, the excursions into folklore and fairy tale, the archaic grandeur, the lapses into seriousness and unhappiness – all these characteristics, to name but a few, are absent from 'Zima . . .' and will have to be considered elsewhere. Nevertheless, this is a good poem to begin with. It is not necessary to summarise the Pushkinian qualities which have already become apparent from the reading of a single poem, but one or two points made generally in chapter 1 are worth brief reiteration. The poem is an enjoyable experience for all of us, poet, general reader, specialist critic, and translator. Its sensual appeal is a strong one on several levels. Most important of all, it gives greater value for money than we have a right to expect because, by virtue of the poet's paradoxical abilities, it reconciles apparent polarities. It is, at one and the same time, democratic and aristocratic, autobiographical and independent of background detail, boring and exciting, filled with magical sounds and yet pregnant with precise meanings, flippant and serious, dismissive of and yet devoted to the literary art. Anyone who works his way through 'Zima . . .', considers the poem in some detail and perhaps learns a few lines from it, can hardly fail to be infected with the spirit of Pushkin and to want to experience more of the same.

3 THE SHORTER POEMS

Noises in the Ear

In a recent broadcast the poet Charles Tomlinson reminded his listeners of an obvious truth which is sometimes forgotten: 'Poetry is first and foremost a noise in the ear.'[1] Much of the pleasure experienced when reading and reciting Pushkin derives first and foremost from 'noises in the ear'. Sheer auditory enjoyment is his greatest gift to us all and particularly to the Russians themselves who, having retained the sensible practice of committing poetry to memory when young, are thus able in later years to recite whole poems and long passages from their national poet – and to do so with relish.

However, to claim that a poet is a master of the art of weaving sound patterns is not always a compliment to him. C.M. Bowra points out that sounds may seduce people into vagueness or even nonsense:

> When Romantic poetry aspires too ardently to become music it tends to leave some of its sense behind. The result is often delightful, but, when we look more closely at it, it reveals a frailty we do not expect in great poetry.[2]

More succinctly he indicates the actual extent of the risks run by 'musical' poets as follows: 'Sound is . . . as necessary to poetry as sight or meaning but it is dangerous to give it too emphatic a place.'[3]

It is not open to doubt that Pushkin, for all his fascination for sound values, does not 'aspire too ardently' for auditory effect. His work does not give sound 'too emphatic a place'. Mirsky explains how he avoids the dangers by referring to 'the fitness of his words and . . . the absolute consistency of the sounds and rhythms.'[4] It is a question of finding the right combinations of sound by some process of instinct and, particularly, of holding back from excess. Elsewhere Mirsky writes as follows:

> One might write an *Alliteratio Pushkiniana* to show the part played in his verse by the repetition of consonants as of vowels. But Push-kin's alliteration is much more discreet and muffled than that of the Roman poets, and the principal consonants employed to bring about his effects are not the heroic r's and metallic g's of Virgil, but the soft and liquid v's, n's and l's. The prominence of these consonants,

together with the play of rhythm and rhyme, contributes in no small way to producing the effect of Pushkin's early mellifluousness.[5]

The Russian poet and critic, Valeriy Bryusov, had much to say on this subject and some of his observations are among the most perceptive and illuminating. Here is a clear statement indicating the importance of sound values for Pushkin.

In Pushkin, as in Virgil, truly *every* line and *every* letter in that line, has been set in its place primarily according to the laws of euphony.[6]

Can it be, perhaps, that sound occupies too prominent a place? 'Sometimes', Bryusov continues, 'it might almost seem that sounds had an overriding significance for him.'[7]

But no, this is only an impression, and it arises only from time to time. Pushkin's remarkable ability is to create patterns of euphony without drawing attention to them.

In Pushkin the sound system is hidden; you have to look closely to spot it. The most complex sound patterns . . . become obvious only when you examine them letter by letter, sound by sound.[8]

Bruysov's final word on this subject is also his most important.

What matters most is that Pushkin knew how to avoid sacrificing any one element of poetry for the sake of another. He did not give precedence to sound over sense, nor to sense over sound.[9]

The success of this balancing act is no accident. It was Pushkin's avowed intention to extract what he could from the acoustic resources provided by his native language without ever using them to swamp the expression of his ideas. His most succinct statement of this method comes in the fragment *Egyptian Nights* when Charsky, Pushkin's alter ego, speaks of 'that blessed state of the spirit . . . when verses lie down before your pen and ringing rhymes run to meet up with a nicely turned thought.' So delicately balanced in Pushkin's mind is the relationship between the idea and its expression by means of captivating sounds that, on another occasion, he mentions the thoughts first and the sounds second:

And boldly thoughts come seething through my head

And easy rhymes come running towards them

(Osen' (Autumn))

Thus, by intention and achievement Pushkin may be seen to have found a perfect compromise between the competing temptations of two of the most important of the poet's special skills. He is a beautiful musician, rightly compared with Mozart in the realm of actual music, and no one should be ashamed to read him aloud and rejoice in the experience of doing so. On the other hand, the ideas, the people, the stories and the everyday objects encountered in his poetry, far from being blurred or repressed by the richness of the sounds emerge with equal rights. Indeed they invariably present themselves with a sharp-edged clarity of focus which, when set against the enchanting mellifluousness used in their expression, brings us once more to the verge of paradox. Beguiling euphony does not seem to be the ideal background against which to attempt the projection of crystal images – but with Pushkin it is so.

There are several ways in which Pushkin's acoustic skill may work upon the reader or listener. Normally, the effect is unobtrusive. As Bryusov points out, you are simply not aware of the clever arrangement of sounds which fall so agreeably upon the ear. It would be possible, for instance, to read stanza IV of Chapter Eight of *Yevgeniy Onegin* many times over, entranced by the spell that it weaves, without knowing precisely what is occurring. Anyone really interested in the underlying technicalities could, if he wanted to take the trouble, learn from a scholar that 'The instrumentation of the first eleven lines in the final text of this stanza . . . is truly remarkable. The alliterations are built around the vowel *a* (which is also the sound of the unaccented *o*) and the consonants *l*, *s*, *z*, *k*.'[10] This comment is followed by a diagram of the stanza based on the recurrence of those letters and including the remarkable sequence 'ka . . . as . . . askala. ka. kaza.' But how many readers are going to bother to look into this? The great majority will simply read the stanza with a generalised, yet real, sense of pleasure. Some may even notice that the key line is, in Russian, 'Kak chasto, po skalam Kavkaza . . .' but there is no reason why many people should linger long even here. The sounds themselves are not assertive. So it is with Pushkin's poetry. A great hinterland exists within it 'from which magic sounds issue in broad patterns but the poet extends no open invitation to explore it and not many passers-by are concerned to do so. All of this territory, it goes without saying, is forbidden to those without a knowledge of Russian, and translators have never even approached its borders.

Such is the richness of Pushkin's achievement in sound pictures, however, that these cannot fail from time to time to obtrude more noticeably. There are two ways in which this is achieved, by the inclusion of a really striking line of verse in an otherwise ordinary context, or by the utter triumph of acoustics throughout a whole poem. A good example of the former appears in the poem *To Chaadayev* (1821) in which Pushkin expresses his gratitude for Chaadayev's constant support particularly in troubled times. This is an insignificant, rather stilted piece of poetry, stiffly proceeding through eighty-four alexandrines end-stopped and scrupulously attired with polished caesuras. Suddenly, however, about half way through, Pushkin ends his opening section with a line of amazing acoustic exuberance,

I tsarskosel'skiye khranitel'nyye seni.

This is the sort of line which stops a reader in his tracks and overwhelms him with its sumptuous effects. The knowledgeable Pushkin lover carries in his memory a dozen or more such lines which, once they have impinged upon his awareness, remain available for instant recall by virtue of their sheer succulence. They crop up all over the place. The celebrated ballad *Utoplennik* (*The Drowned Man*) (1828) includes these two lines:

Al' ograblennyy vorami
Nedogadlivyy kupets?

An early love poem K *** (To ***) (1820) culminates in this sentiment, expressed with an equality of grace and tenderness:

Neschastnyy! budesh' ty gotov
Kupit' khot' slovo devy miloy,
Khot' legkiy shum yeye shagov.

The poem *Napoleon* (1821) presents a good example of Pushkin's ability to fit long, appetising Russian words neatly into an iambic line with results that appeal most agreeably to the ear:

Okrovavlennyye snega
Provozglasili ikh paden'ye

An even better example of this skill appears in the poem 'Zima. Chto delat' nam v derevne? Ya vstrechayu . . .' which we have already considered at some length yet without drawing attention to the lovely languor of line 37, with its sinuous, hyphenated, eight-syllable, caesura-mocking central epithet:

Snachala kosvenno-vnimatel'nyye vzory

Another lovely-sounding line appears in *Vospominaniye* (*Remembrance*) (1824):

Poluprozrachnaya nalyazhet nochi ten'

The 'Little Tragedy' *Kamennyy Gost'* (*The Stone Guest*) (1830) includes these lines, uttered by Laura:

Kak nebo tikho;
Nedvizhim tyoplyy vozdukh, noch' limonom
I lavrom pakhnet, yarkaya luna
Blestit . . .

A well known poem of 1820, 'Pogaslo dnevnoye svetilo . . .' (The orb of day has faded . . .') contains this irregular but hypnotic refrain:

Shumi, shumi, poslushnoye vetrilo,
Volnuysya podo mnoy, ugryumyy okean.

A poem of 1825 shows Pushkin using enchanting sounds in order actually to enchant. He was once given a ring with cabbalistic symbols on it by Countess Vorontsova. Having been deeply in love with her he wore it as a lucky charm after they parted and his poem is intended to cast a spell over their relationship. His last hopes are deposited in destiny guided by this talisman. The poem stands mid-way between a prayer and a magical incantation. What is so memorable about it is the line which opens and closes the poem and concludes four of its five stanzas. This consists of two murmured, hypnotic phrases —

Khrani menya, moy talisman.

The poem is rich in sound effects of many other kinds, but this is the line which lurks in the memory of everyone who has heard it.

There are a few poems — perhaps this is one of them — which commend themselves to the reader first and foremost because of the opulence of their sound effects. No amount of contemplating their meanings will add much to their quality, for they are music in words. Some of them are, moreover, among the best known of Pushkin's poems. Two such are the trochaic tetrameter poems *Zimniy Vecher* (*Winter Evening*) (1825) and *Besy* (*The Devils*) (1830). These poems do have clear meanings but in both cases it is not the meaning that signifies. *Winter Evening* is autobiographical. The poet, under house arrest at Mikhaylovskoye sits with his nurse, who has now grown old, in her little cottage. The storm rages outside, just as metaphorical storms are raging about the head of the poet, and, as she nods by the window, he gives himself up to the pleasures of the bottle and the delicious pain of nostalgia for his own childhood. The heat must have built up in the little wooden shack, the drink now blurs perception, memories crowd in and the storm continues to howl. The *coup de grâce* of this poem is in its last eight-line stanza, which is entirely constructed of lines that have gone before, the opening quatrains of the first and third stanzas. These lines themselves contain wonderful sound effects, particularly in the representation of the storm.

Burya mgloyu nebo kroyet,
Vikhri snezhnyye krutya;
To, kak zver', ona zavoyet,
To zaplachet, kak ditya.

One could make much of the devices used here by the poet. To take a single instance, it is impressive for him to have used an opening line of pure, discrete trochees (Búryă/mglóyŭ/nébŏ/króyĕt) to represent the unceasing pounding of the gale outside. In fact, however, no-one is interested here in technicalities. The storm, the dizzy memories and the bitter-sweet sentimentality fuse together in a succession of enchanting sounds. So unimportant are the actual ideas that the concluding stanza not only avoids the introduction of any new thoughts, it restricts itself to recapitulating the actual words that were used before and the now familiar sounds that went with them — though in a new order.

Apart from the metrical similarities, *Zimniy Vecher* has much in common with *Besy* (*The Devils*). Both poems are set in the Russian winter. Winter for the Russians is a special season, altogether more beautiful and yet more menacing than we in Western Europe can begin to understand. It is depicted continually in Russian literature and, as often as not, it claims a victim. Nekrasov's *Moroz, krasnyy nos (Red-nosed Frost)*, Saltykov-Shchedrin's *Gospoda Golovlyovy (The Golovlyov Family)* and Tolstoy's *Khozyain i Rabotnik (Master and Man)* are but three examples of stories in which humankind falls victim to the Russian winter. Thus, when Pushkin speaks of winter he has in mind a glorious, elemental but brutal force greatly to be respected and feared. These fears are encapsulated in *The Devils*. A two-man team, master and man as it happens, are stranded in a snowstorm. Watching them safely, from afar, we are treated to a magnificent vision of the Russian winter portrayed through the images of Russian folklore. The swirling, howling snows are depicted as evil spirits dancing around the forlorn pair and about to move in for the kill. The actuality of two wretched individuals stuck in a snowdrift amidst a worsening storm and in dire danger of freezing to death is transformed into universality by evoking the deep fears and suspicions, shared by us all, that we are surrounded by malevolent, uncontrollable forces. And it is largely brought about by sound. The urgency of the situation is conveyed once again by means of the dynamic trochaic tetrameter. Again, interestingly enough, Pushkin begins his poem with a line of discrete trochaic feet (Mchátsyǎ/túchǐ,/ v'yútsyǎ/túchǐ). This time that line, and the three that follow it, will be repeated twice, in mid-poem and in the concluding stanza. Thus the vigour, the monotonous insistence or irresistibility and the overwhelming noise of the storm are energetically represented by the metre and the acoustic devices selected for use.

There can be no doubt that what matters most in this poem is not the story, although this stands out clearly enough, not the catalogue of demonic forces listed as threatening the travellers, not, in fact, any of the ideas in the poem, but its total sound picture. Certainly the overall effect of *Besy*, of the sounds and the meaning taken together, is to re-create man's primitive fear of impending extinction at the hands of an alien element and his awareness of a malign destiny, tantalisingly misleading but about to annihilate him, all of which Pushkin believed in with some degree of passion. But the most important ingredient here is the drumming rhythm, together with the hypnotic play of sound. This poem, read with sufficient energy, could almost persuade a foreigner ignorant of Russian to believe in the menacing grandeur of the Russian winter, and it is the system of sound effects that makes this possible.

There are other poems in which acoustic excellence seems to be the most important quality. For example, a Spanish serenade of 1824, 'Nochnoy zefir', as lovely as it is brief, does its best to recapture the atmosphere of an evening in, presumably, Cordoba or Seville, with a gallant gazing up at a Spanish beauty on her balcony. The poem is sensually exciting and rhythmically disturbing. It is hard to believe anything other than that it was written purely on the strength of the sounds produced by the lovely name of the river Guadalquivir. Enchanting though that name may be in Spanish it gains a degree of exoticism in Russian because the two u's have to be transliterated curiously into v's (and there is already a 'v' there waiting for them), thus producing the excellent designation 'Gvadalkvivir'. Just as the poet, when composing his verses must deposit the end of the line first because of the exigencies of rhyme, so, in this case, Pushkin must surely have begun with his concluding word (which ends the refrain stanza used initially, medially and terminally). He built up the poem backwards from that delicious word and the *raison d'être* of the miniature piece — euphonic impact — is still observable in the finished poem. Once again, the music of the refrain seems to be communicable even to those who do not speak Russian:

Nochnoy zefir
Struit efir.
 Shumit,
 Bezhit
Gvadalkvivir.

Pushkin's contemporaries recognised his abilities as a musician in words. His friend Delvig once received a poem from him and wrote back immediately to say 'This is not poetry, it is music, it is the singing of a bird of paradise when you are listening to which you won't notice a thousand years slipping by.'[11] The poem was a free translation of Parny's *Déguisement de Vénus*, entitled *Prozerpina* (*Proserpine* or *Persephone*). It tells a readily understandable story, about the predatory Persephone and her all too physical love for a young male mortal, but, once again, the poem depends for its appeal on a string of lovely sounds. Again, too, proper nouns play a significant role. The opening lines

Pleshchut volny Flegetona,
Svody Tartara drozhat,

are an appetising foretaste of what is to come. Pushkin could not resist repeating them verbatim a dozen lines from the end. In mid-poem we run across a number of beautifully formulated phrases which explain what it was that captivated Delvig's sensitive ear. Perhaps the nicest of all are in lines 8 and 9:

Ravnodushna i revniva,
Potekla putem odnim.

Another obvious exercise in sound conducted by Pushkin for the
sheer love of acoustic experimentation is the poem *Ekho* (*The Echo*)
(1831). It is true that the second of the two six-line stanzas that make
up this little poem indulges itself in a little metaphor. As is the echo, so
is the poet, calling back the sounds of nature and getting no response.
But the true inspiration of the poem is the intriguing business of the
echo and the ringing sounds with which it involves itself. Significantly,
Pushkin here loses all interest in the softer sounds of the Russian language (the v's, n's and l's referred to by Mirsky which do usually attract
him because of their gentleness). Echoes need hard, voiced consonants
and assertive vowels. Hence, the first stanza:

Revet li zver' v lesu glukhom
Trubit li rog, gremit li grom,
Poyet li deva za kholmom –
    Na vsyakiy zvuk
Svoy otklik v vozdukhe pustom
    Rodish' ty vdrug.

The second stanza, too, contains some harsh expressions: 'grokhotu
gromov/ I glasu buri', 'kriku sel'skikh pastukhov' . . . All in all it seems
as if here, too, Pushkin constructed his poem on that basis with no real
attempt to let the concluding, and secondary, idea threaten any serious
detraction from the original purpose.

There are, however, poems in which the battle between sounds and
ideas is more evenly contested. Some of Pushkin's finest productions
overflow with splendid acoustic effects but these are refused predom-
inance because of the urgency of the intellectual message borne by
the poem. Three poems from successive years, *Prorok* (*The Prophet*)
(1826), *Poet* (*The Poet*) (1827) and *Anchar* (*The Upas Tree*) (1828)
illustrate this. *The Prophet* is filled with good sounds throughout. The
final quatrain begins:

Vosstan', prorok, i vizhd' i vnemli
Ispolnis' voleyu moyey . . .

The Poet, also full of interesting devices and rich sounds, includes these
two lines:

K nogam narodnogo kumira
Ne klonit gordoy golovy

The Upas Tree contains, among many others, this utterly memorable formulation:

No cheloveka chelovek
Poslal k ancharu vlastnym vzglyadom . . .

Despite these resounding phrases, which have insinuated themselves irresistibly into the minds of millions of Russians, no-one would even consider describing these three poems as predominantly acoustic. Whereas, in *Zimniy Vecher* (*Winter Evening*) and *Besy* (*The Devils*) and the other poems we have looked at, the general intention was to blur the ideas so that maximum emotional effect could be left to the responsibility of the sounds, now things are different. Each of the three poems cited contains a solidly fashioned concept which must not be allowed to be submerged in a mellifluous sea. *The Prophet* is a lofty statement, but a clear one, of the role of the seer (hence the poet) in human society. *The Poet* is a lucid comparison of the two states all too familiar to writers, the dog-days of uninspired ordinariness and the high-flying moments of artistic inspiration. *The Upas Tree* is a stark comment on the evil endemic in humankind as seen particularly in the widespread thirst for power. These messages are strong and clear. They cannot afford to be lost in a concord of sweet sounds and they refuse to let this happen.

So much for the acoustic effects of this poet. They are strong, subtle and at times overwhelming. No one before or since has manipulated the great resources of the Russian language to better effect. No one has displayed a surer instinct for exploiting, combining and contrasting its characteristic strengths — the sturdy masculine noises akin to those of the languages of northern Europe and the dulcet sounds, so melodiously feminine, which remind us of the south, particularly of Spain and Italy. Two points need to be emphasised. First, it is rare for the sounds of a Pushkin poem, however magnificently orchestrated, to distract from or to distort the meaning. Second, the melodic skills which we have seen exemplified, although somewhat exaggerated in these few poems which have been chosen for that very quality, are not the property of a handful of works. They are present in his earliest works, and were immediately recognised; at the age of fifteen he reduced Derzhavin, the aged doyen of Russian poetry, to tears by a public reading of *Recollections at*

Tsarskoye Selo (1815). At the same time he won over Zhukovsky to such an extent that the latter, then thirty-eight and at the height of his powers, soon began to test his own poems against the acute ear of this astounding teenager.

The same skills were brought to full maturity in Pushkin's first long poem *Ruslan and Lyudmila* which was begun in 1817, with the poet still a schoolboy, and offered to the world in March 1820. Zhukovsky's reaction was to reward the new poet with a portrait inscribed with the sincere message, 'To the victorious pupil from his defeated master.' The outstanding quality of this fairytale narrative was the spontaneous flow of melody which it contained. It was written with apparent insouciance, though actually by means of hard work and scrupulous revision. Its sound effects struck the reading public as magical. These skills were never to desert Pushkin. They remained at the very basis of his reputation as a poet and could be counted on by him at all times. As late as 1836, shortly before his death, he can be seen penning the grandiloquent *Exegi Monumentum* and, slightly earlier, a historical poem with oblique reference to the contemporary political situation entitled *Pir Petra Velikogo* (*The Banquet of Peter the Great*) and containing much evidence of Pushkin's skill as a melodic poet, particularly the construction of the final stanza from constituent parts used previously and variously in the poem. We can say without risk of exaggeration and without risk of debasing Pushkin's reputation that, although at one time, faced with a lack of inspiration on a bleak November day in the country, he may have explained in 'Zima . . .' that his acoustic skills were wanting, nevertheless he was a poet for whom, consistently, the sounds did 'come together'.

A Catalogue of Lovers

From one sensual experience, the pleasure derived from reading and reciting the delicious sounds of Pushkin's poetry, to another, more urgent and more exciting. Two or three dozen love poems of one kind or another written by Pushkin deserve a close look. Several of them are widely accepted as being among his finest works, perhaps among the most expressive and finely wrought love poems in world literature and they appear in every anthology of the Russian poets.

There is nothing remote or theoretical about Pushkin's approach to this subject. His education in sexual matters began early, well before puberty, in his father's library where he had access to the erotic writers of Classical literature and the more recent French school. By the age of eleven he was an eager flirt, though it took him another five years, and much frustrating effort, to cast off the unwanted burden of virginity. Once launched on a libidinous career, he proceeded from one woman to another and rarely stopped to calculate the risks or count the costs — whether in terms of protective fathers, jealous husbands, sexually transmitted diseases or unwanted pregnancies. At least one serf girl was, in fact, impregnated by the poet and dispatched in the time honoured fashion to a rural outpost to avoid embarrassing the *barin* responsible. 'Somewhere in the Nizhni Novgorod district', writes one biographer with a taste for piquant speculation, 'there probably exists to this day a peasant line springing from Russia's greatest poet.'[12]

Another biographer gives us a succinct statement of the importance of sexuality for Pushkin which may appear exaggerated but is not:

> To him, love was an occupation, a *raison d'être*, an art, a profession in itself, on the same level as poetry, and his entire life was to be divided between the two. Or rather, love and poetry were for him divergent manifestations of a single force . . . his . . . 'pure African' sensuality.[13]

Of all the hundreds of writers to have written on the Don Juan theme Pushkin is the only one actually to have behaved like a Don Juan, even to the extent of recording in a young lady's album a 'Don Zhuansky spisok', the Russian equivalent of Leporello's catalogue. His conquests may not quite have amounted to a thousand and three, and they did not extend over all the countries of Europe, but nevertheless Pushkin's character as a woman-lover, a flirt and a seducer became immediately apparent wherever he went. He pursued, persuaded, undressed, caressed and copulated with what must have run into dozens of women, no doubt giving and receiving much pleasure as he did so, and the imprint of this wide experience is on his love poetry.

It is most important to emphasise the sensual, rather than the emotional, attitude adopted by the poet towards his women. Emotional he was, in a superficial sense, and he does seem to have fallen in love in the traditional way on one or two occasions, but none of this should distract us from the essential point about his love matches — that they were physical affairs rather than indications of a search for spiritual solace or even, at a lower level, companionship. Pushkin's only companion throughout the whole of his life was literature. The basis for an appreciation of Pushkin's love poetry is the sure knowledge that, although much of it is addressed to identifiable persons, the addressee simply does not matter. Pushkin loved no individuals, he loved only love, women, their erogenous zones and their sexual parts. An incidental benefit arises from this awareness; it frees us from the dreadful burden of worrying about exactly which poem was addressed to which partner. That can be left to those historiographers who have been described, neatly if sardonically, by E.J. Simmons as 'agglomerators and separators.'[14]

To emphasise the actuality of Pushkin's sexual experience is not to suggest that the whole of his love poetry is salacious. Some of it is, and no one nowadays has to pretend to be immune from the vicarious pleasures offered by libidinous verses. (We shall consider these in a later chapter.) Fortunately, however, Pushkin's well-known capacity for restraint in poetical matters, together with the process of sublimation, has resulted in a large number of love lyrics which epitomise human experiences at a nobler level than that of mere love-play and coition. They gain spiritual sufficiency even as they are created from recognisably base materials. Uplifting in the non-priapic sense, they take the mind away from squalid reality and lead us sometimes to believe in purity, beauty, fulfilment and creativity such as we rarely experience as individuals but love to dream about.

Most of the earlier love lyrics do speak of physical longing. They were written by a young man brimming with red corpuscles and anxious to gain some relief by externalising his physical passion. At sixteen he wrote *Probuzhdeniye* (*Awakening*), a frivolous little piece in which he hopes love will continue to disturb his sleep with its visions and that he might die with them in mind before waking. By the age of nineteen he is in full flow. His poem *To Olga Masson* celebrates, on behalf of himself and his comrades, the venal charms of a notorious lady of pleasure. In *Dorida* he speaks of a fair-haired, blue-eyed beauty; even as he melts in her embraces after one bout of love-making his mind reaches out through the darkness to form a vision of another girl. The poem *Platonizm* is an argument intended to break down the defences of a reluctant partner; it culminates in a sharply angled reminder that Lida's beauty will not last for ever and, in any case, it wasn't created for her to enjoy alone. In 1820 he wrote *K **** (*To ****), a short poem in which he foresees days of parting and anguish ahead. Ah! then he would give anything to hear his dear one's voice or the rustle of her dress. The only thing that detracts from the apparent purity of these sentiments addressed to one of the Raevsky sisters is that five years later the same poem was handed to another girl, his namesake, Sofia Pushkina, with the same intent to persuade her of his undying affection. Also in 1820 he wrote *To Yur'ev* a few lines of congratulations on his friend's success in love with an appended comment on his own experience in the same field. Referring with some exaggeration to his own unprepossessing appearance and his ancestry ('Ugly as I am, of negro descent . . .') he ascribes his success with the fair sex to one thing, the 'shameless fury' of his desire. The following year Pushkin writes *Deva (The Maiden)*, five Alexandrine couplets dedicated to a virgin whose cold austerity remains unmoved by any number of pleas, and 'Moy drug, zabyty mnoy sledy minuvshikh let . . .' (My friend, the traces of forgotten years gone by . . .'), which, by contrast, celebrates the instinctive gaiety of his current partner who was created for pleasure and encourages her to live for that moment of bliss rather than indulge in raking over his past or worrying about their future.

All of these and the other early love poems, although they certainly contain inspired phrases, are by Pushkin's high standards, unexceptional. They have polish, they have enthusiasm and intelligence; they are, however, lacking in impassioned originality. The artist is too clearly in control. For all this talk of ardour he is writing *about* his passion and with some detachment. Where is the evidence that he has been compelled to write by the forces that move him or that he has something new to say on the subject? Perhaps the first sign of this comes in a poem of 1823, 'Prostish' li mne revnivyye mechty . . .?' ('Can you forgive me my jealous daydreams . . .?'), the first of a whole series of poems inspired by Amalia Riznich, all of which rise to new heights of expressiveness. The first twenty-five lines of this poem are conventional. The poet pours out his jealous feelings: why does his beloved act so freely towards other men? He goes on rather too long and comes near to wearying us with his lament. When he refers to her as 'my cruel friend!' this is hardly likely to stir us with its originality or freshness. Suddenly, however, a new passion seems to come over him and the poem ends with a run of a dozen lines which are unmistakably Pushkinian.

V neskromnyy chas mezh vechera i sveta
Bez materi, odna, poluodeta,
Zachem yego dolzhna ty prinimat'?
No ya lyubim . . . Hayedine so mnoyu
Ty tak nezhna! Lobzaniya tvoi
Tak plamenny! . . .
. . . .
No ya lyubim, tebya ya ponimayu.

Moy milyy drug, ne much' menya, molyu:
Ne znayesh' ty, kak sil'no ya lyublyu,
Ne znayesh' ty, kak tyazhko ya stradayu.

At an indiscreet hour mid evening and daybreak,
Without your mother there, alone, half-undressed,
Why must you receive him?
But I am loved . . . Alone with me
You are so tender! Your kisses
Are so ardent! . . .
But I am loved, and I understand you.
My dear friend, I beg you not to torment me:
You do not know how much I love you,
You do not know how terribly I suffer.

This is exciting poetry that truly recaptures the anguish experienced by the speaker. The light unstressed vowels make for an easy, pattering start, the later play of the consonants (especially the m's) add a textural richness and, most important of all, the staid iambic pentameters of the earlier part of the poem are wrenched apart by the vigour of Pushkin's repeated enjambement. The various repetitions, as well as making their obvious contribution to the system of sounds, reflect the pathetic insistence of the unhappy lover. Jealous affection has been movingly depicted and, however complex it might seem when some of the minutiae are called out for analysis, the whole process has been rather simple. This is particularly evident from the last two lines which correspond closely, in a manner which is characteristic of Pushkin, to the patterns of everyday Russian speech.

From now on most of the love poems have something striking about them and one or two attain to sublime heights. The poet, now maturing rapidly, begins to see love from new angles. Two poems which consider the end of a love affair in terms of apparent simplicity are 'Vse koncheno: mezh nami svyazi net . . .' ('It's all over: there is no contact between us . . .') (1824) and the all too well known 'Ya vas lyubil. Lyubov' yeshche byt' mozhet . . .' ('I loved you. Perhaps love still . . .') (1829). These exquisite miniatures are very similar indeed. They bid farewell, with gentle nostalgia rather than painful regret, to a love affair. The fires of love that once burned brightly on both sides have now gone out and both partners will proceed to new experiences. The separation is peaceful, dignified and characterised by the good will which is so typical of Pushkin's general attitude. In the first poem he says in his last lines

'You are still young: you have a lovely spirit and you shall be loved by many others.' In the second he ends with a similar sentiment: 'I loved you as sincerely and as tenderly as, God willing, you will be loved by another.' The tone is tender, the message is uncomplicated, the style is without embellishment. This is Russian at its most sparing, beautifully systematised into simple phrases which seem so close to what people (very civilised people) might say under the circumstances that Pushkin appears to have hit upon the right sentences by sheer good fortune. Sentences like:

Vse koncheno – ya slyshu tvoy otvet.

Ty moloda: dusha tvoya prekrasna,

No pust' ona vas bol'she ne trevozhit;
Ya ne khochu pechalit' vas nichem.

seem to have come straight from an ordinary speaker's mouth without the benefit of assistance from a qualified poet. What is so remarkable is that similar lines fell from Pushkin's pen with effortless regularity. Once again the only meaningful parallel is with the music of Mozart which began its spontaneous flow at a very early age and never ceased. In these two poems almost every line is in this rare category of unforced expressiveness. They are featherweight creations but it is their intention to be so and this is the source of their distinguished quality. Praise for such tiny masterpieces cannot be too high.

Let us return to what is, for Pushkin, the normal expression of his passion. In his twenties the poet, sure of his touch, manages repeatedly the perfect attunement of poetic resources to his amatory ends. In 1824 he writes 'Tumanskiy prav, kogda tak verno vas . . .' ('Tumansky is right in comparing you so aptly . . .'). The unknown female addressee is described as rainbow-like, rose-like and mercurial. Pushkin's shifting line-lengths, varying unpredictably between lines of four, five and six feet (all three of which appear in the first five lines) recreate the impression of light impermanence which is in the subject matter. At that same time he recalls another, more sublime, love from his recent past, Countess Vorontsova, in a poem which begins, 'Nenastnyy den' potukh; nenastnoy nochi mgla . . .' ('The stormy day is done; the gloom of the stormy night . . .'). Two different lines, the tetrameter and the hexameter, are used irregularly here too. To these are added another device, that of omission – rows of dots replace missing lines and the last line begins 'But if . . .'

and gets no further. This sort of thing was new to Russian literature, though its like had been seen before in Western Europe. The fragment, like the half-constructed building knowingly disguised to look like a ruin, was much to the taste of the Romantic artist, anxious to portray the world as asymmetrical, incomplete and unsatisfying. It can be effective, if not overdone, and here Pushkin achieves some measure of impact by breaking off at just the right moment.

Having begun by contemplating the bad weather he proceeds to the sad recollection of his lost, remote loved one. In a curious negative conceit he reflects upon the fact that no-one is with her, no one is weeping, no one is languishing before her, to no-one is she yielding her shoulders, her moist lips, her snow-white breasts . . . That is surely the point at which to break off, overcome with emotion and long-distance carnal desire, and the poet duly does so. The exercise is cleverly conducted but it is not likely that many people will be persuaded to accept this poem as a masterpiece by Pushkin's standards. The lovely sounds and carefully fostered atmosphere are vitiated by the self-conscious artificiality of the poem. It looks like a calculated attempt at the exploitation of new potential; moreover it reads like the work of a poseur. 'Nenastnyy den' . . .' should be read by anyone who wants to see Pushkin at his least Pushkinian, working things out to a preconceived formula (albeit a surprisingly irregular one) rather than allowing verses to flow from him as through a mere intermediary.

A poem of 1826, *Priznaniye* (*An admission*), comes nearer to what we have a right to expect. This is an excited and good-humoured statement of love, or, more properly, passion. The poet is so entranced by the beauty of his addressee (in this case Alexandra Osipova) that he says he does not need love, pity will do: just pretend and he will be happy! He disarms the critical spirit by admitting in mid-poem that his worshipping behaviour is childlike. So it is, in its simplicity, directness and exclamatory tone (the exclamation marks number nine). This poem will not be everyone's favourite but one can forgive a great deal of a poem which contains magical lines like the erotic-onomatopoeic

Kogda ya slyshu iz gostinnoy
Vash lyegkiy shag, il' plat'ya shum,
Il' golos devstvennyy, nevinnyy . . .

and the last resort exclamation of the conclusion, so musically expressed:

Akh, obmanut' menya ne trudno! . . .

Ya sam obmanyvat'sya rad!

Oh, I am easily deceived!
I'm happy to deceive myself!

These five lines alone promote this poem to the advanced category of
the instantly memorable. The last two are also worthy of inclusion in
the verbal arsenal of every aspiring seducer.

To the mid-1820s belong also the two 'Talisman' poems, one of
which has been mentioned earlier. They are similar in intent and effect.
The poet's hope in either case is that the warmth of his earlier relationship — with Countess Vorontsova with whom he may have achieved the
physical relationship which he so desired, but it seems unlikely — shall
be preserved in the future, whatever vicissitudes may come their way.
In particular the poet attempts to invoke upon himself the spirit of
good fortune. He wishes to direct his own destiny into happier ways,
and cannot see why this should not come about since he is bathed in
the benevolent blessing of the lovely donor of the ring. These poems,
'Khrani menya, moy talisman . . .' ('Keep me, my talisman . . .') (1825)
and *Talisman* (1827) are among Pushkin's most mysterious and musical
creations. Once again, successive lines from them are instantly memorable.

A mature love poem, of 1830, presents a good deal of interest. *Pazh
ili Pyatnadtsatyy God* (*The Page* or *Aged Fifteen*) is a deliberate recreation of adolescent infatuation, like that of Mozart's Cherubino. After
the word 'Fifteen' Pushkin adds 'C'est l'âge de Chérubin . . .'. This poem,
intrinsically, is not one of Pushkin's most inspired. It calls out for comparison with Cherubino's famous aria in Act I of *The Marriage of Figaro*
'Non so più cosa son, cosa faccio . . .' or perhaps his even more celebrated love song, 'Voi che sapete . . .' from Act II. In both cases the
comparison greatly favours Mozart and his librettist, the excellent Da
Ponte. Between them they infused the aria with the fluttering urgency
of a breathless, palpitating love-struck teenager and the song with a
delicate balance in keeping with the purity of the sentiments expressed
by an unspoilt lovelorn youth. Aria and song in their words and their
music stand beyond the reach of adverse criticism; they are conceived
and executed to the perfect standards of exquisite art. Ironically, the
lightness, aptness and elegance of these musical creations actually remind us of Pushkin at his own insouciant best. But he is not at his best
in *Pazh*. Here he has made mistakes. Everything in the poem is too long
and therefore too heavy: the title, the line (even though it is only a

tetrameter the great majority of the terminations are feminine (two-syllable) rhymes), the stanza (of five lines) and the poem itself (of six stanzas). It is, of course, well worth glancing at in order to observe the poet working below par. In any case, a comparison between Pushkin and Mozart is usually a useful exercise. The real reason for mentioning the poem here, however, is to draw attention to the very idea of Pushkin writing about Cherubino at this time of his life. At thirty, he is now twice the lad's age, but he still finds his predicament an interesting one. This should remind us of our starting point. Pushkin was in love with the idea of love and its sexual repercussions. In these matters he never matured beyond the stage of a Cherubino.

Actually, this simple idea, although a good general guide to Pushkin's erotic attitude, is something of an exaggeration. In his art, if not in his personal life, he did show some development. This can be seen from the attitude struck in one of his latest love poems, addressed to the woman who had recently become his wife, Natalya Goncharova. In 'Net, ya ne dorozhu myatezhnym naslazhden'em . . .' ('No, I do not value stormy pleasures . . .') (1831) Pushkin speaks of a different kind of physical love. He bids farewell to the writhings, the hot breath and exclamatory enjoyment of his former co-participants in the game of love, he refuses to be discouraged by the coolness or the embarrassment of his new wife, he swears that he actually prefers her less enthusiastic manner and the longer process of arousing her to enjoyment by patient encouragement. This is a poem of tender sentiment which will not leave the reader un-impressed or unmoved. It is, nevertheless, a sham. Pushkin's protestations in this poem are as lacking in sincerity as any of his earlier outpourings of undying love to some transient beauty. The poem itself is, in any case, put together with the same deliberate patience and conscious artistry that its writer intends to apply to his wife's body. His laudable attentiveness is not crowned with rich artistic rewards; one can only suppose that in his real life he failed likewise to achieve the intended pay-off in terms of domestic happiness.

Some months before he had written *Madona* (*The Madonna*) (1830), a poem also dedicated to Natalya, similar in tone and achievement to 'Net, ya ne dorozhu . . .' but without any sexual undertones. (She was then only his fiancée.) This is a curious piece; much may be said about it, for and against. It is both stylised and imaginative, both mechanical and inspired. The message is simplicity itself. The poet states that he has never longed for rich paintings by the great masters — his simple room would be adequately furnished with an image of the Madonna and the Saviour. Now his wish has been granted; the Lord has sent him

Natalya, 'the purest model of the purest loveliness'. Pushkin has chosen a severe formal pattern for this solemn subject, the sonnet, but with hidden variations. The line has been extended by a foot to the length of a hexameter, the rhyme scheme of this apparently Italianate model has been pleasantly distorted (aBBaaBaBccDeDe) and there are several defiant challenges to the authority of the caesura and the line-end. Thus, although the poem sits in majesty on the page, looking and sounding full of noble sentiments, some of the grandeur has been properly subverted so that we know we are dealing with earthlings rather than disembodied spirits. Pushkin even takes time out in his opening quatrain to poke the finger of fun at, of all people, art critics. In what amounts to the most memorable two lines of the poem, speaking of the great pictures he does not want to own, he suggests that people who go in for that sort of thing do so

In order that the visitor might marvel at them superstitiously,
Listening to the grave judgement of the experts.

This poem is a cleverly wrought work of art which deserves a close reading. What seems to detract ultimately from its achievement are the residual traces of artificiality. It is artificiality of an accomplished order but, aside from the fact that unity is put at risk by that digressive opening quatrain, the real impression is that of a skilful artist, like a court poet, giving a command performance. There is no doubt that Pushkin can do this sort of thing more than adequately at the drop of a hat. If this poem, and its like, had been the best he could produce we might have been grateful for its existence. However, our awareness of what he wrote on other occasions, inspired from within rather than prompted by a sense of duty, must colour our attitude to a relatively modest achievement such as *Madona*. Poor Natalya does seem to have been incapable not only of appreciating her husband's poetry but even of inspiring him to go on producing it at the highest level. From time to time Alexander has felt obliged to use his acknowledged skills with her in mind and she, no doubt, was pleased with the result. Posterity sees the position more clearly. To put it bluntly, of all the women to whom Pushkin addressed his love poems Natalya was perhaps the least inspiring.

No better illustration of this could be provided than by consideration of the poem beginning 'Dlya beregov otchizny dal'noy . . .' ('For the shores of a far-off land . . .') which was written in between *Madona* and 'Net, ya ne dorozhu . . .', with another woman in mind. The other woman was almost certainly Amalia Riznich who, unlike Natalya, always

seems to have brought out the best in Pushkin. He speaks of their parting and separation, her death in a distant land (Italy), the disappearance
of her beauty and her sufferings simultaneously and the kiss that she
still owes him, for which he still waits. The emotions are patently sincere, though no doubt they are linked with personal nostalgia for times
gone by which, however troubled, were happier ones. There is not the
slightest trace of artificiality or effort. With fluency and an easy grace
Pushkin treats us to some of his most moving lines, musical in manner,
nevertheless painfully direct because of the simple words chosen for
them, lines such as these from the second stanza:

> No ty, ot gor'kogo lobzan'ya
> Svoi usta otorvala
> . . . .
> Pod nebom vechno golubym
> V teni oliv, lyubvi lobzan'ya
> My vnov', moy drug, soyedinim.

> But you wrenched your lips away
> From our bitter embrace
> . . . .
> Beneath an eternally blue sky
> Under the shade of the olive trees, in our kisses of love
> We shall once more be joined, my darling.

John Bayley describes this poem, not without some justification –
though it is essentially a matter of opinion – as 'the finest of Pushkin's
love poems'.[14] He goes on to express the view that 'the simple vocabulary
of blue skies is as moving as a popular song, and for that reason begins
to generalise a unique experience into that of all lovers.'[15] The process
of universalisation certainly does occur in this poem. All Russians know
it and it is frequently quoted. I have heard it recited by a guide in the
house where Pushkin was taken to die in St Petersburg and, although
Russians tend to invest their reading with a superfluous sentimentality,
the capacity of this poem to survive that unnecessary ordeal and move
the audience was unmistakable.

'Dlya beregov . . .' is usually linked with another putative Riznich
poem, of 1826, beginning 'Pod nebom golubym strany svoyey rodnoy
. . .' ('Under the light blue sky of her homeland . . .'), which is another
thing of beauty, but quite different in tone. Again it refers to the death
of a loved one but, on this occasion, the poet is plunged into a state of

philosophical shock, so powerful is the impact of the awful news that she is dead. 'Where is the agony? Where is the love? . . .' The poet loved her so much that his mind refuses to react in the normal way; it rejects the very concept that such loveliness has perished for ever and it will not celebrate the loss in the time-honoured way, with tears and suffering. The coldness which he feels cannot possibly be indifference, not in someone who had loved this woman recently with 'an ardent spirit, such gravity and strain, such tenderness and enervating languor, such madness and such torment!' To say that he now feels nothing does not convey even the slightest impression of callousness. It is a dramatic, though oblique statement of continuing love. Both of these poems outclass the ones dedicated to Natalya by a clear margin.

Pushkin's best known love poem has been kept to the last. The lyric addressed to A.P. Kern beginning 'Ya pomnyu chudnoye mgnoven'ye . . .' ('I recall a wondrous moment . . .') has become, for good or ill, a classic. It is almost too well known, suffering the danger of slipping into banality through sheer over-familiarity. Yet there can be no doubting its excellence. The poem has an ironic history behind it. When Pushkin first met Anna Kern, in 1819, he was entranced by her but he soon lost all interest and was eventually to refer to her as 'a Babylonian whore'. The collapse of his regard for her, and her power to enchant or inspire him, and the earthiness of his ultimate assessment of her value stand in sharp contrast to the lofty sentiments expressed in the poem. The simple tri-partite structure tells of a first meeting at which the poet was powerfully affected by his encounter with a 'fleeting vision, a genius of pure beauty', then of a period of separation during which he forgot her and lapsed into sterile indifference, then finally of a second meeting at which she re-inspired him and awakened him to a new life. Each section is given precisely two stanzas of Pushkin's favourite iambic tetrameters. All the stanzas are end-stopped and the whole poem has a tidy preciseness about it which is in keeping with the simplicity of the message to be conveyed. The message is that love can transform one's life and make one look upon the world from an entirely new, positive angle. In the event, however, the poem is more complicated than it seems. Its appeal is indirect rather than frontal. It is based upon an intricate series of repetitions. Sounds, words, whole phrases repeat themselves in new patterns, weaving a beguiling web of euphony which represents in musical terms the strange fascination exercised by a lovely woman over a man. She can excite, inspire, energise and animate him but first she has to *enchant* him. She can then make his world seem as complete, rounded, satisfying and perfect as the last stanza of the poem itself which is probably the most perfect example of resolution anywhere in Pushkin's *œuvre*.

The achievement of the last stanza is an amazing feat and it deserves consideration because it is typical of Pushkin at his most natural and his most inspired. He has strained the resources of the Russian language to their utmost and – seemingly by a stroke of luck – got away with it. The penultimate stanza of the poem ends with a repetition, the last two lines exactly repeating the last two of the opening stanza:

> Kak mimoletnoye viden'ye
> Kak geniy chistoy krasoty.

Now comes the virtuosic development of the art of repetition. In stanza four he has used no less than five abstract nouns to show what was lacking in his life when the 'genius of pure beauty' was absent – there was no deity (bozhestvo), no inspiration (vdokhnoven'ye), no tears (sleza), no life (zhizn'), no love (lyubov'). These nouns are of one, two or four syllables; three are feminine, two are neuter. They are all governed by the preposition 'bez' which commands them all to change form by altering their ending to the genitive case (in one case genitive plural). A change like this in Russian has formidable consequences in terms of shifting stress and the addition or subtraction of syllables. They all fit nicely, however, into the last two lines of that fourth stanza, thus:

> Bez bozhestva, bez vdokhnoven'ya
> Bez slez, bez zhizni, bez lyubvi.

But it is surely not possible to take those same nouns, without the preposition, put them all back into the nominative case (keeping the tears in the plural, of course) and still make them fit into two lines of verse? Pushkin achieves this with only the tiniest sleight of hand, merely changing the order of two of the words in the last line:

> I bozhestvo, i vdokhnoven'ye,
> I zhizn', i slezy, i lyubov'.

He seems to have hit upon this possibility by a sheer fluke. Anyone who doubts the difficulty should try to replicate the experiment with any five other nouns. The rules of the game insist that both formulations must result in a natural sequence of words, an utterance as apparently spontaneous as a piece of cultivated prose, yet they must be calculated to conform to the accompanying demands of rhythm and even rhyme.

The intricacy and mechanical soundness of Pushkin's construction stand in an inverse relationship to the easy running of the words as pronounced. It is as Bryusov says; one simply does not notice how complex and difficult the structures are which underpin Pushkin's apparently carefree verses. This is not the only repetition or interesting device in *K A.P. Kern* but it points the way to an understanding of the massive impact this poem has had on the reading public. It is one of Pushkin's most brilliant formal achievements, linked to a lucid, optimistic statement of the effects of beauty and love upon the lucky individual who comes across them. Good luck to this excellent poem; it deserves every ounce of its continuing success.

These are some of Pushkin's love poems. They range more widely than one might expect, treating love from different angles and at different stages. They possess an urgent sense of reality which speaks of a poet who not only knew his subject closely, by dint of long personal experience of it, but actually preferred the reality to any vicarious pleasures obtainable by writing about it. In an early poem, written at the age of seventeen, he wrote

But work is cold and hollow:
A poem can never equal
A smile on sensuous lips!
(*To Turgenev*, (1817))

Pushkin never outgrew this laudable sentiment. Because of it all his poems, and not least his love lyrics, belong to the real world and offer to all his readers a reflection of experience which they will find instantly recognisable. Nevertheless, most readers would claim that, at its best, Pushkin's love poetry reaches sublimity. There are moments when his music combines with and enhances a sudden new perception of the poignant effect of love, or of sexual union, and when these occur he attains the heights of artistic achievement which parallel those instants of ecstasy or enlightenment which make their way occasionally, if all too rarely, into ordinary lives. Certainly there are half a dozen of Pushkin's love lyrics which must count among the happiest creations that have ever been produced by the fertile language of the Russian people. This celebration of femininity is something from which that people will continue to draw sympathetic satisfaction and substantial pride.

The Isolation of the Poet

Much is to be learned about Pushkin's poetry from what he actually wrote about the art itself, not so much in his many theoretical pronouncements in prose on the subject as in the fairly large number of poems devoted to it. From 'Zima . . .' we saw how he placed great emphasis on the coming together of sounds. Other poems repeat this idea and give us also a more rounded view of how Pushkin saw the function of the poet and his own priorities among the various possibilities open to him.

The overall view which emerges from a couple of dozen poems devoted to this subject is complex but consistent. We see the poet's trade depicted as arduous and lonely. He is given little or no support from those around him; any help or approval will come as a pleasant surprise. He will have to do battle against indifference, hostility and the philistine, utilitarian hordes which make up the bulk of society. There will be long periods of alienation, low inspiration, almost despair. Nevertheless the whole business is worthwhile. Poetry offers amusement and, at the best of times, an uplifting of the spirits amounting to ecstasy. In any case, for a born poet participation is inevitable. Finally, there is a clear message personally applicable at least to Alexander Pushkin. The writing of poetry leads to a kind of spiritual detachment from everyone else, particularly from one's enemies; that in turn produces a sense of freedom, even if personal circumstances suggest the opposite, and only through a sense of that freedom — the ultimate kind — is any form of happiness obtainable. These poems, then, taken together, amount to a reaffirmation of the strength of literature, a point of view which needs to be argued through to victory in all societies but which in the Russian context has often been a matter of life and death. Pushkin's line of thought in this field is part of the answer to those who would have us believe he is no more than a clever entertainer.

We shall not spend a lot of time looking at all of these poems individually. For one thing, as one might expect from poems which involve themselves with polemics, the majority of them are simply not in the front rank of Pushkin's achievement as a poet. One or two of them, however, most certainly are and they will have to be discussed in some detail; *Prorok* (*The Prophet*) (1826), *Poet* (*The Poet*) (1827) and *Osen'* (*Autumn*) (1833) are obvious candidates.

Let us summarise one or two of the arguments presented by some of the poems devoted to the subject of poetry itself. One of the most straightforward — and depressing — statements made by Pushkin in this field comes in a rather well known poem of 1824, *Razgovor knigo-prodavtsa s poetom* (*Conversation between bookseller and poet*). The dialogue is one-sided. The bookseller insists on the standards of the material world and blames his own age for being mercenary though most other ages, our own certainly included, have been as bad. The poet explains his sense of alienation and disappointment. The only thing left for him is the knowledge of his own freedom. The bookseller brings him down to earth. 'You can't sell inspiration; a manuscript you can sell.' Utter defeat for the poet, who hands over his manuscript and is prepared to discuss terms. To compound the failure Pushkin employs an unusual device at the end of the poem. After 192 lines of verse shared between the speakers he sets the poet's last short speech down *in prose*.

In *Poet i Tolpa* (*The Poet and the Crowd*) (1828) the argument goes the other way. Scorning the rabble the poet proclaims the ultimate free-dom of poetry which must always stand above the utilitarian demands continually pressed upon it. The closing quatrain is a splendid affirma-tion of this glorious truth, justifiably famous, though subsequently ignored by large numbers of Russian poets especially after 1917:

Not for worldly turmoil,
Not for profit, not for fighting battles
Are we born — but for inspiration,
For sweet sounds and for prayers.

The poet knows he cannot count on much support from outside. In *Otvet anonimu* (*Reply to an anonymous writer*) he thanks an unknown commentator who has given him encouragement and cannot resist cast-ing a passing jibe at the rabble. 'The crowd looks coldly on the poet,' he says, 'treating him like a travelling clown.'

The obvious solution is to turn away from the common herd. It will then be possible to proceed alone or to associate with the small frater-nity of fellow poets to which Pushkin refers in an address *To Yazykov* (1824). 'From ancient times,' he begins, 'a delightful alliance has united poets among themselves.' They are different from the writers of prose. With amused hauteur he tells the prose-writer in *Prozaik i Poet* (1825) that he is wasting his time — any of his messages can be sharpened up and made more effective by poetry. Poetry, moreover, will provide solace when the spirits are low. Adapting Chénier in a poem of 1827, 'Bliz mest, gde tsarstvuyet Venetsiya zlataya' ('Near places where golden Venice reigns'), he compares himself to a gondolier singing for sheer pleasure rather than with some specific aim in mind and says that he too is prepared to go on singing 'without any response' and thinking out his secret verses by way of consolation for the ill-fortune he is suffering. This poem is, incidentally, well worth reading aloud. Pushkin's sound effects are working well and he enjoys playing with sonorous proper names – 'Rinal'da, Godfreda, Erminiyu poyet.'

Sometimes, however, even poetry is a let-down. In 'Rifma, zvuchnaya podruga . . .' ('Rhyme, sweet-sounding companion . . .') (1828) he speaks of her desertion of him and the awful feeling that she will never return. Even as he writes, however, you can see the spirit returning. This turns out to be a light-hearted piece; despite its apparently negative intent it speaks volumes about the capacity of the poet and his sweet-sounding companion to work together in harmony. The inevitability of his continuing to write, and without expectation of reward, is summed up in *Ekho* (*The Echo*) (1831). It is the task of the echo to receive nature's signals and give them back to the world without expecting any further response or acknowledgement: the poet's task is a similar one. Isolation seems to be his inevitable lot but this is no bad thing. If isolation is the price of independence it is a price worth paying.

In 1830 Pushkin composed a noble and defiant self-addressed sonnet, *Poetu* (*To the poet*). It begins with an outright rejection of the need for a poet to court popularity: 'Poet! Set no store by popular affection . . .' Later we read one of the most triumphant assertions of poetic independence: 'You are a King: live alone. Go your own free way . . .' This road, although beset with dangers, leads after all to nothing less than happiness. Six years later, shortly before his death Pushkin returns to the same theme in *Iz Pindemonti* (*From Pindemonti*) (1836) which includes the enjoinder: 'Never be accountable to anyone, serve and oblige no one but yourself . . . This is happiness!' There is a nice irony behind the title. This poem has nothing whatever to do with Pindemonti. It was a tossup whether his name or that of Alfred Musset (sic) should be appended to the poem as a device of obfuscation to delude the censor. Plus ça change, plus c'est la même chose. A well-known Soviet ballad singer, himself no stranger to persecution and the question of independence, used the self-same device for one of his songs only a few years ago. He would be amused at the idea that Pushkin's work, because of its supreme artistry, is sometimes held to be devoid of ideas.

Most of the poems so far discussed in this section belong to the middle or lower range of achievement within Pushkin's work as a whole. Even here, however, there are poems of real and undisputed excellence. *The Poet* was written in 1827 and soon came to enjoy a popularity from which it has never declined. It is a splendid evocation of the powers of inspiration which, from time to time, overwhelm the poet and bear him off on the wings of poetic creativity. The *zvukopis'* of this poem is its outstanding feature, but this is assisted by hidden devices within the rhyme-scheme which have an effect out of all proportion to their apparent slightness. The first section, which depicts the poet in the doldrums, deserted by his muse, consists of eight lines strictly alternating their rhymes and rather monotonously using one rhyme for all four masculine endings (Apollon/pogruzhen/son/on). In the second section of twelve thoroughly excited lines, when inspiration seizes the poet and sweeps him away, not only would such unimaginative rhyming be unthinkable — there is actually a need for something original and positive from the rhymes. It comes in line eleven. The first ten lines have all alternated their rhymes and there can be no doubt that the eye, subconsciously searching out the underlying pattern, expects the alternate rhyme here, that is something to rhyme with the word 'glagol' which ends line nine. No such thing. What looked like an alternating quatrain is dramatically converted into an envelope one by the intrusion of the complex and beautiful word 'vstrepenetsya' which rhymes with the preceding line (kosnetsya). This is at the very point where the meaning of the text is 'The poet's spirit *suddenly starts up* . . .' It is the turning point of the poem in a double sense, the form exactly matching the meaning.

Even in the ponderous process of describing this trick of form it seems necessary to apologise for making so much of it and taking so long. Surely the poet cannot have decided consciously to employ this mechanical device. Need we bother to illuminate it at all? The answer is that the mystery behind the universally acknowledged success achieved by Pushkin in poem after poem is often ascribable to a number of formal devices working together, instinctively invented and conjoined by the poet, and that some exposure of them from time to time helps in some small measure to explain the achievement which is otherwise unquantifiable.

We must resist the temptation to indulge in a protracted analysis of the superb and celebrated poem entitled *Osen'* (*Autumn*) which, as everyone agrees, is an example of Pushkin at the peak of his powers. The poem, which consists of eleven numbered octaves and the first halfline of an ostensibly uncompleted twelfth, appears to be about the season named in the title. Indeed Pushkin does tell us about the seasons — which ones he prefers, dislikes and so on. But the reader is in for a surprise. When he comes to the autumn season we are treated to a brief recitation of the poet's activities before suddenly, in line three of the

tenth stanza, the secret is revealed: 'And poetry awakens within me.'
What is left of the poem is given over to a powerful description of the
effect upon the poet of this sudden onset of inspiration. Then we realise
that all the earlier stanzas, captivating though they are in their own
right, were nothing more or less than a preamble to the real subject
matter: poetry itself.

This poem is so rich in achievement that it almost deserves the extended treatment which we have accorded to 'Zima . . .' Suffice it to
indicate one or two of the more striking features. Stanza VI, devoted to
the late autumn, is Pushkin at his purest:

Kak eto ob'yasnit'? Mne nravitsya ona,
Kak, veroyatno, vam chakhotochnaya deva
Poroyu nravitsya. Na smert' osuzhdena,
Bednyazhka klonitsya bez ropota, bez gneva.
Ulybka na ustakh uvyanuvshikh vidna;
Mogil'noy propasti ona ne slyshit zeva;
Igrayet na litse yeshche bagrovyy tsvet.
Ona zhiva yeshche segodnya, zavtra net.

How can this be explained? It appeals to me
In just the way that a consumptive girl perhaps
Sometimes might appeal to you. Condemned to death,
Poor child, she droops uncomplaining, with no resentment.
A smile is seen on her fading lips;
She is not aware of the yawning abyss of the grave;
A crimson hue still plays upon her face.
Today she is alive — tomorrow she is gone.

There are at least two remarkable forces at work in this stanza, one
of them run-of-the-mill Pushkin, the other, for him, a rarity. On the one
hand the conversational fluency of the first two-and-a-half lines, here
seen exemplified as well as anywhere else with the line-ends and caesuras
treated in cavalier fashion as the verses float past them, is precisely what
we expect from Pushkin. We have seen several examples of it elsewhere.
On the other hand, the extended metaphor employed to give us an impression of the late autumn takes us quite by surprise. Pushkin was no
great believer in metaphor. His predecessors in prose and poetry, at
home and abroad, had so overused it that literature had moved up into
an ethereal realm of conceits and circumlocutions. His true purpose in
literature was to bring it down again to the real world, peopled with and

to be enjoyed by real men, women and children. As a result of this, when he does turn to a metaphor it bursts into his verse with devastating effect, so much so that the moments acquire an unforgettable quality. The metaphor of the deserted house, representing Lensky's corpse in Chapter Six of *Yevgeniy Onegin* and the several metaphors used to depict the River Neva in *The Bronze Horseman* are in this category. The sad beauty of the cheerful, dying, consumptive girl in this stanza is guaranteed to linger in the memory. So, incidentally, is the other extended metaphor used to end this poem. The image of the sleeping galleon suddenly aroused to put on full sail and speed away strongly supports the poet's impression of being borne up and away by the sudden arrival of inspiration. More could be said about *Osen'* but the poem must now be left to speak for itself, preferably, once again, through being read aloud in Russian.

Prorok (*The Prophet*) (1826) is one of the best known Russian poems. It contains the grandest and most sonorous lines ever written by Pushkin and no anthology would be complete without it. The danger in presenting this poem eagerly to poetry-lovers approaching Pushkin for the first time is that they might imagine this impressive purple poetry to be typical of his manner. The only quality in the poem which is typical of Pushkin is its simplicity. Both the message of the poem and the striking devices employed in it are direct and uncomplicated. In the middle of it no less than twelve out of fourteen successive lines begin with the word 'And . . .' This device may rejoice in the grand title of multiple anaphora but it remains one of utter constructional simplicity. The other obvious feature about the poem is its use of magnificently archaic language. In English we may sense the full flavour of this by comparing any ringing passage from the version of the Old Testament in the King James Bible with any of the seemingly squalid modern translations. *The Prophet* is written in 'King James' Russian from first to last. This is appropriate since it tells of the conversion of an ordinary mortal into a prophet of the Old Testament type. The parable is a powerful one. A six-winged seraphim appears before the spiritually impoverished victim and, to the shuddering of the heavens and the movement of the beasts of the sea and the plants in the valley, he replaces his tongue by the forked one of a serpent and his heart by a burning coal. Then the voice of the Lord speaks to him:

'Arise, O prophet, see and hear,
Be filled with my will,
Go forth over the seas and the dry land
Inflaming the hearts of men with the word.'

This is what it seems, a depiction, in allegorical terms, of the inspiration of a prophet. Much of it is borrowed, somewhat garbled, from Isaiah, VI. From what we know of Pushkin and his work it is self-evident that he has in mind another kind of seer and communicator, the poet. This expression of the poet's function in human society, couched as it is in terms of such grandeur, is entirely in keeping with Pushkin's opinion of his calling. From spiritual poverty, through great travail to new, noble heights of perception involving a duty to pass on one's private visions to others through the magic of human speech — this is no more than the story of a poet's personal epiphany. *Prorok* is a unique achievement. Its towering stature has impressed generations of readers and will continue to do so. There are those who consider it to be 'perhaps the greatest of his short poems'.[17] It is certainly the grandest but its most important role is to demonstrate the outer limits rather than the central body of Pushkin's genius.

A few weeks before his death, weary of living continually in proud isolation and filled with ugly premonitions, Pushkin wrote his own epitaph. He took for his model Horace's *Exegi Monumentum* (*Odes* Book III, xxx) which had been translated into Russian by Lomonosov and already adapted by Derzhavin. Pushkin's version is a further adaptation, personalised, democratised and much improved as a piece of poetry. It preserves the grandeur of all its predecessors, as may be seen from its opening line:

Ya pamyatnik sebe vozdvig nerukotvornyy

I have raised up to myself a monument not built by hands

The choice of the word 'nerukotvornyy' is significant. It replaces two words used by Derzhavin 'chudesnyy, vechnyy' ('wondrous, eternal') by one, and one which is stronger, more imaginative and more euphonious. Also, once again in a manner that has the air of a happy chance, it raises the possibility of introducing as a rhyme two lines later the word 'nepokornyy', 'unsubmissive' which is just the epithet which Pushkin will want to use about himself. Altogether a happy choice. There are further touches of individualisation. The fourth line of each stanza is shortened from a hexameter to a tetrameter and, unusually for such a formal piece, the third stanza, as well as introducing us to some very low born people such as the wild Tungus and the nomadic Kalmuck (who will hear of the poet's achievements) actually does so by means of an equally wild enjambement separating adjective from noun.

The five stanzas of this splendid poem tell of the poet's confidence that he will outlive the tsars, gain immortality and extend his reputation, that he has been a man of good will and a defender of freedom. The final stanza enjoins the muse to listen only to the dictates of the Almighty, to ignore equally slanders and flattery and not to take issue with fools. The clear inference is that this is what Pushkin claims to have done. Perhaps the key stanza is the fourth one, which is ironic since it is a substitution for something much more polemical which appeared in the original. John Bayley considers this stanza to be a let-down because of its sudden localisation of the interest from the general to the personal and particular.[18] This is questionable on two counts. First, Pushkin's predecessors seem to plunge into personalised accounts at this stage in the poem without any loss of dignity or impact. Second, the original version included a mention of Radishchev, one of the first Russians to suffer for the radical cause; the specific naming of an individual — the only one in the poem — would certainly have localised the poem. As it is, the clear references to the tsar and the hostile critics who tormented Pushkin, unidentified by name, are allowed to blur into a general picture of those forces which are antipathetic to the poet, not merely in 1836, but at all times. The poem is at one and the same time noble and democratic, specifically directed and universalised, and the fourth stanza makes a useful contribution as it stands. More than that, it states overtly two of Pushkin's aims as a man and a poet. There is the forthright and well known proclamation of his dedication to the cause of freedom, but before that a less assertive, apparently casual statement that he has always used his gifts to arouse 'kind feelings'.

There is much more to this remark than meets the eye and it is fitting that it should be included in this poet's epitaph. There is no poet who better deserves the description of 'a man of good will'. Unafraid to look life's nastiness in the eye, to think about and dwell upon it, he nevertheless conducts his poetic affairs with an irrepressible optimism, wanting to believe in the good and the noble, encouraging us all to do so and, in any case, convinced by his own sheer vitality of the inestimable value of human life. He is wholesome and reinvigorating. He could well have claimed, as Baudelaire did later in the century, 'You have given me your mud and I have transformed it into gold.' 'Kind feelings' are precisely what he does arouse in his readers and a reference to them must certainly be inscribed on his monument — as indeed they are in this stanza:

I dolgo budu tem lyubezen ya narodu,
Chto chuvstva dobryye ya liroy probuzhdal,

Chto v moy zhestokiy vek vosslavil ya svobodu
I milost' k padshim prizyval.

Long shall I be loved by the people
For having used my lyre to arouse kind feelings
And for exalting freedom in my age of cruelty
And calling for mercy on the fallen.

The Poet of Freedom

Pushkin's commitment to the concept of liberty was neither an idle
fancy nor a useful idea to latch on to at the end of his career. It was
something in which he had a genuine interest from his schooldays to
his death and to which he returned continually — perhaps the most important preoccupation of his whole life and career. A Russian observer,
writing a century and a half after Pushkin's heyday, claims that 'Poetry,
love and freedom were fused in his mind into a general entity',[19] which,
although saying a good deal, is scarcely an exaggeration. He probably
wrote more poems devoted in one way or another to the idea of freedom, the restrictions placed upon it and its converse, oppression or
persecution, than to either poetry or love. The *Dictionary of Pushkin's
Language* records almost three hundred uses of the word 'svoboda'
(freedom) and its cognates. In addition there are 133 uses of 'volya'
(and 'vol'nyy') in the specific sense of 'freedom' rather than 'will'.[20]
We do not, however, propose to consider this aspect of his work with
the same degree of attention because, with some few exceptions, it is
overtly didactic and therefore artistically imperfect by the standards
set by the poet himself.

The labyrinth of Pushkin's political poetry is quite complicated
though it is by no means impossible to find a consistent way through
it. Broadly speaking, he began, as a boy and young man, with a clear-
eyed if rather naive view of political freedom, he set himself against the
rule of autocracy and supported radical opinion even to the extent of
endorsing regicide and revolution. Then in middle life (which means in
his twenties) he became disillusioned, not with the basic ideal of freedom for everyone but with the possibility of creating it. At the same
time he found it necessary to compromise with authority and to placate
those who were looking over his shoulder at every word he wrote. Fin
ally, his disappointment turned, in political terms, into something near
to despair and he retreated into a broader, actually more meaningful,

concept of freedom, involving spiritual independence, even at the cost of personal isolation. There is nothing inconsistent in this line of development, given the circumstances of his life in day-to-day terms, and, in fact, he emerges triumphant, with his commitment to liberty intact. His service to the cause of democracy, although it varied from active participation in his early years to ideological support during his mature period, is considerable.

In Pushkin's youth, as one might expect, his commitment was passionate and practical. He was never admitted to the inner circles of the radical movement, as is well known, because of his flippant, unreliable attitude, but he served the cause in such a way, and to such an extent that shortly before his twentieth birthday he was compelled to set off for a period of internal exile in the southern parts of the Russian Empire. And it could have been much worse. His friends Zhukovsky, Karamzin, and others had saved him from a more cruel fate in Siberia.

Pushkin's earliest democratic poems are remarkably well written for a youngster but they possess more passion than artistic achievement. *Litsiniyu (To Licinius)* (1815) is an enthusiastic, if rather wordy, tribute to the man who introduced democracy to Rome and it was followed within a couple of years by *Vol'nost': Oda (Freedom: an Ode)* (1817) which claimed audaciously that no-one, not even the Tsar, was above the law. This poem was circulated only by hand and by letter but it got as far as the Tsar himself and was one of the reasons behind Pushkin's exile. His seditious works also included the satirical *Skazki: Noël (Fairy Tales: Noël)* (1818) and the outspoken *Derevnya (The Countryside)* (1819) which depicted rural life as a haven ruined by the system of serfdom which was everywhere observable: 'Gaunt slavery drags itself down the furrows of the implacable landowner.'

His enthusiasm for the radical cause showed no early signs of diminishing. On the contrary, his messages become all the more pointed in the early 1820s. *Kinzhal (The Dagger)* (1821) and *Docheri Karageorgiya (To Karadjordje's Daughter)* (1820) spoke out in favour of assassination as a political weapon. *André Chénier* (1825) spends its 185 lines in a vituperative rejection of autocracy and culminates in such a proud statement of the poet's involvement in the radical cause, expressed with such vehemence, that for a moment one could almost believe that it was he, rather than the tsar, who wielded all the power. Meanwhile his satirical poems continued with *Ty i Ya (You and I)* (1825), addressed to Alexander I, and his splendid tribute to Napoleon (*Napoleon*) (1821) was viewed with mixed feelings by the authorities: it acknowledged Russia's achievements but was clearly a celebration of Napoleon's anti-autocratic

activities throughout Europe. In 1823 he wrote several poems on the
subject of political freedom. 'Zaviduyu tebe, pitomets morya smelyy
. . .' ('I envy you, brave foster-son of the sea . . .') confuses this general
idea with Pushkin's own sense of constriction and harassment; he ends
with the telling remark, 'O ocean free, I greet you.' A neat little poem
entitled *Ptichka* (*Little bird*) celebrates the Russian peasant tradition
of giving a caged bird its freedom on Easter Sunday. The symbolism is,
and was, rather obvious but the censor was effectively distracted by the
following misleading note appended by Pushkin's publisher: 'This refers
to those benefactors of mankind who use their prosperity to bail innocent people, debtors, etc., out of prison.'

Pushkin's political outlook underwent severe changes in the mid
1820s. He began to record his disappointment at the success of the
radical movement which was naturally compounded by the rout of the
Decembrists for whom he nurtured the profoundest sympathies. Dis-
illusionment conditions what is perhaps the ugliest little poem he ever
wrote, 'Kto, volny, vas ostanovil . . .?' (O waves, who has stopped you
. . .?') (1823). It contains the despairing line: 'O storm, symbol of freedom, where are you?' and, more shamefully, the disagreeable line:

Vzygrayte, vetry, vzroyte vody

which is, acoustically, overdoing things to an unforgivable extent.

In 'Svobody seyatel' pustynnyy . . .' ('Remote disseminator of freedom . . .') (1823) he regrets the lack of response to liberal ideas and
castigates the insensitivity of the masses and then, moving into 1824,
continues the same theme in 'Nedvizhnyy strazh dremal na tsarstvennom
poroge . . .' ('The motionless sentry was dozing on the tsar's threshold
. . .') whereas in *Chaadayevu* (*To Chaadayev*) he rues his own collapse
into inactivity: 'But now my heart, subdued by the storms, knows idleness, peace and quiet . . .'

Pushkin's connection with the Decembrists was of long duration.
Several of the preceding political poems were written with the future
revolutionaries in mind and much prized by them. After the débâcle
in 1825 and the subsequent executions and sentences of exile early in
1826 Pushkin remained faithful to the cause and continued to address
poems to his revolutionary friends. A businesslike little poem entitled
Akvilon (*Aquilon* (*The North Wind*)) is dated uncertainly as 1824 but
Soviet editors doubt this and claim that it must be a post-December
poem.[21] There can be little doubt that they are correct. The poem refers
to the destruction of a mighty oak in a recent storm and the continuing

enmity with which the North wind now lashes even the reeds and piles up the ominous clouds. In a Russian context, even as early as Pushkin, this kind of symbolism is immediately transparent and must surely refer to the rout of the Decembrists. In *Mordvinovu* (*To Mordvinov*) (1826) Pushkin gives voice to public praise for the one sane, brave and intelligent jurist who lent his support to the condemned men. Two celebrated poems have cemented Pushkin's relationship with the Decembrists. In 'Vo glubine sibirskikh rud . . .' ('In the depths of the Siberian mines . . .') he assures the exiles that they are not forgotten and they will soon be free. Some weeks earlier he had written *Stansy* (*Stanzas*), addressed to the new tsar with a clear message: Peter the Great began his reign harshly and continued to rule firmly but fairly – can you not do the same and (by implication) see your way to freeing the imprisoned radicals? This is one of a number of poems which shows Pushkin, the humanitarian who wanted to believe the best of everyone, to have been utterly naive in his day-to-day political thinking. The effect of the poem on Nicholas was like water off a duck's back, and, what was much more serious, Pushkin's friends and admirers were shocked by his apparent justification in the opening stanzas of the harsh reprisals visited upon the radicals.

A year after the Decembrist calamity Pushkin may be seen writing a poem to his exiled friend Pushchin (*I.I. Pushchinu*), more personal than political. Two years after the event he is still keen to renew his association with the unfortunate rebels. The celebrated poem *Arion* (1827) confirms him as the bard of the Decembrist movement, the only survivor of the catastrophe, still singing his hymns of freedom. As late as the year 1835 he is still concerned about his erstwhile comrades. If Peter the Great could hold a banquet to celebrate reconciliation with some of his imprisoned subjects – this was the subject of his *Pir Petra Velikogo* (*The Banquet of Peter the Great*) – the implied question, a full decade after the suppression of the Decembrist coup, was – could not Nicholas bring himself to do the same? Compared with the rebels themselves, in political terms, Pushkin looks like a novice and a nonentity. Each to his trade. We have destiny to thank that he lived on, relatively unhindered, for a dozen years instead of perishing in one way or another with the victims early in 1826. Pushkin's love of freedom was not, as it happens, of the narrowly angled political kind and he has provided a greater service to humanity by expressing it in artistic terms rather than rendering himself up as a sacrificial martyr. That service was provided – though not by his decision, for he would have joined them had he been able – by other, lesser men.

Pushkin's other excursions into political matters are relatively insignificant. His further epigrams directed against Alexander I, such as 'Vospitannyy pod barabanom . . .' ('Bred to the sound of the drum . . .') (1825) are now nothing more than historical curiosities. His sarcastic addresses to the public censor, *Poslaniye tsenzoru* (*Epistle to the Censor*) (1822) and *Vtoroye poslaniye k tsenzoru* (*A second epistle to the censor*) (1824), at once sadly revealing and bitterly amusing, are really in the same category. His poem of 1828 *Druz'yam* (*To my friends*), a pathetic attempt to justify his earlier missives to the tsar which had seemed more to praise him than to criticise, belongs to the realm of historical biography rather than that of art. Even his triumphal poems of 1831 *Klevetnikam Rossii* (*To the slanderers of Russia*) and *Borodinskaya Godovshchina* (*Anniversary of Borodino*) are of marginal interest only, given the surrounding hundreds of poems more worthy of attention because of their artistic content or their greater degree of universality. In them Pushkin writes almost as an unofficial poet laureate deputed to defend or celebrate his nation's affairs. Their didactic spirit is unhidden. Pushkin is writing, according to one critic, '. . . as a patriot . . . as a good political journalist.'[22]

In order to emphasise the sterility of these political pieces it is worth while comparing them finally with two remarkable poems, one virtually unknown, the other world famous among Russian speakers, containing an idea which is essentially political but which is transmuted by sheer poetic quality into something of universal applicability and lasting artistic merit. The first is an untitled poem of 1827 beginning 'Kakaya noch'! Moroz treskuchiy . . .' ('What a wonderful night! The crackling frost . . .'). It consists of fifty-seven familiar iambic tetrameters arranged according to an imaginatively compiled rhyme scheme exactly as in the narrative poems, from one of which, incidentally, this piece has every appearance of having been abstracted. The first eight lines present a scene of tranquillity, a nocturnal urban setting, in winter, with the population abed. The guard dogs barking and rattling their chains in lines nine and ten give us cause to shiver a little for the first time. Now, after a pause, we arrive at what really matters — a scene of the most dreadful carnage, the aftermath of a mass torturing and execution in the days of Ivan the Terrible. The ghastly instruments of agony and death are still there along with the torn and disfigured corpses. Suddenly a horseman enters the square eagerly riding through to a meeting with his woman friend for whom his sexual longing is reaching fever pitch. He must hurry. But to his surprise the horse balks before an object looming up before them. It is a gibbet with a swinging corpse. The rider is amused. He reminds his horse that earlier in the day both of them had been involved in the carnage. Had not the horse actually been used to trample the traitors? Did he not get his hooves splattered with blood? The horse, urged on against his better inclinations, gallops through and away.

This is perhaps the most horrific scene in the whole of Pushkin's work, yet nowhere is his restraint better exemplified. The whole picture is presented at an unusual time of day, from an unusual angle and with every intention of understating the ghastliness. We look upon it through the half light of late evening several hours after the action took place so that the horror has already begun to recede in time and even in its visual impact. The most remarkable quality of the poem is its quietude and stasis. To present such a dynamic occurrence as a few hours of mass torture and execution without colour or movement is a bold, imaginative stroke. The resulting effect on one's sensitivities is similar to that of a painting. Repin or Vereshchagin would have done wonders with the idea had it occurred to them.

Having decided to remove much of the horror in order to avoid the charge of prurience or sensationalism, but to drive home his message by poignant understatement, Pushkin then elected to put much of it back — for the imaginative reader at least — by using an oblique device which Tolstoy would come to employ repeatedly, the depiction of human atrocities against a background of natural beauty and serenity. This provides the true measure of the squalid business of humankind. Without going into detail we might briefly add that the poetic devices in the piece are skilfully called into service. The importance of the rhyme-scheme has been referred to; it is also worth mentioning that both enjambement and onomatopoeia come into their own when it becomes necessary to depict the bridling of the horse. These are some of the key lines:

> Yezdok surovyy
> Pod nim promchat'sya byl gotov,
> No borzyy kon' pod plet'yu b'yetsya,
> Khrapit, i fyrkayet, i rvetsya
> Nazad.

> The stern rider
> Was prepared to ride on under
> But the swift steed bridles under the lash,
> He snarls and snorts and strains
> Backwards.

(Actually he doesn't snarl. Russian is lucky in having at least two entirely different words for snorting which cannot be matched in English.)

This is a splendid piece of imaginative writing which deserves to be better known. Its basic message is a political one. For all the understatement we are clearly required to register shock and horror. Our judgement of the society which permits such atrocities must, of course, be negative. As we reflect on the poem, however, our vision is bound to extend outward centrifugally from that remote square and that evening, now exactly four centuries ago. We are bound to see this poem as a broader commentary on our species and the evaluation of the fundamental nature of humanity cannot stand very high. The only compunction here is shown by the horse and his rider soon cures him of that.

Misanthropy of the same order pervades also the well known poem of 1828, *Anchar* (*The Upas Tree*), a cold, precise calculation of human evil. The Upas tree stands in the desert radiating death by means of the poison oozing from its bark. A slave is sent to collect some of the poison. He returns only to die at his master's feet. The prince then turns his attention to the business of using the poison against his neighbours. This poem has been compared with William Blake's *A poison tree*, from the *Songs of Experience*. There is more than a comparison here: the resemblance is uncanny. The titles, the main theme and many of the details are virtually interchangeable. Both trees have their origin in wrath, they grow, they are heated by the sun and they are rained upon. They are both approached by a human being who is killed by the venomous exudation and who ends up sprawled upon the ground. Both poems affect the simplest of poetic styles, four-stress lines precisely end-stopped in neatly finished quatrains. They have a hypnotic regular tread, avoiding any kind of metrical shocks, and assisted by the regular use of the dully repetitive anaphoric 'And . . .' which introduces nearly a third of Pushkin's lines and half of Blake's. Chilling archaisms, stolen straight from the admonitory prose of the Old Testament, come upon us at key moments. Even an unusual device like the juxtaposition of the same word against itself occurs in both poems (my wrath/my wrath: cheloveka/chelovek). The ultimate message is closely similar: the human species is so steeped in evil that it will look upon the murder of a fellow creature as not merely justifiable but as a necessary, or even enjoyable triviality.

The arresting similarities do not actually make for identical poems. Blake's is the narrower, by a small margin. It is the story of one man's harbouring of a grudge and vicious revenge, though it takes little enough imagination to relate this more broadly to humanity in general. Pushkin's reaches much further out to suggest a poisoned, hostile universe in which we live and a measuring of all-pervading evil which is immediately of elemental proportions. Both poems end in death, and the surviving representative of our species is so odiously portrayed that, having dealt out death, he obviously deserves, and will achieve, nothing better for himself. These poems stand at the end of the universe. They are so black that human mortality seems both merited and desirable. Blake had been here before and would return again; Pushkin never once in his life wrote anything nearly so nihilistic. Unfortunately this, his most atypical poem, is in every way one of his finest, even though it suggests an awful possibility — that not merely the poison tree but perhaps the whole cosmos was born on the day of wrath. This amounts, in turn, to a conclusion that, even if the problem of individual liberty were to be solved on the scale of immediate political évents, man will remain imprisoned within his own irredeemably evil nature and will not deserve to prosper, or even to survive.

Events in the Life of a Poet

Many of the events in the sad life of Alexander Pushkin are recorded in his poetry. Large numbers of poems were addressed to his contemporaries, mainly to his friends but also to his enemies. Later in his career, the habit of writing occasional verse was replaced by a series of contemplative lyrics — the artistic value of which is much more considerable — as he began to review the circumstances of his life and think about the small and unhappy future that lay ahead of him.

During the early part of his career, up to the year 1822, at least half of all his poems have a title which consists of a proper name in the nominative or, more commonly, in the dative case. There is a great scattering of poems long and short written to the people around him, some of them still well known, Karamzin, Zhukovsky, Chaadayev, Delvig, Kaverin, Shishkov, Vsevolozhsky, Baratynsky, Vyazemsky, Glinka and many others. The bulk of this writing need not detain us. It consists of apologies, invitations, expressions of gratitude, exhortations of one kind or another and other such businesslike material. For all the interest which these poems may hold for the specialist there are no hidden treasures waiting to be rediscovered among them. A good deal of this verse is, in fact, respectable doggerel. Anyone who wants to read Pushkin performing at a mechanically reliable level, turning out verses as easily as most people can speak, but without disturbing our aesthetic sensibilities one iota, should turn to poems like *N.N. (To Engel-gart)* or *To Orlov* (both 1819).

As Pushkin matured, however, the poems inspired by the developing circumstances of his life become more interesting, more significant and more moving. A good example is provided by a whole cycle of poems dedicated to Tsarskoye Selo, the lycée where Pushkin spent his school-days, the friends he came to know there and the surrounding country-side. The first one is an innocent song of valediction as the boys leave the school for the last time in 1817. Time has added a touch of sadness and irony to it. The last lines of this poem, *Razluka (The parting)*, dedi-cated to as ill-fated a group of lads as ever left school together, read as follows:

And may (is fate listening to my prayer?)
May all, all of your friends find happiness.

Several years passed and in 1825 Pushkin wrote the first of several poems dedicated to the anniversary of the school's opening, October 19th, a date which the boys had promised to mark with celebrations every year. One of them, Korsakov, was already dead and another, Matyushkin, half way round the world on his third circumnavigation. Pushkin escapes from his current troubles into happy memories and promises to join the group the following year for a joint celebration. He ends on a sad, con-templative note. Who, he wonders, will be the last survivor of the group, left behind to celebrate the day all alone as Pushkin now does himself? In fact it turned out to be A.M. Gorchakov, who was to spend a highly successful life as a Russian diplomat, outlive Pushkin by nearly half a century and eventually attain the age of eighty-four. Year after year on October 19th his thoughts must have returned to his schooldays and he will have read the last stanza of the 1825 poem with recurring sadness.

The poem of 1827 consists of two short but moving stanzas both of which begin with the words 'Bog pomoch' vam, druz'ya moi . . .' ('God help you, my friends . . .'). The events of late 1825 and early 1826 had scattered the generation of 1817 and several of them were now in exile. This tiny poem overbrims with good will and fellow-feeling. Andrey Sinyavsky says 'Never, perhaps, has so much sympathy for others poured forth at one time in one poem of such small size. The goodness of Pushkin brings tears to your eyes.'[23] The mere reversal of the stress at the beginning of that opening line gives it the air of a sobbing attempt to communicate a sympathetic response to the fate of the poet's old friends. Its repetition at the head of the second stanza is a painful experience. Sinyavsky's words are not out of place.

The 1828 poem is merely a passing note of the occasion occupying a single quatrain. In 1829 Pushkin wrote *Vospominaniya v Tsarskom Sele* (*Reminiscences at Tsarskoye Selo*), an imitation of the very first poem which he had declaimed in public and had published in 1814-15. It deals with the memory of 1812 when Russian soldiers marched past the schoolboys on their way to defend the fatherland. It is of little consequence and of less artistic merit than *Tsarskoye Selo* (1823), a poem of two octaves in which memory is brought into play more gently, re-creating the woods, the poetry, the days of idleness and the lovely walks of his adolescent years spent in that beautiful place. The last two lycée poems are far more moving. Written respectively twenty and twenty-five years after the opening of the school they are set-pieces with a difference, personalised and emotional outpourings redeemed from the touch of maudlin sentimentality by their honesty, their carefully disciplined formality and the genuine nature of the gathering collective tragedy. By 1831, when he writes 'Chem chashche prazdnuyet litsey . . .' ('The more our school celebrates . . .'), Pushkin has to record the sad fact that no less than six of their company are dead – with the survivors scarcely into their thirties. What he did not know was that a seventh, S.F. Brogilo, had also perished some years before in the same battle for Greek independence that had drawn Byron to his death. This poem contains a poignant premonition of his own demise, although that was still six years away. It was, incidentally, one of only six poems completed by him in that disturbed and unhappy year. The last one in the series, 'Byla pora: nash prazdnik molodoy . . .' ('Time was when our young celebration . . .') (1836) was scheduled to be read out by the author at the annual reunion of the old classmates. It consists of eight octaves tracing the memories of their schooldays and the great events which they were privileged to witness. Events in Pushkin's life had brought him to his lowest ebb; he had never felt more isolated, unhappy and discouraged. The sadness of the occasion overwhelmed him. The minutes of the meeting record the fact that, having begun to recite, he forgot his words and was obliged to admit that he had failed to complete the promised poem. What really happened was that he was too overcome with emotion and tears to continue. Thus ends a cycle of poems which excites our deepest sympathy and admiration for Pushkin and his comrades. It is true that they are both personalised and overfilled with rich feelings to which we as outsiders have no direct access. Except, perhaps, for 'Bog, pomoch' vam . . .' they cannot be compared seriously with the many nobler achievements by the same writer. Nevertheless they belong intimately to this poet and they touch his deepest interests. There can be no doubt that, even if we need biographical details to assist us with them, these poems deserve our highest regard.

It remains for us to glance at a handful of poems also directly related to the circumstances of Pushkin's life, one or two of which had achieved deserved acclaim. Two poems with the same title *Primety* (*Signs*) present some interest because they reveal aspects of Pushkin's personality which as yet remain underacknowledged. The first one, written in 1821, is a country poem which asks us to look very closely at the various signs offered by the natural world so that we may be able to read the countryside and the climate more intimately. This is an indication of Pushkin's own deep affection for country life and his awareness of the primitive, though enviable faculties of country people. The second poem, written in 1829, deals with signs also written in nature but of a different kind. The poet sets off to see a woman friend but delays because the moon rises on the wrong side. All poets, he claims (rather dubiously), are subject to superstitious ideas. Pushkin certainly was quite capable of aborting carefully laid plans simply because of an unlucky portent such as a hare crossing his path. This is, strangely enough, all part of his quest for ultimate freedom. For most of his adult life he worried about civil, political and spiritual independence. This was sufficient for most of the time to distract him from an even greater worry. Supposing men were guaranteed basic liberties in the ordering of their daily lives are we not still ruled and directed by a force of destiny, capricious but predominantly malevolent? This idea, which would provide a major part of thematic interest in such mature works as *The Bronze Horseman* and *The Queen of Spades*, is hinted at in the second poem entitled *Primety*.

Philosophical speculation is not Pushkin's forte; he is not one of Russia's metaphysical poets. Lomonosov, Derzhavin, Baratynsky, Tyutchev — these are the Russian poets who join together to address their collective wisdom to the eternal questions as presented by the natural world. The most we are to expect from Pushkin is an occasional flash of philosophical insight, usually prompted by adverse circumstances, usually pessimistic. An example of Pushkin attempting not too successfully to make such a contribution to our thinking comes in an early poem *K **** (*To ****) (1817) where late-adolescent blues impel him to contemplate human happiness and to conclude that it is short lived. The poem has nothing of interest or originality to offer. In later years the poet will achieve more. By 1823 he was capable of *Telega zhizni* (*The Waggon of life*) which is a lively and light-hearted speculation about the finite human condition. Life is a waggon driven by time.

In early youth we tell the driver to get a move on. (Here Soviet editors get themselves into a terrible mess because of their prudery: what Pushkin actually says is 'Get fucking going!'). In middle age we begin to notice, and to fear, the great hills and abysses and we ask him to slow down. Alas, as we nod our way through old age the driver still refuses to slacken the pace. This is really a bit of philosophical flummery but the verse itself is rollicking good Pushkin. It introduces, for instance, one of the marvellously complex Russian verbal formations which are so dense with meaning: the single word 'porastryaslo', with its double perfective prefix, makes a meal of suggesting that life has 'knocked us all about a good bit' by middle age. On the other hand, one should not take this poem too seriously – it is merely a wry observation about what we all complain about, the speedy passage of time. It was given undue prominence in 1947, when, in translated form, it appeared as the title of a short anthology of Russian poems.[24] In reality it typifies neither Pushkin nor Russian verse.

In 1828 Pushkin sat down on his birthday in a philosophical mood and wrote a sardonic little lyric beginning 'Dar naprasnyy, dar sluchaynyy . . .' ('Gift given in vain, gift given by chance . . .'). The gift in question is the gift of life itself. Our poet asks the eternal question: who or what called him up out of oblivion and why? He can see no aim in life and finds the whole business of it very tedious. Although delightfully composed of three successive questions and two short statements, and as light as a soufflé – which is most surprising in view of the gravity of the issues hinted at – this is another slender piece. Pushkin is still only half way along the road to full expressiveness as far as his poems of philosophical awareness are concerned. We must turn, in conclusion, to three poems where this aim is properly achieved.

In 1829 Pushkin wrote a meditation on death which has become well known, 'Brozhu li ya vdol' ulits shumnykh . . .' ('Whether I am wandering down noisy streets . . .'). As well as containing rich sound patterns which make it a pleasure to read and to quote, this piece introduces us to useful reminders of human mortality without indulging in the slightest hint of self-pity, unnecessary agonising or morbid fascination. A lyrical sadness pervades the poem but the overriding impression is not of our progress towards a bleak terminus but of the *continuation* of life in other ways. The great oak will outlive the poet (it is probably still there and will outlive us too), the baby whom he caresses is generously accorded the right to take the poet's place in the world and the finest gesture of all is reserved for an excellent concluding stanza. Having said that, although it doesn't matter very much, he would prefer to think of his body decaying on home ground, (which, of course, it now is) he goes on to insist that 'young life shall play' at the very entrance to his tomb and that nature shall continue always to decorate it. The opening line of this final stanza is a miniature masterpiece

I pust' u grobovogo vkhoda . . .

The recurrent heavy vowels impart a light touch of lugubrious enjoyment as a suitable background to the ambiguity of the meaning: 'at the entrance to the tomb' can indicate both a location and an awareness of impending death. Here is a poem with which, unlike the earlier ones described, every reader will wish to identify with all his spirit. It is an example of Pushkin's ability to deal with disagreeable subjects and still arouse the 'kind feelings' of which we have spoken.

A second poem which is personal in intention, occasioned by immediately adverse circumstances, yet universal by implication is the one which begins with the sad call, 'Pora, moy drug, pora! Pokoya serdtse prosit . . .' ('It's time, my friend, it's time. My heart seeks peace . . .'). It is well established that this was written to his wife in 1834 as an externalisation of the disappointment felt by the poet when his request to be allowed to retire to the country was turned down. It contains no more than four Alexandrine couplets though rather more than that was planned. We may consider it a blessing that not another line was added. Pushkin's intention to go into further detail would have personalised what is, as things stand, a universal experience. The poet speaks, once more in lines of the most enchanting fluidity, of his weariness. Time is speeding away and life's rich rewards are escaping. The moment we begin to see how to live everything is snatched away by death. A famous line follows:

Na svete schast'ya net, no yest' pokoy i volya

There is no happiness on earth but there is tranquillity
                    and there is freedom.

That tranquillity and that freedom are what the stricken poet now desires beyond all else. Who does not? These lines can only be read with the utmost sympathy, for Alexander Pushkin, for oneself, for humanity. Do we not all seek what the poet seeks and what he expresses in one of his most beautiful lines? He seeks to retreat

V obitel' dal'nuyu trudov i chistykh neg.

To a distant home of work and pure delight.

Never has the lovely soft '1' of the Russian language been put to better service than in this last line.

Finally let us consider a poem which, if it had been written later and in the absence of the better candidate *Exegi Monumentum*, might well have been taken for a suitable epitaph. *Vospominaniye* (*Remembrance*) was written (at first called *Bessonnitsa* (*Insomnia*) and then *Bdeniye* (*The Vigil*) which titles were sensibly rejected as tending to narrow down the meaning of the poem) in 1828. Richly endowed with some of Pushkin's most enchanting patterns of sound, the poem weaves a background tapestry of euphony as complicated and colourful as the long scroll of the poet's life itself which he now unrolls. Sitting in his room in St Petersburg, unable to sleep, haunted by the shadows of the White Night outside which will not allow darkness to descend, he contemplates first the deserted city, then his own agitated mind, his remorse, his anguish and the whole of his loathsome past. Comes the final quatrain and his meditative tone is suddenly transformed into a bitter outburst, amply supported by the spitting sound of the strongest Russian sibilant 'shch' which intrudes so violently after the third syllable in lines thirteen and fourteen ('s otvrashcheniyem' and 'trepeshchu'). The poet reviews his life with utter revulsion. Where can he go from here? Something dramatic is clearly to be expected: madness, suicide, a sudden conversion of some kind? The concluding line, after the bitter complaints and the bitter tears of line fifteen, comes as a surprise, rather like the concluding couplet of many a Shakespeare sonnet (Nos. 12 and 19 are good examples) which overturns all that has gone before:

'Yet I do not wipe away the sorrowful lines.'

There is a lot of wisdom, soundly based on experience of life's hardships, in this final line, and it is Pushkinian wisdom. It instructs us that life itself is a hard experience, that reason shows it is not worth while, that remorse and anguish are our lot, but then, at the eleventh hour, it reminds us that this is after all, only one side of the picture. The other side, we may be thankful, is amply portrayed elsewhere in Pushkin's work. From first to last, and often despite himself, Pushkin constantly reminds us that notwithstanding any amount of evidence to the contrary, simply to be alive on this planet and to go about our normal human business is a privilege beyond our comprehension and a pleasure so exquisite that we need our poets to help us with the expression of it.

4 NINE NARRATIVE POEMS

The Narrative Poet

Narrative poetry occupies an honourable station in the literature of every country. Its roots may be traced deep into history, to markets, taverns and other places where people gathered together, exchanged news and gossip, and learned to entertain each other long before the advent of literacy. Poems with stories in them have always been popular — in both senses of the word — and it is safe to predict that, even in the western world where this art form has recently been eclipsed by others, they will return one day to favour and high achievement. The Russians yield to no-one in the pleasure and pride deriving from their narrative poetry and Pushkin's contribution to the tradition is of signal importance. He cultivated the narrative poem from the beginning of his career almost to its end. He completed ten *poemy* ranging from *Ruslan and Lyudmila* which propelled him into renown at the age of twenty to *The Bronze Horseman* which crowned his fame once and for all in 1833 (though its actual publication was delayed until four years after his death).

At the height of his popularity, in the early 1820s, he could count on large sales for his story poems. *The Captive of the Caucasus* earned him five hundred roubles in 1821. Two or three years later he was able to inform his brother: 'Pletnev writes to me that *The Fountain of Bakhchisaray* is in everyone's hands.'[1] So it was, and this poem brought in no less than three thousand roubles. A quarter of Pushkin's total output, roughly ten thousand out of forty thousand lines, was given over to narrative poetry — and this does not include *Yevgeniy Onegin* which alone takes up another seventh.[2] There is no period of his activity (other than the last three or four years when he was writing little poetry of any kind) during which Pushkin could resist for long the impulse to return to narrative verse. His career as a narrative poet not only overlapped with the protracted writing of *Yevgeniy Onegin*; it began four years earlier than that eight-year stretch and ended three years after it. Throughout all that time Pushkin matured and refined his technique until he was able to create, in *The Bronze Horseman*, one of his undisputed master works, a *poema* which brings the genre to perfection. It has every claim to be considered one of the finest narrative poems ever written. The purpose of this chapter is to indicate the path taken by the poet in preparing himself for that singular achievement, to set down the basic characteristics of his narrative poetry and to show how, in exemplary fashion, he was able to profit from yesterday's misjudgements when preparing tomorrow's successes.

Compression and Diversity

Pushkin's longer poems are characterised by a fluent narrative manner which is kept in check by a series of restraining forces which preserve him from garrulity or any of the other excesses which await the over-confident story-teller in verse. Length itself is an important matter. Where Byron − to take the obvious point of comparison − luxuriates in his use of language and allows most of his narrative poems to ramble on well beyond a thousand lines (in the case of *Childe Harold's Pilgrimage* well beyond four thousand) Pushkin starts with 777 lines in *The Captive of the Caucasus* and sees to it that every narrative poem afterwards gets shorter still. The significance of this comparison is sharpened by the cardinal exceptions which infringe the general rule for both poets. On the one hand, Byron's *The Prisoner of Chillon* limits itself to 392 lines and enhances its quality by doing so; it is one of his most powerful stories, described recently by John Jump as 'the harrowing recreation . . . of the experience of a man long denied his freedom',[3] and a tale 'notably free from the characteristic faults of the Turkish series' in which 'Bonivard's simple account of his sufferings amounts to an indictment of injustice more forcible than any polemic could have been.'[4] On the other hand, Pushkin's *Poltava* moves in the opposite direction. In writing the work too quickly he allowed it to escape and run away to almost 1500 lines. If anything the critics have been too kind to it but most of them admit nevertheless that this poem is, in Mirsky's words, 'as a whole not flawless'.[5] Walter Vickery's judgement is that '*Poltava* must by all standards be reckoned a considerable achievement. There are, however, valid reasons for finding fault with it.'[6] We shall consider these reasons in due course; for the present it is enough to establish a link between them and the sheer length of the poem in which they appear. Brevity is Pushkin's hallmark and when this quality deserts him trouble arises. In order to underline the point still further we should recall that Byron normally uses a longer line than Pushkin's, as is the case when we compare *Don Juan's* 16,000 lines with *Yevgeniy Onegin's* less than six thousand. It is by such simple figures that garrulity and laconism are brought face to face.

Economy of means is one sure way of making sure that the reader of a narrative poem does not become bored. Another one is variety. It is important not only that the overall length of a poem should be controlled but that a similar limitation should be placed on the small subsections of which it is comprised. We shall see later, when discussing *The Bronze Horseman*, how cleverly and with what tantalisingly good taste Pushkin modulates from one incident, character, mood, description or observation to the next. This skill (at its least evident in *Poltava*) sustains the interest and pricks the imagination. It is supported by another principle of diversity (again at its least evident in *Poltava*) which functions unobtrusively, below the level of the reader's immediate awareness, but has a significant part to play in ensuring the triumph of versatility over monotony: his deployment of rhymes throughout the poems. Having decided at an early stage to eschew the stanza as a basis for his narrative verse – a policy from which he departed only in the case of his amusing poem *The Little House in Kolomna* – Pushkin saw the need to go even further, to deny even the principle of regularity in his rhyming. His rhymes look regular but they are not. Many mistakes have been made by critics who have glanced at the rhyme schemes and formed an incorrect impression of their simplicity. Boris Unbegaun cannot have looked carefully at the opening five lines of *Andzhelo*, which rhyme AbAbb, before suggesting that the poem is written in rhyming couplets.[7] Peter Henry is inaccurate in his description of the rhyme-scheme in *The Gipsies* as 'a combination of alternating rhymes, rhyming couplets and sometimes pairs that are further apart. Occasionally there are three rhyming lines.'[8] The first part of this definition is an oversimplification; the second is wrong – there are triplets in Pushkin, but not in *The Gipsies*. Similarly oversimplified are John Bayley's descriptions of 'the rhyme pattern of *abab*, alternating – but not regularly – to *abba*, and interspersed with occasional couplets . . .'[9] which are supposed to run through *Ruslan and Lyudmila* and 'the alexandrines rhymed in free quatrains'[10] which are claimed as the basis of *The Gabancaliad*. (In the second instance even the alexandrines are out of place: the poem is written in pentameters.) Not for the first time we have come upon a Pushkin phenomenon which is more complex than might be suggested by casual appearance.

What actually happens in all of Pushkin's narrative poems (except *The Little House in Kolomna*), whatever the line-length, is that a long chain of rhymes is put together which pays no attention to any pauses in the narrative but simply goes its own way throughout the poem. The links in the chain are normally quatrains. These are predominantly alternating quatrains (abab) but envelope ones (abba) crop up not infrequently and according to no set pattern. The beginning of *The Fountain of Bakhchisaray*, for instance, consists of the one followed by the other: *vzor, dymilsya, dvor, tesnilsya; dvortse, chitali, pechali, litse.* Things become more complicated when occasionally a fifth line is added, anywhere within the quatrain, to produce a different-sized link which imparts a nice shock of surprise. It is also common for a couplet to drop in unannounced. Less frequently, the rhyme group is extended to six lines or, on one or two rare but notable occasions, well beyond that. Triplets are brought in from time to time, but always when the subject matter is less than serious for they usually amount, in Pushkin's poems, to a little joke. On rare occasions there is a direct correspondence between the intrusion of one of the longer rhyming groups into the overall scheme. We shall draw attention to some such examples in due course. For the moment these exceptional moments do not signify. The importance of the diversity created by the strange succession of differently constituted rhyming patterns is diversity itself. The reader's inevitable ignorance of what is actually happening down among the line-ends is reflected by the errors committed even by seasoned critics when summarising the complex formations. The shifting patterns of the rhyme-schemes in Pushkin's narratives impart a pleasingly varied flavour to the telling of the story which, taken together with the brevity already mentioned, insures the poet against any weakening of interest on his reader's part.

The variations in rhyme provide a feast of material for the formalist critic. True enough, Pushkin did not calculate his permutations with a conscientious effort; nevertheless, his capacity for variation is a sure guide to the level of his inspiration and achievement. The tedious life of the harem described in *The Fountain of Bakhchisaray* and the luxuriant wordiness of the poem as a whole are reflected in a low level of rhyming diversification. The weakness of *Poltava*, and the hastiness of its execution, are amply demonstrated by the paucity of its rhyme changes; in his longest narrative, precisely when variations are most urgently required, Pushkin's skill in manipulating them deserts him. In *The Bronze Horseman*, Pushkin's finest narrative poem by a clear margin, just as everything else — the story, the characters, the issues discussed or implied — arrive at a rich fulfilment of the poet's genius, so, too, do the formal devices of the poem. The rhyme scheme presents one or two substantial surprises which will be described in the next chapter. Equally important, however, is the fact that in this masterpiece the rhyme scheme is at its most varied. This poem enjoys the lowest degree of formal orthodoxy and thus the highest measure of diversification. It is not necessary to *calculate*, in formal terms, the means by which *The Bronze Horseman* outdistances its predecessors in achievement — its excellence may be established in more straightforward and more appealing terms — but such calculations are available for the eager scholar who might like to pursue them.

A final word about Pushkin's rhyming. It needs to be compared with Byron's in order to point up once again the differences between the two poets. Here is a quotation from the end of Byron's *The Giaour*:

> And thank thee for the generous tear
> This glazing eye could never shed.
> Then lay me with the humblest dead,
> And, save the cross above my head,
> Be neither name nor emblem spread
> By prying stranger to be read,
> Or stay the passing pilgrim's tread.

Note the rhymes: 'shed, dead, head, spread, read, tread' — six of them together. Pushkin at his lowest ebb could never have brought himself, for any reason, to rhyme six successive lines with the same sound. The very idea would have been offensive to him, a tawdry display of the first and easiest of the poet's skills. In the whole span of approximately nine thousand lines of Pushkin's narrative poems only on a few isolated occasions, and only for a good reason will the company extend membership even to a *triple* rhyme. There could be no more pointed reminder of Byron's negligence and Pushkin's sensitivity in matters of poetic form.

The False Start

The first of Pushkin's *poemy* is a false start. *Ruslan and Lyudmila* was begun when the poet was only eighteen and being paid by the government for doing nothing but enjoy himself in St Petersburg. The poem grew into a long one, of nearly three thousand lines divided into six cantos. It took all but three years to bring to completion and its best known section, the thirty-five lines of the Prologue beginning

> U lukomor'ya dub zelenyy;
> Zlataya tsep' na dube tom . . .

There is a green oak-tree by a bay
And on that oak-tree is a golden chain . . .

was not added until another eight years had passed.

This poem is quite different from its successors. It tells a peripatetic, questing fairy-story having no relationship whatsoever with the real world. It is a forerunner not so much of the later narratives as of the several immaculate *skazki* (fairy tales) in verse which Pushkin wrote in his prime, the finest of which according to general opinion is *Tsar Saltan*. However, *Ruslan and Lyudmila* is described generically as a *poema* and its formal properties, particularly the metre, do prefigure the narratives and not the *skazki*. It is properly discussed in relation to the *poemy*.

The story, crudely simplified, goes as follows. On the wedding night of Ruslan and Lyudmila the bride is spirited away by an ugly dwarf-magician, Chernomor. Ruslan and three rivals, Farlaf, Rogday and Ratmir, set off on a quest to find her. The action alternates between Lyudmila and Ruslan. A more resourceful figure than many another abducted heroine, she avoids Chernomor by stealing and using his cap of invisibility. Ruslan eventually tracks her down after overcoming a series of obstacles. He defeats a mysterious knight who turns out to be Rogday, a severed giant's head belonging to Chernomor's brother, numerous other enemies and finally Chernomor himself, by clinging to his beard as he soars into the skies and winning a trial of strength which lasts for several days. This brings us, however, only to the end of canto four. In the next canto Ratmir and Farlaf reappear and the latter appears to bring the tale to a bad end by abducting the unconscious Lyudmila once again and stabbing her husband to death. Canto six restores the necessary happy ending. Ruslan is revived by magic water. After winning the city of Kiev and resuscitating his bride he pardons Farlaf and they all live happily ever after. The story is rounded off by a famous incantatory couplet, the same one with which it began:

Dela davno minuvshikh dney,
Predan'ya stariny glubokoy.

The deeds of bygone days,
The legends of deep antiquity.

Thus, by one of the repetitive devices beloved by the narrators of folk poetry, a gigantic ring is closed and we know for certain that this time the adventures are complete.

Ruslan and Lyudmila was the first major landmark in Pushkin's career; it sold well and made his name. It was a landmark also in Russian literature; with the possible exception of Bogdanovich's *Dushenka* (1783) the reading public had seen nothing like it. The poem still reads like a delightful, dizzy mixture of individual brilliance and a wide range of literary borrowings, imitation and parody. Russian folk sagas (*byliny*), Russian chap-books, Ariosto, Voltaire, Parny, Wieland, Bogdanovich and Zhukovsky have all been identified as contributors to the tone and style. There is no doubt, however, about its originality. The unconstrained current of melodious verses which flowed forth in hundreds, borne along by a natural talent, buoyed up by humour, marked the appearance on the literary scene of a young genius. The poem was written, and intended to be read, with a sense of unfettered enjoyment. It was obviously a light-hearted entertainment, yet it had style and polish. It had been put together with true skill. The sense of occasion which characterised earlier Russian poetry, and particularly the longer poems even of distinguished writers like Derzhavin, had been filtered out of *Ruslan and Lyudmila*. What replaced it was a sense of exact appropriateness. The poet seemed to know instinctively how to make poetic language sound natural, when to call for special effects, when to turn them off and when to avoid them entirely. The beginning of the first canto illustrates the new skill. For over a hundred lines Pushkin sets the scene steadily with sparing use of his potent devices and nothing but a gentle undulation in the rhyme-scheme. Then comes the abduction scene of which John Bayley says 'The moment is genuinely uncanny.'[11] How is it managed? Simply by unleashing the dogs of poetry, which have so far been restrained, allowing them to vent their full fury and then quickly recalling them. The actual onslaught lasts for exactly ten lines. These are preceded by a mouthwatering description of the lovely moments when the newlyweds retire at last from the company and make their way to the bedroom where 'the gifts of love are being prepared' in dimly lit and luxurious surroundings. Nothing must disturb the strong young man and his lovely bride at this time. Pushkin instructs his rhymes to behave themselves and make no obtrusive gesture; they obey — AbAb, AbAb . . . Yet another AbAb group of rhymes lead us unwittingly into the key section which begins with the lovers' gentle ministrations and ends with all hell let loose:

1   Vy slyshite l' vlyublennyy shopot,
     I potseluyev sladkiy zvuk,

I preryvayushchiysya ropot
Posledney robosti? Suprug
5 Vostorgi chuvstvuyet zarane;
I vot oni nastali ... Vdrug
Grom gryanul, svet blesnul v tumane,
Lampada gasnet, dym bezhit,
Krugom vse smerklos', vse drozhit,
10 I zamerla dusha v Ruslane.

1 Can you not hear the tender rustle,
The sweet sound of kissing
And the trembling murmur
Of the last vestiges of shyness? The husband
5 Senses the delights to come.
Now they get down to it ... Suddenly
Thunder struck, light flashed in mist,
The lamp guttered, smoke coursed through,
Everything fell into darkness, everything shook
10 And Ruslan's spirit froze within him.

The uncanny air is created by the most ordinary of poetic devices, the titillating enjambement between lines 4 and 5 (the first infringement of good order), the disastrous, banging enjambement two lines later (Vdrug/grom gryanul ...), the sudden outpouring and pile-up of alliteration, assonance and onomatopoeia, the jerking of the reader's attention backwards and forwards between tenses (present, present, past, past, past, present, present, past, present, past — all necessarily translated into English by a past tense), and, undermining everything, an unadvertised subversion of the rhyme scheme which reads: AbAbCbCddC. All of this must have tumbled out on to paper pell-mell under the urgency of the exciting moment; it lacks any appearance of dogged calculation. Nevertheless the disruption of the nuptial scene is reflected in a disruption of the formal properties of that part of the poem. Pushkin's unique instinct for matching subject and form, for doing it briefly and then switching back to normality, has expressed itself in no uncertain way.

The atmosphere of *Ruslan and Lyudmila* is one of levity. In fact we know that Pushkin achieved his apparent spontaneity by hard toil and scrupulous revision. The seeming insouciance of Pushkin's manner is belied by the innate formal conscientiousness demonstrated throughout the poem and exemplified in the abduction scene. In a similar manner every other potential fault of this poem is neutralised by a countervailing saving grace. The childishness of the subject matter is offset by an adult eroticism, conversely the epicurean spirit is never allowed to become immoderate, the pseudo-seriousness is enlivened by humour, the precocious self-confidence is controlled by a mature hand, the digressive spirit, while allowed a free rein, is disguised by the sheer charm of the actual excursions and their narrators, the overall sophistication of the poem is rescued from self-congratulation by gaiety.

Much more might be said, and frequently has been said, about *Ruslan and Lyudmila*. The poem is, after all, a protracted and complex literary innovation. On the whole, however, given the broad extent of Pushkin's achievement in other, more serious fields, over-generous attention to this poem seems misplaced. For all its sparkle it remains a work of slight significance. It is no more than a beautifully executed, gaily painted object of play. Mirsky has its measure when he describes it as 'a highly elaborate and artistic toy' and 'an agreeable poetic pageant'.[12] The poem has nothing to say, it provokes in the mind not a single thought beyond admiration for the skill that produced it. It leads nowhere. The acid test of Pushkin's finest achievement distinguishes what may be described as universal, profound and communicable to non-Russians from what is not. *Ruslan and Lyudmila* communicates nothing to outsiders which is of greater significance than the dancing phrases of its entertaining transposition into musical form by Mikhail Glinka.

Four Southern Poems

Next came the period of indebtedness to Byron. Four narrative poems written in as many years, *The Captive of the Caucasus* (1820-1), *The Robber Brothers* (1821), *The Fountain of Bakhchisaray* (1822) and *The Gipsies* (1824) demonstrate the impact of the English poet upon Pushkin and illustrate how quickly and successfully he worked through it. The first of them, appearing at the same time as Zhukovsky's splendid translation of *The Prisoner of Chillon* (1821) (the excellence of which is a sad reminder of the mediocrity of Pushkin's English and American translators), was enough to turn the new, modish interest in Byron into a temporary national obsession. As in other countries this interest was linked no less with the personality and activities of the English lord than with his work. Despite a rapid cooling from boiling point Byron's popularity declined in nineteenth-century Russia more reluctantly than elsewhere and, to a reduced extent, exists there today in literary circles, matching a certain revival of interest in Byron in our own country.

All four poems deal now with a putative real world, rather than fairy-land, but it is not yet the real world of *Count Nulin* and *The Bronze Horseman*. It is that of the displaced, alienated hero so beloved of European writers of the period. Three of them treat unhappy love and all four deal with persecution. The leader of the group, *The Captive of the Caucasus*, tells of a Russian prisoner taken by Circassian tribesmen to a remote camp in the hills. A local girl falls in love with him. He cannot return her love because he has been soured by (vaguely intimated) earlier experiences and he will not pretend. She liberates him notwithstanding and, as he swims across a river to safety, she plunges to her death in the same waters. The second story, *The Robber Brothers*, part of an intended longer work but nevertheless a complete entity, is the pathetic confession of a brigand who tells of his imprisonment along with his brother, their exciting escape and his brother's death soon afterwards following illness and delirium. The third one, *The Fountain of Bakhchisaray*, is an Eastern poem set in the Crimea where Khan Girey falls in love with a new captive in his harem, Princess Maria, and rejects his old favourite Zarema. Tragedy is inevitable. Maria cannot return his love, Zarema cannot contain her jealousy. Zarema accordingly kills Maria and is executed in her turn by the Khan who then goes off to forget himself as best he can in battle. The fourth one, *The Gipsies*, depicts Aleko, a fugitive from some kind of legal or political persecution, who joins up (as Pushkin himself apparently did on one occasion) with a troupe of gipsies. He wins the love of Zemfira and for a while they live happily together. However, reverting to type, Zemfira discovers that she cannot meet his alien standards of connubial fidelity. She takes a gipsy lover. Aleko finds out, kills them both and is banished from the gipsy camp as his only punishment. We leave him as a lonely, now doubly alienated figure, abandoned in the wilderness.

The stories of these poems have certain similarities and share underlying themes. The influence upon them of such poems of Byron's as *The Corsair*, *The Giaour* and *The Prisoner of Chillon* is reasonably obvious and has been generously documented. However, they relate to Byron in different ways, revealing a diminishing dependence upon his work to the extent that, while *The Captive of the Caucasus* does read like a kind of Byronic tale with an unusually passive hero and unusually precise poetic manner, *The Gipsies* has original qualities which are beyond the English poet. All four poems have Romantic, more specifically Byronic, heroes. Exoticism and alienation are the order of the day and the chief preoccupation in all of them is the same – the question of personal liberty overlaid with interesting moral considerations arising from an awareness of personal responsibility. The settings are remote, unusual places, the backgrounds are spectacularly wild and beautiful, the denizens of these places are fascinatingly strange creatures. We visit in turn the wild Caucasian mountains with their bloodthirsty warring tribesmen, a secret hideout beyond the Volga where all kinds of criminals, riff-raff and outcasts congregate, an eastern harem in the Crimea several centuries ago and a gipsy camp wandering over the plains of Bessarabia. This is the escape into exoticism so highly favoured by the Romantics and it links the four narratives. It will need to be, not partly, but fully outgrown before Pushkin produces anything like a masterpiece in the genre.

The Byronic tale in verse, whether by Byron himself or by his imitative successors, has rather obvious qualities and certain striking defects. It tells a lively adventure story, often with bloodshed, a murder or some other violent death thrown in, against spectacularly unfamiliar background. The heroes are outlandish and their motivation is sometimes vague. Extravagance and mystery predominate at the expense of everyday reality and clarity. Reality and clarity arc, of course, the stock-in-trade of Pushkin and he has even managed to infuse them to some degree into these poems despite the unpromising situations, circumstances and settings selected for the occasion. Soon he will be employing them to the full. At this early stage his works, when subjected to the kind of scrutiny demanded if we are to pursue the poet's claim to a reputation of international stature, are seen to possess some of the weaknesses which attend a good deal of the literature appearing in Europe during the early nineteenth century – diffuse political thinking, confused and over-simplified sociology and melodramatic characterisation. A mellifluous style, a capacity for restraint, a keen eye for relevant detail, a sense of place leading to luxuriant descriptive passages – these are real Pushkinian qualities but they are not enough entirely to redeem any of the first four narratives.

There are clear signs, however, that within this Byronic period the poet's sense of his own true purpose and direction is maturing. The differences between *The Captive of the Caucasus* and *The Gipsies* are more remarkable than the similarities between them. Pushkin has turned from the small epic to the smaller narrative and from static narration to dynamic representation of incident. Compared with its forerunner *The Gipsies* is compressed, variform, imaginative and altogether more interesting, with real issues of human psychology and morality for us to ponder. In practical terms this means that the 777 lines of the earlier poem have now been shortened to 578, names have been given to the characters which fact alone abbreviates the distance between us and them, and the story has been broken up into seven dramatic scenes (some with actual stage directions), two songs and an epilogue. Thus variety has been added, the interest has been sharpened and the passage of time is nicely recaptured by the several happily timed breaks in the narrative and changes in style. The treatment of the main theme, freedom, remains rather heavy-handed, the words *volya*, *vol'nyy* and *svoboda* cropping up with tedious regularity, and some of the language is stilted. There are too many unnecessary archaisms and poeticisms; this is the last narrative in which anyone will be permitted to say, *'Ostav'te, deti, lozhe negi'* ('Leave, children, your couch of bliss') instead of 'It is time to get up'. (At the end of *Poltava* Charles will awaken Mazepa with the words 'It's time! Get up, Mazepa. Dawn is breaking' (lines 1432-3).) *The Gipsies* stands as a classic example of a transitional work but there can be no doubting that it contains some excellent passages. Two of these are to be found where they count most, at the beginning and the end. Like a film-director the poet zooms down and in from a long-distance aerial shot of the wandering gipsies and then approaches their camp from a curiously oblique angle by drawing attention to their glittering camp fires as seen from outside through the waggon-wheels. Within moments we are whisked into the midst of one family and the story is under way. This is imaginative narration of a high order. It is matched by the zooming up and away at the conclusion of the poem as we leave Aleko's solitary waggon in the middle of the steppe, equated, in one of Pushkin's sparingly employed metaphors, with a wounded crane who cannot fly south with the rest of the flock. In *The Gipsies* Pushkin's touch is becoming sure. His knowledge of when to start and stop, when and when not to digress and qualify, when to describe and when to leave actions or dialogue to tell their own story, his whole narrative technique has undergone perceptible refinement. Imagination, originality and control over his resources are already enabling Pushkin to outByron Byron.

The Supremacy of *Count Nulin*

An awareness of the limitations of the earlier narrative poems enhances the inevitable sense of admiration evoked by his mature ones. *Count Nulin* (1825) and *The Bronze Horseman* (1833) produce a double sense of wonderment, first that they sound so perfect, with every poetic means exactly attuned to the desired ends, and, second, that so much is included in so small a compass. Not a syllable seems to be wasted or wrongly deployed. It is significant that neither of them contains a wisp or a whiff of anything associated with Byronism or Romanticism. They are set in the modern world and no kind of allowances have to be made for characters or events which are less or more than real. *Count Nulin* is not in the same league as *The Bronze Horseman* for reasons which will become clear, but it is still one of Pushkin's most perfect, appealing and enduring creations. It has all the gaiety and flashing wit of *Ruslan and Lyudmila* but the emptiness of purpose, the out-and-out irrelevance of that early work, together with its protracted story-telling, have been replaced by solidity of content, purpose and method.

The story centres around a bored rural landowner's wife, Natalya Pavlovna, who is neglected by her husband because of his penchant for outdoor sport. One day, when he is out hunting, she observes a carriage break down just as it passes her estate and invites the travellers in. There are two of them: Count Nulin, a dandified déraciné Russian just back from abroad and on his way to show himself to St Petersburg, and his man, Monsieur Picard. Nulin and Natalya spend a delightful evening, beguiling each other with fancy conversation. There is not a little flirting and, on retiring, Nulin begins to think he may have missed a fine opportunity for a sexual conquest. Perhaps it is still not too late. He steals into Natalya's room and gropes at her counterpane. Alas for his hopes. Natalya slaps him across the face and he beats a retreat to the yapping of her maid's miniature Pomeranian. The atmosphere next morning is less embarrassing than he feared; in fact the conversation goes so well that Nulin feels his earlier ardour returning. However, Natalya's husband returns from the hunt and Nulin makes a hasty departure. Natalya derives much pleasure from recounting her nocturnal adventure to her husband and to everyone else in the locality. The husband, of course, goes about fulminating, but the strongest reaction − ironic laughter − belongs to someone else:

> Who laughed? Their neighbour Lidin, − he,
> A landowner of twenty-three.[13]

For all her apparent prudery and self-righteousness Natalya has after all been enjoying a nice taste of infidelity with the young man next door.

It should be apparent even from this simple summary that the poem overbrims with humour from start to finish. The comic entertainment operates on several levels and it is both straightforward and sophisticated. The former kind is self-evident, the latter depends on outside knowledge, of the poet's original intention, of a not too familiar piece of Shakespeare and of a little Roman history. Pushkin's note on this poem reveals a good deal:

> At the end of 1825 I was living in the country. Re-reading *Lucrece*, a rather weak poem of Shakespeare's, I thought: what if it had occurred to Lucrece to slap Tarquin's face? Maybe it would have cooled his boldness and he would have been obliged to withdraw, covered in confusion. Lucrece would not have stabbed herself, Publicola would not have been enraged, Brutus would not have driven out the kings, and the world and its history would have been different . . .
>
> I was struck by the idea of parodying both history and Shakespeare; I could not resist the double temptation and in two mornings had written this tale.[14]

Let us celebrate this happy conjunction of a classical education, an inventive mind and an artistic spirit. It produced in two mornings and three hundred and seventy lines an unblemished masterpiece which may be safely handed both to those approaching Pushkin for the first time and to those who need persuading of Pushkin's true quality as a writer of world standing. The poem is not actually a parody *tout court*, either of history or of Shakespeare, but our knowledge of this starting point enriches the already appetising flavour of the story. It invites us into the same kind of fanciful speculation about the funny workings of history and human affairs in general. It invites us also to reread Shakespeare's tedious poem *The Rape of Lucrece* in order to discover how much parody there is in *Count Nulin* and how good its quality may be. The answer is — not much, but what there is can only make us regret that the poet did not indulge himself in this direction more frequently. Pushkin's parody of Shakespeare exemplifies the art to perfection: it is exactly imitative, reductive in terms of length and tone, yet devoid of malicious intent. Tarquin and Nulin are both welcome guests in the homes of Lucrece and Natalya Pavlovna. They dine and talk late. On retiring the two men lie abed restlessly thinking of their lovely hostesses. Each remembers the way in which his hand has been pressed, the flushed face of a healthy young woman, the meaningful gaze . . . they both set off through the darkness, in the one section of Pushkin's poem which actually distorts Shakespeare's version into an amusing mirror image. Tarquin is filled with Machiavellian scheming, weighing the risks of his conduct against the demands of his passion, seriously torn between dread and desire. Nulin is scared but hopeful, tense but terribly amusing. Tarquin is described solemnly as 'this lustful lord'; Nulin ironically as 'our ardent hero'. Their actions, on setting forth, form an amusing contrast. Tarquin throws 'his mantle rudely o'er his arm' (and he will need it to protect him against the cold in the castle) whereas Nulin dons a gaily decorated silk dressing-gown. Tarquin, lighting his torch, performs a manly deed:

> His falchion on a flint he softly smiteth,
> That from the cold stone sparks of fire do fly,
> Whereat a waxen torch forthwith he lighteth . . .

This is in keeping with his stallion-like nature and in one line here Shakespeare cleverly calls up ten of the strong monosyllabic words in which the English language is particularly rich in order to avoid feminine mellifluousness and create an impression of bold, strong-striding masculinity. Nulin's corresponding action is rather different. He bumps into a chair and knocks it over in the darkness before stumbling off, ready-for-anything (we are told), in groping search of his latter-day Lucrece. The original protagonists are actually mentioned at this point, as a gentle reminder of the parodic intent:

> And swiftly, flinging o'er his back
> His dressing-gown silky and gay,
> Upsetting a chair in the black,
> In hope of sweet rewards, away
> Moves Tarquin to Lucrece anew,
> Set to see all adventures through.

Each man, proceeding through the darkness, is conscious of the noise of his movements and the risk of exposure. Tarquin fears the doors creaking, Nulin the floors squeaking. Each one pauses at the chamber door and much is made of the lifting of the latch or the squeezing of the handle. Once inside with his noble hero Shakespeare establishes an elevated tone and sustains it throughout a dozen corpulent stanzas before Tarquin acts; he then moves forward and places his rough hand on the sleeping maiden's bare breast. Pushkin takes the opposite course by pricking the bubble of tension immediately with a sly little joke:

> The hostess is in sweet repose,
> Or feigning sleep most excellently.

In a matter of seconds Nulin's hand, too, begins exploring where it should not but at this point Shakespeare's cruel, heroic story is exploded into bathos. This is the end of the parody, except for one or two slender borrowings which Pushkin has distorted for his own purposes (the role of the maid, references to the night, etc.). Among these one stands out as worthy of mention. Before Tarquin does his worst with Lucrece he allows her long moments of reflection and pleading. All to no avail:

> Yet, foul night-waking cat, he doth but dally,
> While in his hold-fast foot the weak mouse panteth:

Perhaps Pushkin's imagination was captured by this cruel image. He appropriated it for his own use, deciding, however, to extend the feline implications and use them to depict his own hero. Nulin, after knocking over the chair, is represented by the following slightly extended metaphor in which the cat, for all its predatory intent, is somehow emasculated by comparison with Shakespeare's:

> A sly cat sometimes set off thus.
> A maid's spoilt pet, of mincing walk,
> Down mousing from the stove he'll stalk.
> Slow-moving, inconspicuous,
> Eyes screwed in half a squint, advancing,
> He'll coil into a ball, tail dancing,
> Spread paws from sly pads, and anon
> Some poor, poor mite is pounced upon!

This is fine parody; *Count Nulin* contains 40 or 50 lines of mock heroics rapidly inflated to something like the broad dimensions of the original and deflated even faster with a chance down-to-earth remark, the process being repeated several times. Pushkin strips everything away from Shakespeare, changes his characters into their opposites and ends up telling only a superficially similar story in his own way. For the well-informed he also manages to imply that the original poem is overblown to the point of absurdity. Its turgidity is ridiculed by Pushkin's attitude to Shakespeare's 265 complex Chaucerian septets of the type known as rhyme royal (rhyming ababbcc), consisting of five pentameters rounded off with a hexameter couplet, which comes to 1,325 pentameters accompanied by 530 hexameters, no less than 1,855 lines in all. Pushkin rendered them down to 370 freely flowing, freely rhymed tetrameters with a joke in every line.

Elsewhere, however, the poem does more than serve as a grotesque mirror of a grand, largely forgotten poem. The story has been Russified, ruralised and modernised, taken over by Pushkin as his own to such an extent that, if we were to remove the two or three references to *Lucrece* and with it Pushkin's well-known note on the poem, only the lynx-eyed or imaginative would see any connection between the two. This poem contains more satire than parody. Nulin himself is an absurd fop but he represents a type not unknown to contemporary society and worthy of a satirical shaft or two. He has something in common with the 'superfluous man' soon to become a traditional figure in nineteenth-century Russian literature, though he is spiritually too shallow and sexually too dynamic to pass for an adequate representative of the species. A pretentious gallomaniac, he has lost all contact with his native country. His come-uppance is merited and we rejoice in it. His significance is expressed in his name, the English equivalent of which would be Count Nullity. The other two characters, Natalya and her husband, are portrayed sketchily but with full conviction. They tell us much about the rural landowning class, adding to the store of knowledge to be gleaned elsewhere in Pushkin, not least in 'Zima . . .' (see Chapter Two) and *Yevgeniy Onegin* (Chapter Eight). Their boring lives, trivial pursuits, dismal distractions, inadequate personalities and spiritual impoverishment are encapsulated in this small narrative poem the sociological content of which, although presented in an offhand manner, is a matter of consequence. What is depicted here is that vulgar emptiness of character described by Gogol as *poshlost'*, yet there is no jaundice in its description. There is little enough malice anywhere in Pushkin and not an iota in *Count Nulin* which is as light-hearted as a summer's day.

The appeal of this poem rests upon its ordinariness. Natalya Pavlovna has mushrooms to pickle and geese to feed. When she looks out of the window she sees urchins laughing at the yard dog who is having a go at the billy goat. Ducks and turkeys waddle around and washing is strewn on the fence. She fluffs her hair in a fussy femininity when a guest is due to arrive. We are presented with tiny details of the accoutrements possessed both by her husband and the Count. The poem is filled with palpable objects: bounding borzois, a tightly laced Cossack coat, a Turkish knife, a rum flask, a horn on a bronze chain, frock coats, waistcoats, hats, fans, capes, stays, pins, cuff-links and lorgnettes, a couple of novels (titles supplied), a broken carriage, a travelling trunk and so on. These minutiae of everyday life carry both conviction and appeal. The poem is nicely described by one of its own lines (59) as 'lacking Romantic fancies'.

The achievement of this poem seems, therefore, to depend upon ordinariness, clever narrative skills applied to a good story with a nice twist at the end, and several degrees of humour. Is that all there is to it? It is certainly dangerous to begin to read into such a delicately presented work any real seriousness of purpose. This is why *The Bronze Horseman*, which achieves its own narrative perfection and has grave messages too, must outrank *Count Nulin*. On the other hand there is always the danger of undervaluing Pushkin by accepting only his immediately obvious presentations and assuming that nothing serious or permanent lies behind them. Repeatedly his readers are beguiled into thinking that his sounds, his forms, his stories and his ideas are simpler than they really are. The poet's insouciant manner suggests frothy levity; in actuality his works teem with ideas worthy of consideration even if they are often expressed *in statu nascendi*. This is one reason why so many other writers have developed his concepts into more substantial studies. What Russian writer has *not* done so? The superfluous man, the little man, the superman, the strong heroine, the brooding presence of St Petersburg — these are a few of the fundamental themes handed down with such apparent negligence by Pushkin. It seems almost adventitious that they were developed so substantially and successfully but with hindsight we are now in a position to appreciate the full richness of his legacy and the virtual inevitability of its productive capacity. With this in mind it scarcely seems too heavy-handed to distinguish even in *Count Nulin* at least a number of whispered suggestions about human conduct, morality and inadequacies. Are there not at least hints about social and family problems, awkward psychological truths and even ethical dilemmas? Each reader must decide for himself whether this is so but he or she should do so armed with the knowledge that Pushkin generally pays his readers the ultimate compliment, assuming in them a cultivated familiarity with world literature and a capacity to seize on to the tiniest hint and appreciate its full implications. He does not spell out his messages for illiterates, nor does he like to be seen communicating messages at all.

Limited Achievement in the Later Narratives

In October 1828 Pushkin wrote *Poltava*. It is his longest narrative poem by a large margin, at 1,487 lines almost twice the length even of *The Captive of the Caucasus*, or four times as long as *Count Nulin*, and it was produced rather quickly. Walter Vickery tells us it was written 'in the short space of about three weeks'[15] and John Bayley 'in a fortnight, an astonishingly short time'.[16] Actually two or three weeks is not all that desperately short a period for a poet of Pushkin's fluency: a fortnight's writing at an average of a hundred lines a day (and Pushkin was capable of multiplying that work rate by two or three at least) would have seen the thing through. Were not *Count Nulin*'s 370 lines penned in two mornings? It is not the overall span which surprises but the lack of forward planning, the obvious haste of the writing itself and, most unusually, the absence of any rigorous revision. Procrustean efforts have been made repeatedly to persuade us of the merits of this poem which was castigated by contemporary critics and disregarded by the reading public. It is true that the modish popularity of the narrative poem as a genre was well past its peak and that there were certain critics, like Nadezhdin, Bulgarin and Polevoy, whose *ad hominem* strictures could never be relied upon for objectivity. That being said, the poem has many faults, particularly the lack of unity between its two stories; this was pointed out immediately by Ivan Kireyevsky and Pushkin praised him for the acuity and intelligence of his article in *The Moscow Messenger*. Re-readings of the poem merely confirm the unhappy first impression that it is misconceived and melodramatic.

In one sense *Poltava* represents a step forward in Pushkin's technique. It is his first historical narrative poem, anticipating *The Bronze Horseman* (and other works) by its enthusiastic portrayal of Peter the Great and anticipating both that work and *The Captain's Daughter* by its attempt to insinuate personal tragedies into the depiction of great historical events. In another sense it reverts disappointingly to the period of the 'Southern poems', with its crudities of characterisation, motivation and construction. It is not a poem by means of which one would care to attempt the transmission of Pushkin's reputation to an audience the world over.

The plot is quite complicated. The first two cantos tell a tragic love story. The aged hetman Mazepa (a grown-up version of Byron's youthful Mazeppa) falls in love with his god-daughter, Maria Kochubey, and she with him, despite the forty-five-year age-gap between them. (Pushkin took the implausibility of this in his stride, pointing out to critics that the literary world is full of unlikely love matches like, for instance, the one between Othello and Desdemona. For all his protestations this improbable love-match remains a fundamental weakness of the story.) Marriage is out of the question because of parental opposition, so the pair elope. Maria's father plans revenge. He decides to expose Mazepa's plottings against his ally Peter. Mazepa hopes to bring the Ukraine round to the support of Charles XII so that the combined forces may defeat the Russian army under Peter. This is the truth but Peter refuses to believe it, thus enabling Mazepa to turn the tables on his enemy by having him arrested and then, in the second canto, executed. When Maria learns of her father's fate she goes out of her mind. In the third and final canto we move up into the realms of real history. Mazepa has joined Charles XII openly and together they confront Peter's army, only to be defeated at the battle of Poltava. Only after the battle does Mazepa discover Maria's madness.

Those who have wished to promote the interests of this poem are not without ammunition. There are redeeming features. The description of the night scene in the memorable lines beginning

Tikha ukrainskaya noch'.
Prozrachno nebo. Zvezdy bleshchut . . .

The Ukrainian night is still.
The sky is clear. The stars shine bright . . .

(so appetising that Pushkin repeats them verbatim), the clinical economy of the execution scene and the enthusiasm of the Russian troops greeting their tsar after an instant of uncanny silence — these are moments worthy of Pushkin and they remain in the memory. The characters, however, are overdrawn and poorly motivated. Extravagance attends every incident in the poem; one crude measure of this is that, at a quick count, it includes no less than eighty-two question marks and sixty-seven exclamation marks, almost all of them used as rhetorical devices. The various interests of Maria, her father, Mazepa, Charles and Peter, which are obviously irreconcilable or irrelevant to each other in the narrative sense, resist all coalescence into artistic wholeness. The very title of the poem is largely irrelevant to the first two-thirds of its content. The relationship between the patchy *Poltava* and *The Bronze Horseman* is similar to that between *The Captive of the Caucasus* and *The Gipsies*. In both cases the former work goes to literally greater lengths in dealing with a subject similar to that of its successor but looks by comparison like a rambling experimental essay.

Two narratives remain before we reach the grand climax. Both are exceptional and atypical in several ways. They stand right outside Pushkin's normative line of development and are difficult both to assess *per se* and to relate the overall scheme. They are *The Little House in Kolomna* (1830) and *Andzhelo* (1833). One way to look at them is to consider them a return to pay final tributes to two of Pushkin's greatest sources of inspiration, Byron and Shakespeare.

The Little House in Kolomna is an insubstantial tale, again rather too long for its subject matter, running to forty *ottava rima* (abababcc) stanzas. Both the stanza and the line (iambic pentameter) are long ones. They bring Lord Byron instantly to mind and the connection between this poem and his *Beppo* is well documented. The story concerns a middle class family in Kolomna consisting of a widow and her daughter who solve a domestic problem by hiring a new cook. All goes well for a time. The cook's culinary clumsiness is balanced by her surprising disinclination to demand a proper wage. One Sunday morning, however, the mother returns from church early, suspecting the cook of robbing them, only to find her/him sitting before the mirror shaving. Parasha, the daughter, takes the confusion in her stride and Pushkin is not so indelicate as to accuse her of anything. Nevertheless it is clear that her lover has been living in with the family and that only an accident has exploded the nice little arrangement. This is another genuinely amusing story, akin in spirit if not in technique to *Count Nulin*, and it is a source of real pleasure. The *coup de grâce* lies in the ending with its shock of surprise and its skittering suggestion of the improper relationship. This redeems all that has gone before, and redemption is needed for the reader cannot avoid being puzzled by the opening, an *art poétique* excursion lasting for a fifth of the whole poem in which Pushkin discourses on his reasons for abandoning the tetrameter and taking up the octave, and by the further digressions which bamboozle him as the story, such as it is, progresses.

A good deal of exegetic research has gone into this little tale. Mirsky and Bayley[18] remind us of the ingenious arabesques of criticism which have been woven around it. It is a revelation of the inner life of the poet (Gershenzon), of diabolical intervention in human affairs (Khodasevich), of the dark sexual sources of Pushkin's poetry (a professor left discreetly unnamed by Mirsky). This innocuous nonsense need not detain us though it provides a salutary lesson in how *not* to pick up hints and ideas in Pushkin's work. The strength and the weakness of this poem, its whole character in fact, derive from something much more obvious and simple. *The Little House in Kolomna* is a flexing of Pushkin's *literary* muscles, an enjoyable work-out for him in an unfamiliar field. The poem begins by saying 'I am fed up with the four-foot iambic; everyone writes in it . . .' and ends with a literary joke in which the poet discusses the need for a moral at the end of the story and comes up with one: hiring an unpaid cook is a dangerous business;

it is unnatural for a man to dress up as a woman; he will have to shave and that is not a womanly thing to do. The concluding words are, 'You won't squeeze any more out of my story.' From first to last he is toying with the literary illusion, a common enough practice for this poet. Little literary jokes abound. In stanza IX, for example, he addresses his frisky muse like a schoolmaster settling his class down before the lesson starts; stanza XXVI contains one of his most whimsical enjambements which involves the splitting of a name and patronymic, Vera/Ivanovna. The poem struggles somewhat against its own stanza. With the notable exception of *Yevgeniy Onegin* (for reasons discussed in Chapter 8) Pushkin's outward-pushing genius and thirst for flexibility could not be accommodated within stanza forms when a long story needed to be told. On the other hand, there is a good deal of entertainment in *The Little House in Kolomna* which is a poem to be reread with pleasure. On the first occasion it is likely to be perused with impatience but rescued by the brilliance of its ending. After that the reader will be able to relax and enjoy the professional jokes and digressions in their own right instead of regarding them as obstacles to his progress through the story. This narrative poem is a treat for the literary-minded. It has been too often rewarded with the heavy hand of the exegete or dismissed as an insignificant lightweight. Those who cannot identify with its spirit have a long way to go before claiming to appreciate Pushkin. Literature, sexual naughtiness and amusing entertainment are all to be found at the *fons et origo* of his genius and all three are strongly represented in *The Little House in Kolomna*.

Pushkin's problem poem is *Andzhelo*. No one knows what to make of it. There is virtually no received opinion as to its quality. Critics always have to admit either that it is an excellent attempt at something difficult which has a number of drawbacks or that it is a misguided attempt at something impossible in which there are some leftovers of Pushkinian quality. The nonplussed attitude universally adopted towards this poem is best summed up by Mirsky who explains that it 'met with the cold and disappointed amazement of contemporaries and has fared little better with posterity. It has scarcely even profited by the general Pushkin idolatry of our own time (1926).'[19] Since that time opinion has, if anything, hardened against it. John Bayley says *Andzhelo* 'has no flavour',[20] Walter Vickery that 'it leaves behind a certain feeling of distaste for the human kind'[21] and Tatiana Wolff that 'Pushkin extracted the kernel of the play . . . but in doing so he sacrificed its life.'[22] On the other hand Mirsky thought highly of it and, more to the point, so did Pushkin himself. Moreover, the writing of *Andzhelo* coincided with the composition of Pushkin's undisputed masterpiece *The Bronze Horseman* and was thus created in his maturity and at an inspirational high point. For these reasons alone it deserves a close scrutiny.

For some reason Pushkin decided, when writing *Andzhelo*, to plunge off into a quite new direction. It comes as no surprise that he should revert to Shakespeare but the choice of the shapeless, unnatural *Measure for Measure* is scarcely what one might have expected. John Wain's assessment of this work is typical, sane and charitable: 'This play is no doubt Shakespeare's most interesting failure, but a failure, all things considered, it is.'[23] A possible explanation for the strange choice has been put forward by Walter Vickery in a recent article. His thesis is that 'Pushkin's interest in *Measure for Measure* had its basis in Pushkin's own feelings of vulnerability and jealousy caused by the Tsar's attentions to his wife.'[24] This may help a little but it solves none of the artistic problems arising in *Andzhelo*. Certainly Pushkin reduced and refined his material as always, but he turned away once more from the recognisable modern world in which all his most successful works are set, ignored even the documented past and entered a remote fictional territory. The setting is actually Italian but nowhere and no one in it is at all familiar. He turned also to a line that was quite new for his narrative poetry, the lengthy and dangerous hexameter dominated by a tyrant of a caesura − though at least he retained his flexible chain of rhymes. Why did Alexander Pushkin, at this advanced stage of his career, suddenly turn to this alien form, an awkward and stylised line of verse? Why did he tackle a subject lacking any kind of verisimilitude and contemporary relevance?

The story is that of the main plot of *Measure for Measure* with the characters mercifully reduced in number from twenty-five to nine. Andzhelo is given the regency by a duke who rules a town grown lax in its standards and discipline. He rakes up and enforces all manner of ancient statutes including one which, archaically for a non-Muslim society, condemned to death anyone guilty of fornication. One Claudio is the first to be sentenced under this old law. He sends his sister, Isabella, a nun, to plead with Andzhelo who promptly falls in love with her and offers to free Claudio at the price of her honour. Finally Andzhelo is tricked by the substitution of his own ex-wife for Isabella and the duke, who has learned of his evil and hypocrisy, confronts him with the truth, exposes him, threatens him with execution and then finally forgives him.

On the one hand Pushkin adjusts and simplifies Shakespeare's story, much increasing its verisimilitude, especially at the climax and denoue-

ment which Shakespeare drags out unforgivably for a whole act, con-
voluting the plot into still further torments for Claudio. On the other,
there is nowhere near enough truth-to-life for him to present this as a
straight story modernised like *Count Nulin* or made to seem like real
history. It seems mistaken to accuse Pushkin of a lapse of taste or an
inaccurate aim at this late stage in his development as a narrative poet.
Certainly he must have known what he was doing and must have done
it in the way he originally intended, in view of his repeated defence and
approval of the poem notwithstanding the antipathy or indifference of
his readers. The story, and the form in which it is recounted, are both
of them stylised, rendered artificial, removed from the norm governing
both everyday life and most of Pushkin's literary experience. This was
a conscious step. That, in turn, must be the helpful clue in evaluating
Andzhelo. It must not be compared with the bulk of his other poems
for the comparison is without profit. The same criteria can hardly be
applied. It should be set apart, judged differently and considered as far
as possible *in vacuo*. It is not meant to effervesce with narrative interest
like *Count Nulin* or *The Robber Brothers*, nor to recapture the true
spirit of a past age, remote area or alien people, like *Boris Godunov* or
the four Southern poems, it is devoid of satire and parody, for all its
closeness to the original play, and it certainly does not tell a story for
its own sake.

Andzhelo is replete with ideas concerning human conduct — the
poet is particularly interested in the need for personal responsibility in
ethical matters, the revolting business of hypocritical behaviour and the
more uplifting quality of magnanimity — and they are presented here
in a way which is unique in Pushkin but not unknown to literature in
general. The poem is best seen as a formalised and graceful morality
piece, deliberately stilted from the first few noble lines and the start of
the entirely unbelievable story. Thus it belongs to a fairly rare category
of literature, strangely poised between didacticism and art, which includes, for example, works like *The Clerk's Tale*, Cervantes' *Exemplary
Novels* and some of Tolstoy's later stories (*The Three Old Men, What
Men Live By* etc.). In all of these works simple but unreal stories are
told in a formalised way with the aim of proclaiming a useful moral
purpose. Unreality, stiltedness, stylisation, stiff formalisation — not
only does the presence of these forces fail to detract from the enjoyment and the instruction, they actually add to the impact in a circuitous
manner. The very unreality of the events and the narrative actually
underscores the moral truth which is always the same: that good sense
and natural love are more important than rule-making, that honesty and

sincerity may be expressed only in what people do, not in what they say — in general terms that common sense, altruism, simple goodness of spirit and human nature must triumph over stupidity, officiousness, inordinate self-seeking and duplicity. The more unreal and stylised are the behaviour of the characters and the presentation of the story, the more the writer emphasises the gulf between the everyday world of common sense and the inane posturings which are a potential development of human behaviour realised occasionally by some individuals who lose their sense of reality. This complicated idea may be assisted towards simplification by reference to a different art form, the painting of icons. Here, too, we encounter stylisation and such defiance of the laws of verisimilitude that in certain instances they are actually inverted. Perspective, for instance, is often reversed in an icon so that parallel lines are seen to diverge as they depart from the viewer. The intention here is obviously not to represent the real physical world but to encourage the mind and spirit to soar upwards and outwards in a state of receptivity. At the same time simplicity concentrates the attention by eliminating distractions. This is why the faces on icons which look to the untrained eye like gloomy or solemn countenances are intended to be merely devoid of expression. Thus the hand of the devoted artist prepares the mind of the onlooker for a spiritual experience. By not dissimilar methods a fictional writer may sometimes create a simplified, unrealistic work in order to impress an idea upon his readers. In all such cases the essential ingredient is consummate artistic skill without which the idea collapses into absurdity.

This line of argument takes us to the outer reaches of Pushkin's universe, far away from the comforting criteria to which we have become accustomed. For this reason it is impossible to pronounce an unequivocal verdict on *Andzhelo* as a work of art. *Poltava* is relatively unsuccessful, for the reasons given above. *The Bronze Horseman* is a masterpiece because it eliminates the faults detracting from *Poltava* and the other narrative poems and for a number of positive reasons which will be considered shortly. How can one say whether *Andzhelo* is 'successful' or not? Everything depends upon the reader's readiness to accept the methods and standards of a new medium. This work stands so far away from its fellows that a comparison between them is like bringing together a Gregorian chant and a Mozart symphony or paintings by Rublev and Repin.

Towards Fulfilment

When we consider the general pattern of Pushkin's career as a narrative poet there emerges a resemblance to the progress of his work as a whole. What we are faced with is the usual Pushkinian process whereby he takes note of an important source, imitates it, refines it, improves upon it and abandons it for something else. Occasional flashes of out-and-out originality, as well as occasional lapses into inferiority occur as by-products. Russian folklore, the Byronic narrative, William Shakespeare's plays and poetry, Russian history all provided source material in different ways and were subjected to modification at his hands. Byron he was particularly interested in and hard on. All these poems impress in different ways. All of them, likewise, contain perceptible shortcomings or, at least, lack profundity. What is missing from the series, if we are to apply the very highest critical standards, is an out-and-out masterpiece, one redoubtable narrative poem which might amass the sundry virtues and discard the failings of these various preparatory works. That, no less, is the achievement of *The Bronze Horseman*.

5 THE BRONZE HORSEMAN

The Statue and the Poem

One of the finest of Leningrad's tourist attractions is the two-hundred-year-old equestrian statue of Peter the Great (1672-1725) commissioned by Catherine II and executed by a French sculptor, E.M. Falconet. For all its splendour this statue, known universally as 'The Bronze Horseman' after Pushkin's narrative poem in which it appears, is a curious work of art. It was intended as a tribute to Peter, and in particular to his almost superhuman achievement in building a new city on the inhospitable swamps of northern Russia. A spirit of dynamism and domination, consciously infused into the scheme from the earliest sketches, was perpetuated through the enormous difficulties which Falconet himself overcame during the twelve years of design and construction, and it survives in the resulting monument. Nevertheless, a closer look at the statue cannot fail to reduce the sense of admiration with which it is at first approached. To begin with, three incompatible visual metaphors are mixed together. Peter is depicted, astride his massive Orlov charger, riding uphill and about to surmount the crest. This hardly corresponds to the base of the statue, a 1,500-ton granite block called 'The Thunder Stone' which has been hacked into the shape of a breaking wave. Neither of these images squares with the swamp serpent which the horse is trampling in mid-gallop with its hind hoofs. This necessary constructional device was introduced at a late stage to provide an extra anchorpoint and it looks like what it is, an irreconcilable afterthought. Besides this, the tsar himself has been given some less than regal attributes, a squat figure, a puffy face, a quizzical gaze and a puzzling right-hand gesture about which there has been much speculation. How far is Peter really in control of his mount? Is he about to fall back, recover himself, even soar up into space? Is he urging the steed on or restraining it in the face of some catastrophic hazard?

Whether by accident or design Falconet has created an ambiguous monument which qualifies its praise of the addressee even as it is bestowed by calling attention as much to the tsar's human deficiencies as to his transcendent qualities. This ambiguity evidently held a special appeal for Pushkin for he has used the selfsame property as a source of enrichment for his poem *The Bronze Horseman*. Pushkin's ambiguity owes nothing to vagueness, indecision or *force majeure*; it is a deliberately chosen policy based upon a desire to set out a series of antitheses in such a way that their ultimate irreconcilability should be disguised. The idea worked so well that the poem exactly matches the statue in its ironical combination of conflicting interests into an appealing and harmonious whole. The reconciliation of opposing forces on a number of different levels is the greatest claim to fame of *The Bronze Horseman*.

So high is this pinnacle of fame that there is now nothing controversial about the greatness of the poem. Critics, when they pronounce upon it, find that their main task is to avoid repeating already used superlatives. The least that is normally said of the poem is that it is Pushkin's finest; it is commonly rated the leading poem in the Russian language and John Bayley has overtopped all his predecessors by describing it as 'the most remarkable of nineteenth-century poems',[1] presumably in any language. The praise may seem extravagant to non-Russian speakers and Walter Arndt, perhaps with that remark in mind, describes *The Bronze Horseman* as 'overpraised by some' and then only as 'perhaps the most significant of Pushkin's narrative poems'.[2] The warning against an excess of enthusiasm is useful, but the limitations implied here by the word 'perhaps' seem as excessive in the opposite direction. There is no real case for reducing *The Bronze Horseman* in rank. From all points of view and by any standards this is an exceptional piece of poetry deservedly occupying a distinguished place in Russian literature and outstanding in the context of Pushkin's own work.

Sources of Inspiration

Much energy has been spent determining the sources of this masterpiece. This kind of research will not show how, or by what distance, the poem outclasses its rivals but the multiple sources are important for a full understanding and they call for a brief rehearsal. *The Bronze Horseman* was a long time maturing in Pushkin's mind and there were one or two false starts, fragments of which have been preserved, in particular *The Genealogy of my Hero* (1836) and *Yezersky* (1833). His preoccupation with Russian history and specifically with Peter the Great was of long duration; *The Bronze Horseman* clearly relates to *The Negro of Peter the Great* (1827), *Poltava* (1828) and the unfinished *History of Peter I* (1831-6). The animation of the statue in the Don Juan legend, as re-created by Pushkin in *The Stone Guest* (1830), might have suggested the similar event in his greatest narrative poem, especially since the statue in each case communicates first by a movement of the head. It is also true that the names Yevgeniy and Parasha are not unique to this poem. Thus there are many reflections elsewhere in Pushkin of some of the features of *The Bronze Horseman*. It has also been demonstrated that further ideas, great and small, as well as certain phrases and even whole lines were borrowed by Pushkin from other writers, including Batyushkov, Vyazemsky, Gnedich and Shevirev. Ryleyev's name may be added to the list for there are a number of borrowings from his poem *Voynarovsky* (1824-5). Certain contemporary anecdotes concerning incidents during the St Petersburg floods of 1826 and the historical account of these catastrophes by V.N. Berkh (wrongly described by Pushkin as V.I. Berkh in his foreword) were also in the poet's mind as he wrote. Much the most important of the external sources, however, was a long work by the Polish poet Adam Mickiewicz entitled *Forefathers' Eve*. Mickiewicz was well known to Pushkin and they are reported to have held a long conversation one day beneath the monument itself. Parts of Mickiewicz's poem, especially that section of Part Three known as the *Digression*, contain overt criticism not only of Peter but also of the city and empire he created. At one point, for instance, Mickiewicz suggests that while Rome was built by men and Venice by the gods St Petersburg was the product of Satan. It goes without saying that this work was banned in Russia but Pushkin certainly knew it well. Although he agreed with some of the sentiments he retained the right to refute such criticism when it was voiced by a foreigner. His apotheosis of Peter and St Petersburg in the Introduction to *The Bronze Horseman* is obviously some kind of reply to Mickiewicz.[3]

These are some of the main sources which have been identified. However, the accurate pinpointing of them does not even begin to explain why the resulting work should be so highly esteemed. What happens in the poem? What meanings does it possess which make it so important? What formal qualities distinguish it from its predecessors and rivals?

The Story

There are three sections to *The Bronze Horseman*, an introduction and two numbered parts. The introduction describes Peter the Great's conception and then creation of a city on the northern swamps which became so grand that it outshone even the capital. Pushkin extols the city and its activities for about 80 lines, congratulating Peter on his domination of the harsh elements. Part One reintroduces the city in an ugly situation amid worsening winter weather and presents another hero, Yevgeniy somebody-or-other, a poor clerk upon whom most of our attention will be focussed from now on. (Half the total lines of the poem are devoted to Yevgeniy.) We learn of his simple dreams for domestic happiness with his fiancée Parasha. A high point of this section is Pushkin's furious description of the flooding of the city which even the tsar can do nothing to resist. In Part Two, once the waters have begun to recede, Yevgeniy, helped by a chance encounter with a ferryman, makes his way over to Parasha's house but everything there has been destroyed and washed away. Yevgeniy's mind cannot stand the strain. He loses his reason and begins to roam the city. One night he comes across Falconet's statue. Blaming Peter for having created the city in the first place he threatens him. The huge idol seems to look round at him. Yevgeniy runs away and keeps on running; all night he seems to hear the clanging steed thundering behind him. After this experience he always slinks unobtrusively past whenever he has to cross that same square. But he doesn't last much longer. His dead body is washed up on a little island, discovered on the threshold of Parasha's wrecked home itself and buried.

A Multiplicity of Themes

This simple but tragic story is tightly packed with a number of competing themes, some Russian, some universal. One of the first secrets of its success is the sheer density of *The Bronze Horseman*. As well as being the last of Pushkin's narrative poems it is also the shortest of the serious ones; none of the various versions exceeds five hundred lines which makes it one third the length of *Poltava* and only just over half as long as *The Captive of the Caucasus*. It is the only one (excluding the less serious *Count Nulin* and *The Little House in Kolomna*) with a contemporary, recognisable situation and it possesses even a brief foreword emphasising the reality of the events described. Thus, at a stroke, Pushkin has updated, intensified and authenticated his material.

The meanings of *The Bronze Horseman*, overt and inferential, can scarcely be pinned down; they add to themselves and contradict each other, run off into new directions and find constant renewal, prompted by all manner of references. These range from straightforward statements and questions about human affairs to a quite new system of symbolism, itself covering a broad range with the immediately obvious (like the symbolic horseman himself) at one end and minute half-hints of other worlds and deeper issues at the other. The ideas are grouped in a way traditionally beloved by the Russians, in polarities. Most of the main antithetical preoccupations of Russian history and culture are included in *The Bronze Horseman*, either as stark confrontations or merely as embryonic comparisons. The age-old, still unresolved Westernising/Slavophile question is represented in Peter's whole concept of St Petersburg as a window into Europe; Russia's westward movement is shown to bring about both good and evil consequences. This controversy sharpens its focus if it is narrowed to the local, but also long-lasting problems of Russia versus Poland. The hidden polemic with Mickiewicz shows that Pushkin had Russo-Polish relations in mind (perhaps the Polish uprising of 1830 in particular) though he is more concerned with aggressive defence of his homeland than with the more awkward international issues involved. Other political events alluded to surely include the Decembrist uprising of 1825 which had taken place under the very eyes of the Bronze Horseman in Senate Square (now Decembrists' Square) and during which shots were fired into the crowd from alongside the very ornamental lions which crop up twice in Pushkin's poem. A further Russian question raised in passing is that of the competition between Moscow and St Petersburg for pre-eminence as the capital city.

A French scholar has suggested that the whole poem is an allegory of the relationship between Pushkin and Nicholas I.[4] A better known American one, Edmund Wilson, emphasises the poem's long-lasting relevance to Russian politics by drawing a parallel between Peter the Great and Joseph Stalin.[5] In this context it seems preferable to set personalities aside. Pushkin's poem invites consideration of a general political issue which has bedevilled his countrymen for centuries, that of the autocracy *vis-à-vis* the common people. The problem here is that Russia seemed to need a strong, decisive leader. Such a man could make things happen and direct the destiny of Russia into greatness. On the other hand, what about the rights of ordinary people under a dictatorship? Pushkin leads us first into admiration for Peter and his grandiose achievements, then, like Falconet, makes us wonder how certain and secure things are by undermining the tribute with hidden ambiguity.

> Fearsome in all the darkness now!
> What contemplation in that brow!
> What strength and sinew in him hidden!
> And in that horse what fiery speed!

Where do you gallop, haughty steed?
Where will those falling hoofs be ridden?
O mighty overlord of Fate!
With iron curb, on high, like this
Did you not raise on the abyss
Our Russia to her rampant state?

At the same time we are persuaded into ever deeper sympathy for
Yevgeniy and are forced to weigh the interests of the petty individual
against those of the great overlord. There can be no facile resolution of
such a fundamental political problem and Pushkin is not simple-minded
enough to suggest one. We are left with the two opposing principles,
autocracy and democracy, attempting to fill the same space.

This is the point where the significance of *The Bronze Horseman*
begins to extend outwards into universality. Yevgeniy may be seen as
a Russian victim protesting against his maltreatment at the hands of the
autocracy. So vast is the background of the poem and so anonymous
is Yevgeniy that he may also be taken to represent any ordinary man
caught up in the great movements of history. His destiny is controlled
for him and his simple dreams are destroyed like those of any common
citizen drafted into an army, or those of any refugee or war widow. One
of the great questions posed inferentially by the poem is this: how do
you assess the contrary claims of whole countries, states and political
systems on the one hand and of ordinary, innocent, peace-loving subjects on the other? The state must grow and prosper — Pushkin does
not doubt that — but many innocents will be ground to pieces in the
wheels of progress and it is impossible to withhold sympathy from
them. Pushkin's contribution to their cause, lest they be forgotten, is
to record the pitiful, meaningless protest of one such victim.

These are some of the social, historical and moral questions raised by
The Bronze Horseman. Even judged on this level, taking into account
also the excitement and pathos of the story itself, it stands out as an
important Russian poem. The true distinguishing feature of the work,
however, is that it incorporates a further theme of such sublimity that
these lesser questions are made to appear trivial, local and short-lived.
Pushkin recalls for us at the opening of the poem, at its end and at
several points during the story, that before societies of any kind came
into existence there were at work the great forces of nature. *The Bronze
Horseman* is a reminder of those elemental powers which operate all
round us. What is man's position in relation to nature? Has he the right
to confront her with his own interventionary schemes? How successful

will these be if he does? Here we see Peter turned inside out, which is one of the miracles of such a short narrative poem. To Yevgeniy, as to Pushkin, he appears as a looming, menacing figure invested with maximum power. To Mother Nature he, and his pitiful successor Alexander I, look quite different. Peter and Alexander are mere humans. They may win the occasional battle against the elements but nature is not to be subdued for long. She will claim her own. That message is clear throughout the poem but it is pointed up with peculiar irony at the end of the introduction when the narrator states his confident wish that the defeated elements will make their peace with Peter and discontinue their futile enmity. Almost without pausing for breath he goes on to recall a very recent disastrous occasion when the elements showed beyond any doubt that they were not defeated, nor was their enmity futile, nor had they the slightest intention of leaving Peter to his everlasting sleep. This is one of the most telling juxtapositions of contrary ideas in the whole poem. Moreover, nothing in the course of the story will suggest that this is the last fling of a vanquished enemy. Everything speaks of the temporary subjugation of the seas; nature will come again.

The issue raised here is a very large one, nothing less than a consideration of man's ability to dominate his environment. This enables *The Bronze Horseman* to take rank alongside some of the great myths and legends of the past. Peter's outrageous, superhuman act, the construction of a city where climate and topography said it was not possible, renders him a worthy comparison with Icarus, Prometheus and Canute. The saddest incident in this poem is neither Yevgeniy's tragic discovery that his sweetheart is dead, nor his persecution, nor his death; it is, if we can bring ourselves to think in broader terms about the true capabilities and limitations of men, that pathetic moment when Tsar Alexander I puts in his appearance at the height of the flood, the people having turned to him in their panic.

> Then out came he,
> Sad, stricken, on the balcony.
> 'The Tsars,' he said, 'may not contest
> God's elements.'

If not the tsars, then who?

Such are the chief preoccupations of this magnificent poem. Beginning with the sad tale of Yevgeniy they take the mind in an upward and outward spiral from the local to the eternal. All manner of other ideas are, incidentally, tossed off in passing, bits of food for the intellect or

spirit. Is there such a thing as destiny? Peter invokes that force himself
and is related to it more than once by the narrator. Yevgeniy seems
destined for tragedy throughout, his Fate is said to await him as he
approaches Parasha's annihilated home, and it can only be as a result
of some malevolent kismet that his corpse and the wreckage of her
house are washed up together on the same tiny island. There are interesting hints at the contradistinctions between paganism and Christianity
borne out in the subtle juxtaposition of non-religious and religious
images. (These latter two points will shortly be considered in more
detail.) Finally, the poem includes a clear suggestion that to distinguish
between reality and unreality (in one of its several forms: sleep, dreams
and madness) is not so easy as it might seem. Perhaps Pushkin is sending
us back to Calderon and Plato; perhaps Cervantes is also in his mind,
since it is as a madman that Yevgeniy finds sudden understanding.

   The Bronze Horseman is the most mature, the most serious, the most
speculatory of all Pushkin's works. It is at the same time a *tour de force*
of compactness and harmonisation, introducing and uniting so many
disparate notions in such a short space. The next task is to discover
some of the ways by which all this is achieved.

Similes and Sounds

Despite its thematic saturation *The Bronze Horseman*, by playing upon
diversity and relying upon hints and symbols, manages not to appear
overcharged. The same is true of the poetic contrivances employed;
although numerous and multicoloured they are not permitted to cloy.
The safeguards in this case are brevity and an instinct for modulation.
Consider, for example, Pushkin's use of simile, metaphor and sound
effects, which are hard to separate because they so often come together.
The poem is crammed with similes and metaphors, sometimes swirling
along in an eddying current not unlike the river itself.[6] In fact, the river
and the flood use up most of them, and some extend over several lines.
The river is like a sick man tossing and turning in his bed, a spitting
cauldron, a wild beast, an attacking army, a villainous gang scurrying
out of a sacked village and strewing plunder down the streets, a hostile
simmering liquid over a hot fire, a panting warhorse retreating from
the field. These unpleasant images, used in the purple patches of *The
Bronze Horseman*, are usually accompanied by other devices; a scudding
run of couplets takes over from the *andante* movement of quatrain
rhyme-groups, violent enjambement wrenches the tetrameters into a

kind of rhythmic prose and a torrent of acoustic effects is let loose. This might mark the downfall of a lesser poet. The vital things to know are when to turn off the whole machine and what to say afterwards; Pushkin does know. The flood scene provides a good example. The rise of the river is traced from the previous night, onomatopoeia and alliteration are employed to depict the fury of the flood, an exclamatory climax comes in the breathless recitation of all the objects seen swimming down the streets (twenty-one words without a single verb, long and sonorous ones fitted three and four to a line in a way that English would be hard put to match), a wail of panic from the people creates the briefest possible transition and then — silence. Out comes the solitary tsar in the sad moment described above. The whole business has taken thirty-five lines.

Another instance occurs at the start of Part One. Nine lines are devoted to a description of the menacing river, the clouds, the cold, the wind and rain. Without warning and with only the words 'At that time . . .' as a hinge Pushkin swings into a quite different tone with the casual introduction of Yevgeniy. He soon proceeds into out-and-out flippancy when considering with the reader what parts of Yevgeniy's biography should be included and what left out. Shortly after this will come Yevgeniy's reflections and then the storm and the flood. These examples are not exceptional. The whole poem subdivides into thirty or so short paragraphs — the grand paean addressed to St Petersburg is the longest of them all and it occupies only forty lines of the introduction — but the changes in tempo and tone occurring both within and between them are innumerable. Crises and climaxes multiply in a mercurial procession and all the time the Russian language oscillates between different poles, the archaic and the modern, the poetic and the realistic, the grandiloquent and the down-to-earth, the dignified and the colloquial, conforming with exact appropriateness to each momentary need. It is this kind of easy modulation from subject to subject and mood to mood, engineered with fluidity and perfect timing, based upon the flimsiest of transitional remarks, which is the saving grace of this dense work with its serried sections.

Resourceful Rhyming

With Pushkin clearly at the height of his powers we are impelled to look for further merits in his finest poem. There are some interesting surprises in his rhyming. Apart from a couple of agreeable, but accidental-looking, half-rhymes (*neyu* with *svirepela/revela* and *sledov* with *zlo/voshlo*), there seems to be little unusual about the rhymes of *The Bronze Horseman*. Pushkin had no interest in the obvious poetical pyrotechnics achievable by revolutionary departures from canonised metres or rhymes. That goes for the rhymes themselves but the disposition of them is something different. In the previous chapter we saw something of the complexity and significance of this system. The changes are rung mainly in the interests of diversity and they are part of what is often loosely described as Pushkin's 'flexibility' or 'plasticity' of form. On rare occasions the variation bears a clear relationship with the surface meaning of the poem so that it is possible to reveal a subtly hidden and exciting device by which the form of the poem reinforces the story-line. A suspicion that this poem of so many other unusual qualities will prove exceptional in this regard is vindicated by an examination of the rhymes.

One outstanding feature of the rhyme-scheme is the extent to which that staple unit, the quatrain, is subordinated. Groups other than quatrains have a field day, especially couplets and the asymmetrical five-line groups. Virtually half of this reduced proportion of quatrains, moreover, belongs to the envelope type (abba). This makes for an inordinately high incidence of couplets and an increasingly high expectation of them in the reader's mind. From that flow both the speedy movement of *The Bronze Horseman* and the sense of shock and disturbance when, at key points and on several occasions, the poetic fabric is apparently torn apart and the narrative leaps forward rapidly and jerkily, performing wild tricks with enjambement, rhyme-patterns and everything else that comes to hand. The flood, Yevgeniy's descent into madness and the chase scene provide the best examples of this.

There is one startling occasion when the rhymes simply refuse to settle into any small, complete pattern. They go on repeating and falling over themselves in a section which is irreducible to anything less than nineteen lines. It is the description of Yevgeniy half way through Part Two, beginning 'But my poor, poor Yevgeniy . . .' which contains this unadvertised and protracted disruption. The nineteen lines are constructed upon seven rhymes (three feminine, four masculine) which are intermingled with only a loose background of logical order to begin with and chaos at the end. The scheme reads: AbAbCbCddCeeFgFgCgg. It sets out with all the appearance of normality, AbAb . . . but the reappearance of that 'b' rhyme in line six (*um, shum* and now *dum*) sounds the first false note. The scheme now proceeds into increasing derangement, ending with an almost nonsensical (for Pushkin) six-line unit which introduces a new masculine rhyme 'g' (*dobrom*), repeats the preceding feminine one 'F', repeats the 'g', harks absurdly back to the thrice-used 'C' last heard from seven lines previously and then thumps down two more 'g's, making four in all. Only now can this rhyming group be said to be complete.

Pushkin is neither a capricious nor a self-indulgent rhymster. Such a jumble is therefore unimaginable without some underlying cause. Not that the phenomenon, let alone the reason for it, is directly noticeable on the level of consciousness. Remarkable though this passage is there is no evidence that it has attracted any attention; even the few verse translators, who must have seen it when following the rhyme-scheme, have disregarded Pushkin at this point, lengthened the section and superimposed their own, better organised, groups of rhymes. Despite the absence of any blatant signals, however, this departure from normality is an important one. At some subconscious level of appreciation the eye darts about in an attempt to make sense of that large group, to establish at least a hypothetical norm against which the deviations might be sensed as enjoyable eccentricities. There is no such sense of order. This simply could not happen in Pushkin if all were well up on the surface of the story. What is happening there at this stage is that Yevgeniy loses his reason and we are told (in that very section) of the first demented wanderings of his body and mind. As he rambles around in increasing bewilderment and alienation so does the rhyme-scheme which is used in the telling of his story. There are a few further instances of this kind of parallelism in other narratives. We have drawn attention to one of them in the abduction scene at the beginning of *Ruslan and Lyudmila*; another long group of twenty lines occurs in *The Gipsies* immediately following the murder (lines 487-506) but this is the best example of the story-line finding supporting expression in the formal deeps beneath that level.

Nor is that the only unusual trick of form. Take, for instance, the opening ten and a half lines of *The Bronze Horseman* which are as well known as any in Russian.

Na beregu pustynnykh voln
Stoyal on, dum velikikh poln
I vdal' glyadel. Pred nim shiroko
Reka neslasya; bednyy cheln
Po ney stremilsya odinoko.
Po mshistym, topkim beregam
Cherneli izby zdes' i tam,

Priyut ubogogo chukhontsa;
I les, nevedomyy lucham
V tumane spryatannogo solntsa
Krugom shumel.

On a shore beside the desolate waves
He stood, filled with lofty thoughts,
And gazed into the distance. Before him
The broad river coursed along; a poor skiff
Moved down it all alone.
Here and there along the mossy, swampy banks
Black huts could be seen,
The homes of wretched Finns;
And the forest, unknown to the rays
Of the sun hidden in the mist,
Made its murmur all around.

No one seems to have noticed how strange they are, these celebrated lines describing Peter standing silently on the northern swamps and what he sees. The odd thing here is that those ten lines fall into a clear, repeated rhyming pattern which is not only not repeated again in *The Bronze Horseman* but which does not appear anywhere else in Pushkin. Why should it be so? There are at the famous head of this famous poem two identical five-line groups rhyming aaBaB. This is some sort of catch. At first sight it looks almost as if the poem might be in couplets. That theory holds good until the end of line four which fails to produce the expected 'B' rhyme (with *shiroko*). By the end of line five we think we have it; there is a complete five-line unit aaBaB. How satisfying when that same unit repeats itself. And yet, seen in context, this phenomenon is a strange one. In Pushkin's poems five-line groups rarely accompany each other and virtually never start the narrative off even singly. When they do follow each other they are usually different five-line groups. And here are two of these groups right at the start of the poem. By line ten the subconsciously seeking eye distinctly expects a third such group. Perhaps this will be a whole poem written in strange, unseparated and disguised stanzas? This theory is quickly demolished. The second line of the next group fails to fit the pattern. A group of aBaB is formed and we are then off into the usual stream of quatrains with occasional variations. How can we explain this anomalous beginning? Is it merely a question of formal frivolity? This seems unlikely in view of the seriousness of the poem and the absence of similar examples elsewhere in

Pushkin. Indecisiveness or a change of mind? Certainly not in a Pushkin
at the peak of his powers when his sureness of touch is at its least
questionable. Some kind of trickery? There seems no point in that.
There has to be a more sensible explanation.

The real clue lies in the fact that the short opening section is markedly
offset in formal terms from what follows. If it can be shown that the
sense of that section is also somehow offset then we shall have established a meaningful parallelism. There is indeed such a distinction. At
first Peter surveys an almost primeval world, an alien element, incomprehensible to him in its naturalness, its wastage and its poverty. He will
see it almost immediately through the prism of its potential but before
that he must be allowed to glimpse and take in the pristine scene, to
assess it as it now is before he changes it. That pristine scene is what
occupies the first ten lines of the poem the form of which is equally
alien and mystifying. Line eleven changes everything. Peter snaps out
of it, begins to think clearly and lays his plans for the future. The tenor
of this and the next nine lines is quite different from the opening. Peter
is already beginning to impose his order on the alien scene. Naturally as
he does so the opening 'stanza' effect disappears and Pushkin imposes
his own familiar order on an alien-seeming rhyme-scheme. Thus as Peter
assumes control of the wasteland he takes charge of everything at once,
both in the natural scene being described and in the devices used to
describe it. Once again it is possible to indicate a subtle and unusual
formal property working to good purpose in *The Bronze Horseman*.
One of the remarkable aspects of this one is that for once the true
mode of chaining together the rhymes is postponed for ten lines and
the exception to that rule is given first. The variation thus precedes the
theme, the syncopation comes before the standard rhythm, which adds
poignancy and emphasis to the opening of the poem.

There is in addition a slight taste of irony behind the whole method
used here. The exactitude of that opening pattern aaBaB, so carefully
chopped off at line five for emphasis, so meticulously repeated up to
line ten, suggests an underlying sense of meaningful order which belongs to the natural world as described therein. Peter cannot see it. He
must change it, imposing his own rhythms and constructions upon the
apparent chaos before him. How wrong he was, both in failing to com-
prehend the self-enclosed logic of that natural scene and in attempting
to destroy it – this is the burden of the whole subsequent story, or
a large part of it. If it is not being too fanciful, one might claim that
those opening 'stanzas' help reinforce the message that nature has her
own ways upon which she will insist and to which she will return despite

the best efforts of men to change them. Incidentally the end of the poem has a rhyme scheme of four quatrains with one interpolated couplet. There is no attempt to suggest nature's return by recreating the opening five-line groups, for which we may be thankful. Whatever else one may decide about these tricks of rhyming it is certain that Pushkin did not preconceive them mechanically. Had he been of the mentality to organise the ending deliberately into a formal reflection of the unusual opening he would have lacked the very spontaneity which created the whole poem in the first place.[7]

Structural Cross-references

The varied themes and moods of *The Bronze Horseman* are integrated and harmonised in several ways, Pushkin modulating from one to the next with inimitable fluency. The shortness of the poem helps too; there is no time for it to run out of control. Another unifying force is the rather complicated system of interrelated references within the poem. The darkness, the wind, the rain, the proud Idol with its outstretched hand, the house in Senate Square with its two lions standing on sentry guard, all these, and other details too, are mentioned on more than one occasion. Such cross-references within the poem help stitch the thing together tightly. However, this system is seen at its most effective not in such random instances but in the way that the beginning of the poem relates to its ending and the way that the ending looks back not merely to the beginning but elsewhere within the poem as well.

First the beginning and the end. They share a close association, which is a force for good, encircling the poem in a cyclic structure significant for both form and meaning. We are finally returned to a place remarkably similar to where we began, removed from Peter's city, another deserted shore. It is surprising how many images and even specific words are common to both scenes, not merely the plentiful obvious parallels – water, the river, the bank, the waves, the beach – but more unusual ones too; 'uninhabited', 'poor', 'black', 'dilapidated', 'fisherman', 'shack' are all words which, with some slight shifts in meaning, reappear at the end to remind us of the beginning. (Some of them appear elsewhere in the poem too.) Both scenes are alike in their stillness and remoteness. Individually and together they suggest the eternal presence of nature which we have argued to be the most serious theme of the poem. Man, in so far as he appears at all, seems like an insignificant, anonymous intruder. The murmuring forest and sportive waters have a more dynamic role in these moments than Peter or Yevgeniy or either of the fishermen.

As well as providing a back reference to the point of departure, this special ending seems to have another function. Its air of finality, of true deathliness, comes not only from the barrenness of the little island but also from a strange intermixture of pagan and Christian images which together suggest a remote after-life into which dead souls may proceed. The crossing of water before the body can come to rest, together with the mention of a boat and its coming to moor on the island, appear vaguely to recall Charon's ferrying of souls across the Styx. Perhaps this would be too vague if that was everything, but it is not. A sharper focus is achieved if we recall Yevgeniy's earlier crossing of the waters just after the storm. It was an absurdly unreal occurrence in the midst of events taken from cruel actuality. A boat suddenly appeared out of nowhere ('like a godsend') and he was transported across by a carefree ferryman who charged him a *grivennik* (ten kopecks, only a small sum) despite the great difficulties, hardships and dangers of the journey. At that time it is most unlikely that Yevgeniy would have met any ferryman still plying his trade, let alone doing it with good cheer, and one who would 'willingly' take grave risks for a derisory fee without waiting for other passengers. This figure is beyond doubt a reminder of Charon, even down to the low-value obol which his clients had to pay. His appearance in the story is otherwise unwarranted. So, incidentally, are the coffins which float down the street washed out of their cemetery by the floods. It is possible that these coffins are, and probable that this latter-day Charon is nothing other than a gratuitous *memento mori*, a grisly prophecy of Yevgeniy's inevitable tragedy. The grotesque arrival and behaviour of the untimely ferryman is a solemn prediction of his death. That death almost comes immediately when the boat all but capsizes. There is a moment of anguish and 'finally . . .' (the word *nakonets* comes at a line-end and we hasten forward to find out what happened) – 'it reached the shore'. Yevgeniy is apparently safe, but there is the irony of it. He might as well have perished. In fact, even in surviving he does still perish, for all that awaits him now is a slow decline, after a terrible shock and the sadness of bereavement, through madness, wandering and persecution to death itself. This first crossing is the true one. Charon, having received his nominal fee, completes his task by delivering Yevgeniy into hell. All of this is gently recalled by the closing scene of the poem which involves another crossing of the water.

And yet the ending is actually a Christian one. In that closing scene the word *Voskresen'ye* is mentioned. Not only does this word evoke that holy day Sunday, reminding us of churchgoing, but it also carries with it still some vestige of its original meaning, 'Resurrection'.

> Or else a civil servant comes,
> Boating on a Sunday,
> To this deserted island.

Yevgeniy was just such a civil servant and here he is transported at the end of the story across the waters to the remote island. His cold corpse was buried there *radi Boga*, a phrase which means loosely 'out of charity' though its literal meaning is 'for the sake of God', a Christian or semi-Christian, touch with which the poem ends. Greek and Christian mythologies work here in double harness to draw out the little island into a symbol of the after-life. This is not, as it happens, the only occasion when Greek and Christian references occur in close juxtaposition. Towards the end of Part One at the height of the flood St Petersburg (elsewhere Petrograd and Grad Petrov) is suddenly rechristened Petropolis and compared to Triton, a Greek merman-god. Only a few lines later the people are shown to be in dread of the wrath of the Christian God and the tsar himself refers to his own impotence in the face of God's elements.

There is, however, even more than this in the ending of *The Bronze Horseman*. Working away at the same time is a convolution of irony which is at once sadly amusing and profoundly disturbing. In the first place Yevgeniy was washed up on to the island with a ruined little house. Whether they arrived together or separately does not matter; either way their arrival here is remarkable. What does matter is that this is clearly Parasha's house. Earlier this was described as 'a ramshackle little house' (*vetkhiy domik*); now it is virtually the same (*domishko vetkhiy*). Yevgeniy's corpse is found not just anywhere but lying on the very threshold, with all the connotations that the phrase has, in any language, of an impending stride into new and exciting experiences – if you are allowed across. So near and yet so far. The inference is not merely that Nature (or Peter or Fate) has demolished Yevgeniy, but that she (or he or it) has first been cruel enough to allow him tantalisingly near to the realisation of his modest ambitions, to the very threshold of a new life, before destroying him. This sad and cruel irony is confirmed if we look back to the ruminative soliloquy of Yevgeniy in Part One which is sometimes omitted because it was struck out in the manuscript but is often reinstated nowadays because editors and public like it so much.[8] This twenty-one line passage, beginning, 'Me, get married? Well, why not . . .', is well worthy of inclusion both *per se* and as a key piece in the system of cross-references. It is introduced by the words, 'What was he thinking about, then?' which recall the solemn, 'And he was thinking . . .' introduction to Peter's grand schemes; how ordinary and modest Yevgeniy's plans appear by comparison. It also contains a reference to trips out on a Sunday, which identifies Yevgeniy again with the Sunday/Resurrection reference at the end. More importantly still, it predicts a happy life coming to a serene end in a domestic burial scene with the grandchildren seeing them off lovingly into the grave. There is a painfully ironic distinction between this day-dreamed idyll, ending 'And our grandchildren shall bury us', and the actuality 'His cold corpse/Was buried out of charity'. The warmth and love of a hoped for family burial is brutally replaced by a bleak anonymous interment.

All these thoughts, symbols and back references come together, packed tightly into the last eighteen lines. The ending thus provides a moving summation of some of the main themes of *The Bronze Horseman* and it certainly emphasises the ironic smallness, insignificance and impotence of human endeavour when set against the great movements of nature. Isn't this what life is like? — the poem seems to ask at the end. You dream, you act, you build, but it is all without meaning and value. If you happen to be born a tsar your grandiose schemes may take on an air of deep purpose and permanence but they are swept aside by the destructive forces of nature as easily and as soon as she chooses. If you are less lucky and are of low birth even the most modest of plans are liable to instant demolition from any of several quarters. Not only that, but nature seems to take a cruel pleasure in dangling before us the ironical promise of success, achievement, happiness, significance and permanence before atomising our schemes. Pushkin makes an accusation similar to that of Gloucester in Act IV Scene I of *King Lear*,

As flies to wanton boys, are we to the gods;
They kill us for their sport.

The Overall Achievement

As an object lesson in building on past successes and simultaneously learning from past mistakes, *The Bronze Horseman* would be difficult to surpass. This narrative poem succeeds in recreating what was of value, disparately spread, in all Pushkin's earlier serious narratives — an exciting tale, convincing evocation of place and character, a sense of the

dramatic, an instinct for variety, an awareness of history, the incorpora-
tion of a moving personal story, the posing of moral questions – and
adds to all that a new dimension of serious political and philosophical
speculation. At the same time every one of the earlier defects is discarded, the vagueness, lack of verisimilitude, the constrictions provided
by the Romantic hero and his plight, the tendency to go on too long,
the inner fragmentation which works against unity. The meanings are
many and profound, the form is a blend of spontaneity and authority
perfected to a degree unusual even for such an instinctively disciplined
master as Pushkin. So great is the distance between this poem and its
confrères within the genre that one scarcely wonders that it has been
so lavishly praised.

6 STORY-POEMS IN THE POPULAR TRADITION

We have looked at a large number of Pushkin's shorter poems and traced his development as a narrative poet. Between these two extremes stands a group of poems, longer than most of the lyrics and shorter than the narratives, which must not be disregarded. They belong in the main to the popular traditions of bawdy verse, fairy stories, folk tales and ballads. The first of these subjects touches inevitably on sexual matters and also on religious sensibilities.

(The Subject Cannot Be Even Hinted At)

This heading, now mercifully untrue, is taken from Prince Mirsky.[1] His parenthetical comment on Pushkin's *Tsar Nikita and his Forty Daughters*, written in England more than half a century ago, is a reminder of the difficulties to be encountered when approaching the subject of Pushkin's bawdy poems. In the west these difficulties have dwindled away to almost nothing. We can now speak frankly about sexual matters and even use in public those short Anglo-Saxon expressions known to everyone but unusable until recent times except between close friends. The Russians still have far to go in these matters, being at present well short of Mirsky's position of reticence in the England of 1926. This means both that Soviet editions even of such major figures as Pushkin are still edited down to exclude indelicate expressions, so that definitive texts are hard to come by, and that adult Russians freed from such restrictions are so racked with embarrassment that they prefer not to think of their literary idols as having sullied themselves with what may be seen as obscenities. To take one example, Andrey Sinyavsky is an enthusiastic Pushkin-lover, a well educated man, an artist of some renown and an intelligent editor and critic. For all that his misrepresentation of Pushkin on this one subject is so remarkable that, in the following quotation, he is guilty of some of the most unforgivably inaccurate comments that have ever been made about the poet:

> Let us repudiate as irrelevant and unworthy of Pushkin the heavy-handed obscenity of these gutter creations in which the shortage of

135

any grace and intelligence is made up by straightforward plebeian bawdiness.[2]

Even with an effort of will it would be difficult to pack more inexactitudes into one sentence about Pushkin. The proper way to deal with this statement is to rewrite it, replacing most of the main words with their antonyms. Pushkin's bawdy verse must be accepted as an integral part of his overall achievement. There is simply too much of it to ignore. It is normal, natural and healthy as well as abundant. Not that it is always edifying. The quality which always shines through Pushkin's indelicate poetry, redeeming it from the trappings of true obscenity which attract the normally attendant epithets 'abominable', 'filthy', 'disgusting' and 'offensive', is his humour, the one quality which the sensitive Sinyavsky himself lacks and fails to discern in his admired poet. Anthony Cross, discussing the subject in some detail, refers to 'a characteristic Pushkin touch — the ironic smile which comes from an awareness of his own self-indulgence, that healthy reaction which saves Pushkin increasingly from the temptations of a pornographer.'[3] This comment bears upon *Ruslan and Lyudmila* — the abduction scene which is discussed in Chapter 4 — but Cross makes it clear that the same quality attends Pushkin's bawdy verse as a whole. To judge by his extensive correspondence Pushkin's day-to-day Russian must have been richly salted with lewd expressions. Enough of these have crept into his works and afterwards been excised by editors or censors for an émigré publishing house to make up a whole volume of them entitled *Pushkin without censorship*.[4] It makes amusing rather than prurient reading.

The humour and the degree of explicitness range widely. In a little poem 'Christ is risen' (1820) the poet wishes his Jewish friend, Rebecca, a happy Easter, sends her a kiss and promises to adopt her faith in the future if she will return it. He ends with the naughty remark, 'I am even ready to hand you the one thing by which you can tell a true Jew from an Orthodox'. Notwithstanding the obvious implication Soviet editors do print this poem. They are more reticent as the sexual references become more explicit. They prefer not to remind us of *A comparison*, Pushkin's neat little typographical joke against the castrated French writer, Nicholas Boileau (-Despréaux):

Darling, Would you like to know
The difference between Boileau and me?
Despréaux only had a   ,
But I've got   : and a   ,

They emasculate many of Pushkin's sharpest epigrams by removing the bit that matters, such as the last line in this octave directed against General M.F. Orlov

> Orlov and Istomina lay in bed
> In abject nakedness
> The undependable general
> Had not distinguished himself in the ardent affair.
> Without any offence to her dear friend
> Laisa took out a magnifying glass
> And said, 'Let me have a look
> At what you've been fucking me with, my dear'.

They sometimes rescue a poem from outer darkness by making a prudent, though prudish, substitution of an unacceptable embarrassment. A good example is in the poem *To a beautiful woman taking snuff*. For twenty-seven lines the poet describes the sort of people he can accept as tobacco-users — pompous old professors, young soldiers and wrinkled harridans. But surely not his addressee — she is too lovely. Still, if she must indulge she must, and he allows his fancy to stray in a different direction. How nice it would be for him to be ground into a powder, kept in a box and then administered all over her person, stealing under her silks on to her breasts and . . . even . . . Here Pushkin gives it us straight: '. . . between her legs' (*mezhdu nog*). Russian editors, anxious to preserve the poem as a whole, remove those words and replace them by the phrase *mozhet byt'*, meaning '. . . perhaps'. Sometimes if there is a very bad word they simply leave dots. This occurs in an early poem 'Going home from vespers . . .' where one lower-class woman, arguing with another about the men they have been seen with, rather crudely twists a Biblical saying into an *ad hoc* folk proverb:

> You can see a straw in somebody else's cunt
> And you can't see a beam in your own.

Examples like these could be multiplied easily. Pushkin rejoiced in literature, sex and humour; it was inevitable that the three of them should come together. The resulting poems are amusing diversions, not among his most serious creations, but amounting to a minor genre still capable of providing pleasure for those who can bear to contemplate it with the fig leaf off. Much more significant are two of his longer poems in the same field. *The Gabrieliad* and *Tsar Nikita and his forty daughters.* These are works of true style and accomplishment well worthy of Pushkin's name. They ask to be associated with *Ruslan and Lyudmila*, the original version of which had a strongly erotic content, as well as *Count Nulin* and *The Little House in Kolomna* which are erotic by implication at least. The light-hearted spirit of story-telling runs freely through all of them and they are united by a discreet intelligence which allows all of them to run risks without incurring the consequence of bad taste.

The Gabrieliad runs a double risk, being both blasphemous and erotic. In its day it caused the author much trouble and repeatedly he had to deny that it was his. In point of fact, Pushkin's style and even his autobiographical imprint on the poem are unmistakable. Rather bored with church observances and revolted by the pious hypocrisy all round him he sat down at the end of Lent in 1821 and wrote this satirical amalgam of several of the Church's most revered dogmas, the Annunciation, the Virgin Birth and the Fall of Adam and Eve prominent among them. He tells the story of Mary, a beautiful young Jewess neglected by her old husband but soon destined to lose her virginal innocence. The Lord appears to her in a dream but, visiting his court, she takes a stronger fancy to the handsome Angel Gabriel. Before either of them can take matters further the Devil presents himself to Mary as a snake, seduces her spiritually by explaining how unfairly history has treated him – did he not *save* Adam and Eve by introducing them to physical passion? – and then, turning himself into a handsome youth, he carries the seduction to its logical physical conclusion. Gabriel drives him off and repeats the debauchery. Only God is left. Mary lies naked on her bed, dreaming of Gabriel when a white dove descends upon her, works gently at her intimate parts and eventually, after many a gasp, quiver and coo, falls away satisfied, delicately shading 'love's flower' with his wing.

The sexual content of this poem is strong. The various suitors are described fumbling their way under Mary's clothing until they discover what they are after. Gabriel defeats the Devil only by biting him in his most vital part. Eve is aroused to awareness by a rather obvious symbol, 'Two apples dangling from a wondrous bough' and her newly awakened husband loses no time exploring between her legs. In one of his numerous digressions the poet recalls teaching an old love of his how to bring herself physical relief as she lay in bed at night without him. There are, however, no disgusting crudities – all the obvious 'four-letter' words are excluded from the poem – and it is the agreeable, exciting, climactic and satisfying aspects of human sexuality which are celebrated. Most pornography exploits and demeans women. Not this poem. Mary, who is aroused to a hitherto unknown sexual pleasure, who gets her man and goes on enjoying his services after the poem has ended, is the heroine of the story and much the happiest character in it. After her triple adventure she considers her position:

A weary Mary, as he flew away
Thought, 'Ah, what fun and games I've had today!
That's one, two, three. They're really not too bad!
I've weathered it, I think I can record.
Together in a single day I've had
The devil, one archangel and the Lord.'[5]

We can only hope that Pushkin, skilled as he was in the erotic arts, left most of his women as contented as this literary heroine. Elsewhere in *The Gabrieliad* he demonstrates a deep understanding of femininity, albeit jocular in its expression, and the poem imparts a clear suggestion that the author's obvious interest in women amounted to sympathetic affection and attentiveness.

As always the sexuality is constantly undermined by humour. A further link between this poem and *Count Nulin* is its parodic intent. Full enjoyment depends upon a close knowledge not only of the original events described in the Bible, but of the actual texts. At one point there is an obvious parody of the *Ave Maria*. Offensive as this may well be even today to some of the faithful, to the uncommitted it has the appearance of clever burlesque executed by a skilled parodist. The extent to which Pushkin restrains himself in the face of great temptation is epitomised by one of his formal devices. *The Gabrieliad* is written in rhymed iambic pentameters. The rhymes course along in the manner described in Chapter Four. Early in the poem Pushkin introduces a triplet, rhyming *tron*, *on* and *zvon* successively (lines 60-62). The effect of that intrusive third rhyme is always amusing. In this poem more than any other there would be justification for a string of triple rhymes. Pushkin, however, limits himself to one only in 552 lines. Gone now are the days when Pushkin had to disclaim this splendid piece of poetry. 'I can only express my regret', he wrote to the tsar in 1828, 'that such a shameful and miserable work should be ascribed to me.'[6] We may now claim on his behalf not only that he wrote *The Gabrieliad* but that the poem adds much to his credit.

The poem with a subject which could not even be hinted at by Mirsky was *Tsar Nikita and his forty daughters*. This consists of 235 lines of irrepressible sexual fun. John Bayley refers to it as 'a wonder-fully obscene little tale'.[7] Wonderful it is, obscene it is not. Neither is it, in Simmons's words, 'out-and-out pornography'.[8] Pushkin had a clear concept of obscenity.

> An obscene work is one whose aim or action leads to the undermining of the rules upon which social happiness or human dignity is based . . . But a jest inspired by heartfelt gaiety and a momentary play of imagination can appear immoral only to those who have a childish or obscure idea of immorality confusing it with didacticism . . .[9]

Although the content of *Tsar Nikita* is wholly sexual it is fully in-sured against concupiscence by its ringing innocence. It is as light as thistledown and all the dirt, if there is any, must accrue in the mind of the reader, not the dispassionate, amused story-teller who is frequently embarrassed to have to continue what his obligation as a chronicler forces him into.

This most delicate of indelicate stories goes as follows. The rich Tsar Nikita lived a life of happy luxury. Only one thing spoiled it. He hap-pened to have forty daughters, from various mothers, and they all shared the same defect. Between their legs they had no . . . that is, they were born without a . . . How can such an embarrassment be put into inoffensive words? The poet struggles for inspiration and finally finds a way of telling us:

> Aphrodite's lovely breast,
> Lips and feet set hearts afire,
> But the focus of desire,
> Dreamed-of goal of sense and touch,
> What is that? Oh, nothing much.
> Well then, it was this in fact
> That the royal lassies lacked.[10]

At last a means of curing them was found. A messenger was dispatched to an old witch who persuaded the devil to come up with a varied selec-tion of the necessary objects. There were all sorts and sizes of these 'things we all adore', including curly ones and coloured ones. The witch counted out forty of the best, wrapped them in a napkin, locked them in a box and sent the messenger back home. Inevitably, unable to con-tain his curiosity, he opened the box and watched in panic as the 'little birds' soared up and settled in the trees. How to get them back? Crumbs were no use as a bait. ('Evidently they feed on something else.') An old crone, passing by, knew what to do. 'They'll come back if you just show them your . . .' — again no actual mention of anything indelicate. The trick worked and he returned home with the priceless articles. Rewards all round and great celebrations followed.

This poem propels the reader's imagination into unmentionable immodesties but does so with protesting innocence. There are no sniggering innuendoes but there are plenty of little sexual jokes. What are we to make of the one characteristic of his precious cargo which attracts the messenger's curiosity and pricks his interest? Applying himself to the casket he can see or hear nothing, but when he sniffs he soon guesses what he is carrying. If the words 'familiar scent' mean anything to the reader then he must be to blame for any impure thoughts they might provoke. The poet places no emphasis upon them. The speed of the narrative hastening along with its happy trochaic lilt, does not allow him time to do so. There is no luxuriating in long descriptions or mature reflections. Urgent business is afoot and everyone's duty is clear: the messenger must carry out his assignment with alacrity and the poet must report him doing so. If the reader cares to think his own thoughts and come to his own conclusions that is his affair. The folkloric style, echoes of Pandora's Box and the use of the magic number forty, widely occurring in the scriptures and in folk tales, enhance the poem's spurious sense of respectability, by suggesting vague affinities with greater narrative traditions such as Greek mythology and popular legends of antiquity. In fact it is an extended tight rope which the author teeters along for two hundred and thirty-five lines talking all the time about women's and men's sexual parts without once naming them. We must regret the false shame which has kept this poem for so long from its public. Anthony Cross writes this unfortunate summary of its history. 'It has received . . . little or no attention from critics and literary historians, although the late B.V. Tomashevsky . . . had more ideas on *Tsar Nikita* than he ever committed to print.'[11] It is certainly a delight to read. Anyone who does read it may do so with the clearest conscience: *Tsar Nikita* is ninety per cent humour and ten per cent titillation.

The Kingdom of Thrice-nine

Pushkin's *Tale of the Golden Cockerel* begins in a strange location 'Somewhere in the kingdom of thrice-nine, In the state of thrice-ten . . .' This is one of the traditional formulas used like 'Once upon a time . . .'

to begin a Russian folk tale or fairy-story. The poet spent some considerable time in this kingdom and his adventures there, occurring in his full maturity, proved remarkable. He returned from it like one of the heroes of such stories, laden with exotic treasure. More precisely he wrote five famous *skazki*, or fairy tales (though this term is misleading — Russian folklore is devoid of fairies as such) between 1830 and 1834. Despite the apparent triviality of the genre these are commonly held to be among his very finest creations. The extent of his achievement in this area is astonishing. What nation other than Russia can look back over only a century and a half to the inventing of some of its best known, best loved and now traditional fairy stories? Invented they were. Later in this chapter we shall look at a good number of Pushkin's borrowings and adaptations from world folklore but these were to help him with his ballads. The fairy tales all came from his own imagination.

The test of a fairy story is in its appeal to children. Pushkin's tales pass this test with honour. Beyond that they have not failed to excite the admiration of all educated adults who have come across them. This is an area in which we depend greatly upon the evidence of native Russians and Mirsky is, as usual, forthcoming on the subject of the *skazki*. He tells us that, 'The child (I speak from personal experience) is admiringly absorbed in the process of narration and in the flow of rhyme as is the sophisticated critic in the marvellous flawlessness of the workmanship and consistency of the "style".'[12] The striking quality of these poems, one which is barely detectable by a non-native speaker if he is honest, is their authenticity. There is not a false note in them. Children and sophisticated Russian critics would have told us by now if there were. On the contrary, their every last detail places them to the general satisfaction in the centre of the Russian folk tradition. Indeed we are told that 'some of Pushkin's works written in the folk spirit (e.g. 'Songs of Stenka Razin') have been taken by researchers to be transcriptions of genuine folk songs.'[13] It is easy to see why. A single example of a narrative device used by Pushkin in a manner indistinguishable from the anonymous Russian narrators of antiquity may stand for many. In *The Dead Princess* Yelisey travels far and wide in search of his poisoned and entombed bride. No one can help him so he turns in despair to Mother Nature:

Then at last the warrior turned
To the Sun who redly burned·
— 'Sun, our luminary, pacing
Yearly round the skies . . .

In the wide world hast thou ever
Seen a young princess? . . .'

The sun cannot help but recommends the moon:

    – 'Moon, thou Moon, good friend of mine,
Horned and gilded, who dost shine
In the misty deeps . . .
In the wide world hast thou ever
Marked a young princess? . . .'

The uninformed moon recommends the wind:

    – 'Wind, O Wind, so strong and proud,
Chaser of the flocks of cloud . . .
In the wide world has thou ever
Marked a young princess? . . .'[14]

The wind, as we might expect, solves his problem. It is instructive to compare these procedures with similar ones occurring widely in the Russian folk tradition. That most famous of ancient Russian poems, *The Lay of Igor's Campaign*, which dates back, it is supposed, to the twelfth century, about six hundred and fifty years before Pushkin wrote his *skazki*, contains much the same thing. This time Igor's second wife Yaroslavna laments the defeat of her beloved and, in the familiar tradition, addresses her sorrows to the elements:

> Yaroslavna, early in the morning, laments on the rampart of Putivl saying: 'Wind, O Wind! Why, O Lord, do you blow so hard? Why do you carry the . . . arrows on your light wings against the warriors of my beloved? . . .
>> Yaroslavna, early in the morning, laments on the rampart of the city of Putivl saying: 'O River Dneiper . . .! You have battered your way through the rocky mountains . . . Carry, O Lord, my beloved back to me . . .
>>> Yaroslavna, early in the morning, laments on the rampart of Putivl saying: 'O bright and thrice-bright Sun! You are warm and beautiful to all. Why, O Lord, did you dart your burning rays against the warriors of my beloved? . . .[15]

Vladimir Nabokov, writing about *The Lay of Igor's Campaign*, refers

to 'An array of animals . . . playing a changeful double role in the structure.' He points out that 'the diverse expressions of the theme enter
into a subtle arrangement of calls and recalls, with every step having its
reverberation and every echo its arch.' He mentions an 'all-pervading
sense of magic so vividly conveyed by flora and fauna' and draws attention to 'interlinked themes . . . intonational refrains and recurrent types
of metaphor.'[16] These characteristics, and numerous others, far from
being unique to *The Lay* are widely encountered in many Russian (and
foreign) folk tales. Pushkin's ability to recall and imitate such time-
honoured and widespread features of folk literature, without a trace of
effort or artificiality, is certainly one of his highest achievements.

The tales themselves may be simple but the story behind them is not.
Pushkin's preparations were long and complicated, beginning, of course,
in childhood when he listened like other youngsters to recitations of
Russian folk tales, and continuing on a more serious basis in adult life
— particularly during his enforced stay at Mikhaylovskoye (1824-6) —
when he caused his old nurse, Arina Rodionovna, to recite them again
so that he could make a conscious study of their workings. There is also
some intrusion into his own tales of non-Russian material, the best
known example being Washington Irving's *Tales of the Alhambra* one
of which formed the starting point of Pushkin's *Tale of the Golden
Cockerel* (1834). This was the last of the series which had earlier produced *The Tale of the Priest and his Workman Balda* (1830); *The Tale
of Tsar Saltan* (1831); *The Tale of the Fisherman and the Little Fish*
(1833) and *The Tale of the Dead Princess and the Seven Heroes* (1833).
An interesting feature of this group of poems is their formal diversity.
We might have expected the poet to have struck up a successful formula
and simply repeated it. Not so; the lengths of the tales and the metres
employed vary considerably. Three of them, *Tsar Saltan*, *The Dead
Princess* and *The Golden Cockerel* are written (like *Tsar Nikita*) in
trochaic tetrameter, but their lengths are, respectively, 996, 552 and
224 lines, the first of these being four-and-a-half times the length of
the last. The other two tales are metrical anomalies and, moreover,
very interesting ones. *The Priest and his Workman* consists of 189 extremely varied lines. They range from three to no less than fourteen
syllables and yet these remarkably unequal lines are made to rhyme
in couplets. The effect is electrifying. The rhythm spurts and jumps
where it will but the supervising rhymes chase about bringing order as
best they can. This creates a sense of formal uncertainty which plays
against the normal repetitiveness of a folk tale, enlivening and colouring
the whole story as well as underscoring the uncertainty of the hero's

ultimate success. Everyone has his own favourite among these stories — Mirsky goes enthusiastically for *Tsar Saltan*[17] and Bayley for *The Golden Cockerel*[18] — but this tale must surely have its own right to pre-eminence. It has the strongest claim to individuality because of its formal inventiveness which is so well attuned to what Oliver Elton describes as 'The admirable rough-and-tumble of the business'.[19] *The Fisherman and the Little Fish* is different again, varied but less so. It is governed by no kind of regularity, neither by line nor by rhyme. The lines are, however, all between nine and eleven syllables long so that the occasional jerkiness of *The Priest and his Workman* is no longer apparent. Occasionally a strategically aimed couplet settles things down with even greater certainty. The surprising fact is that each of these five tales must be accounted a success in its own way. It is almost as if Pushkin's adaptation of his various sources, and his deep identification with them, guarantees authenticity whatever formal pattern might be imposed. We must remember that the very decision to tell such stories in verse is an innovation; the great majority of their antecedents existed in a prose version.

A word or two about the actual stories will not be out of place. *The Tale of the Priest and his Workman Balda* ultimately concerns the theme of greed. A priest hires a workman on strange terms. The man will do all he requires if he can hit the priest over the head three times at the end of a year. The priest cannot resist the temptation of a year's free service and his new workman performs even better than expected. As time draws near he dreams up an 'impossible' task so that he will not have to fulfil his nasty half of the bargain but Balda, using his wits, achieves it and the wretched priest has his brains knocked out. Rough justice, but a clear message is conveyed by the last line: 'Priest, you shouldn't have gone rushing off after cheapness.'

The most famous of these tales, the longest by far and the one with the longest title is: *The Tale of Tsar Saltan, of his son the glorious and mighty knight, Prince Guidon Saltanovich and of the fair Swan-princess*. While Tsar Saltan is at war his wife bears him a son. Through the machinations of her rivals, however, the pair are cast out to sea in a barrel. The son, Guidon, breaks out and, almost immediately saves a swan from death at the hands of a predatory hawk. She rewards him by setting him up in a glorious palace and kingdom of his own. After a number of setbacks he and his mother and father are reunited and the evil-doers are pardoned. The swan, unsurprisingly, turns out to be a beautiful princess whom Guidon takes for his bride. An interesting feature of the story is that, at several points, it becomes necessary for Guidon to traverse the seas hidden in a boat and he does so by changing himself into a bumblebee. This little detail, picked up by Rimsky-Korsakov in an otherwise little known opera, has become known to the world at large in the miniature showpiece entitled 'The Flight of the Bumblebee'.

The theme of greed returns again in *The Tale of the Fisherman and the Little Fish*. A fisherman catches a magic fish. Because of his mercy she grants him a wish and he asks only for a new trough. Scolded repeatedly by his wife, he returns and asks for more, a new cottage, a palace and servants, a whole empire, and finally dominion over the seas and the fish herself. When he returns he and his wife have lost everything. Even the trough is broken. Hence the phrase, in the modern Russian language, *ostat'sya u razbitogo koryta* which means 'to be no better off than you started' — a good example of a bit of Pushkin that has passed unnoticed into the popular idiom.

The Tale of the Dead Princess and the Seven Heroes needs little recapitulation. Give or take a few details (such as the transformation of homunculi into heroes) it is the familiar story of *Snow White and the Seven Dwarfs*. Vanity, jealousy and violence destroy those who turn to them and the reader enjoys the triumph of innocence, beauty and youth. It will be difficult for any English-speaking person to read this story without the intrusion of Walt Disney into the experience.

The Tale of the Golden Cockerel is, however, something quite new. Tsar Dadon (mysteriously transliterated into Dodon in some English versions) is worried in his declining years about the protection of his kingdom. An old astrologer recommends a golden cockerel which will warn of any danger. The tsar accepts the offer with gratitude and promises to grant the astrologer any wish. After a long interval danger does threaten. Dadon's two sons ride off to combat and the father follows, only to discover a slain army and both his sons dead — they have, apparently, killed each other. His grief is quickly assuaged by a glamorous queen who then appears. Infatuated, he takes her home only to be confronted by the astrologer who now claims his wish — the queen herself. Dadon laughs him to scorn and has to kill him off when the fellow persists. Alas for him. The cockerel, descending, ends his life with a peck through the skull and the mysterious queen disappears. This is a cruel affair, taken by some to be an oblique comment on the abuse of power known only too personally by Pushkin himself. Here is John Bayley's comment:

> The origins of *The Golden Cockerel* and its hints of political meaning give it a special place. More remarkable than any specific reference

... is Pushkin's use of the *skazka* to create a gruesome little tableau of the nature, in any age, of power: its irresponsibility and its blindness ... it would not be absurd to class *The Golden Cockerel* with Tolstoy's *Hadji Murad* and *The Bronze Horseman*.[20]

No one can say for certain that this kind of judgement is wrong but it does seem to stretch rather too far both the political implications of this unsubtle tale and the extent of its achievement. The misuse of power, along with other human shortcomings, is a common theme in folk tales. In *The Priest and his Workman*, for example, the priest's wish to control his man's destiny and Balda's exercising of his inexorable power over his master provide the whole story. In *The Golden Cockerel* the power happens to be invested in a tsar but this is scarcely enough to politicise the poem. It is a mistake to read any localised meanings into the five *skazki*. It may be true, on the broadest level of meaning, that, in speaking to our primitive fears and desires, they give us some instruction towards the improvement of character and conduct, but even this is vague and doubtful. They are stories in the purest sense. This debars them from serious consideration alongside *The Bronze Horseman*, *Yevgeniy Onegin* and the best of Pushkin's lyric poems because they contribute so little to our thinking. It is in terms of sheer artistic achievement that they merit the attention and high praise which has often come their way.

Balladry

Among his many other skills Pushkin can lay claim to mastery of the art of balladry. His attraction to the genre is twofold. On the one hand, he had a deep sympathy for the common people of the countryside and a deep love of their traditional stories some of which appeared in ballad form or were readily adaptable to it. On the other, he could scarcely fail to be attracted by the literary challenge offered by the popularity of ballads among poets of the Romantic period all over Europe. In the event two or three of his best ballads, it is widely acknowledged, came to equal anything produced outside Russia at the time. Several interesting points emerge from a study of this aspect of Pushkin's poetic art. He wrote more ballads than is probably realised (at least two or three dozen), they are, of course, among his longer poems, they drew his attention away from the beloved iambic tetrameter to several other metres, particularly the trochaic tetrameter, and they are extremely varied in their provenance, borrowing ideas from widely scattered places: England, Scotland, France, Moldavia, Poland, Serbia, Lithuania, the Ukraine, and elsewhere. Of great significance is the fact that balladry is not a youthful pursuit of Pushkin's, it comes upon him properly in his middle twenties and stays with him. To take the most extreme example of a year's work, in 1833 he devoted half his total output of shorter poems (not that there were many at all) to this kind of story in verse.

An early poem *Domovomu* (*To my house-spirit*) (1819), which is not a ballad as such because it has no narrative interest, gives an indication of the skills which will serve Pushkin well in another decade or so. A kind of incantation asking the house-spirit to bless his home and garden, it is put together with the fluency, variety and euphony which would shortly make him famous. The most noticeable feature of the poem, however, is its nice blending of the supernatural and elemental with the everyday. A protective spirit is invoked, primitive fears of the rain, the wind and the snow are voiced, but in the next breath the poet asks the *domovoy* to keep an affectionate eye on the secluded vegetable garden with its decrepit gate and tumbledown fence. Thus the simple details of day-to-day living are mixed up with mysterious, transcendental forces. The formula − not dissimilar to the method employed in his best prose story *The Queen of Spades* − will work wonders in the later ballads.

Before we get carried away with Pushkin's successes it is worth glancing at his worst attempt at balladry, also an early piece, *Chernaya Shal'* (*The Black Shawl*) written in 1820. Here is an arresting example of the mediocrity into which he was occasionally seduced by new possibilities laid out so enticingly by European Romanticism and which one day he would transcend with triumph and consistency. Based on a Moldavian folk song it recounts the murder of an unfaithful girl and her lover. The teller of the tale catches the two of them *in flagrante delicto*. The killing is described in the lurid terms which we have come to associate with the excesses of passion to which unrestrained Romanticism was prone to lead and which scarcely epitomise the Pushkin whom we now accept as the fountain-head of Russian literature.

> I entered the chamber in that remote place;
> The false maid was in the Armenian's embrace.
>
> My head swam, and then . . . to my dagger's refrain
> In mid-kiss the blackguard was taken and slain.

I stamped on the man's headless body and stayed,
Pale-faced and unspeaking, my eyes on the maid.

There is always a market for that sort of thing and this unspeakable extravaganza came rapidly to enjoy popular success. One of Pushkin's contemporaries, Vladimir Gorchakov, speaks of its early popularity with General Orlov in Kishinev.[21] Musical versions embellished, if that is the word, fashionable drawing-rooms.[22] There are several to choose from, solo songs and duets, a cantata, even a one-act pantomime-ballet.[23] In later years it fell from grace and is now largely disowned. Mirsky described it as 'one of the crudest and least Pushkinian things he ever wrote'[24] and Nabokov as 'some indifferent couplets in amphibrachic tetrameter',[25] though more recently Bayley has implied that we should accept *The Black Shawl* as an efficient and equable exploitation of contemporary taste.[26] In fact, although the poem does possess two easy virtues, an agreeable euphony and folkloric formal simplicity, these properties would not have been beyond the powers of any amateur poetaster of the period. To the twentieth-century ear it sounds unnecessarily outlandish and meretricious, all too eager to lay stress on what is sensational and sentimental.

When Pushkin came into full flow as a balladeer he would never again be guilty of such excesses. He worked in four main fields, a religious one in which he depicts monks or knights going about their duties in mediaeval times, a historical one dealing with real historical events, an ethnic one providing him with stories from other national traditions, and a purely fictional one in which he retells stories from Russian folklore. An example of the first may be seen in 'Zhyl na svete rytsar' bednyy . . .' ('There once lived a poor knight . . .') (1829) which depicts a religious knight's tranquil, saintly progress through his worldly life. Unfortunately he dies without the last rites and this presents a problem to the administrators who sort out the details of one's life after one is dead. The devil blackens his character in an attempt to claim his soul but he is defeated by the intercession of the Virgin Mary and the knight duly enters heaven. The fourteen simple faithfully end-stopped quatrains reflect the honest orderliness of the good man's life on earth. This is a tranquil, justifiably mechanical little story possessing great charm.

The historical ballads score one or two notable successes. *Pesn' o Veshchem Olege* (*The Lay of Oleg the Wise*) (1822), a popular recitation piece, is written in lively amphibrachs and an irregular stanza form. A sorcerer warns Oleg that his beloved horse will be the death of him so

Oleg, full of regret, has the beast killed. He insists on seeing its bones and this proves his downfall, for a serpent flashes from the skull and stings him to death. The poem, with its seventeen sestets, may be a fraction too long – a criticism from which several of the ballads are not entirely immune – but its story line is strong, the emotions are patently sincere and the cruel, tragic ending imparts a powerful shock. In 1826 Pushkin set down three *Songs of Stenka Razin*, the details of which he learned from his nanny, Arina Rodionovna, the verses of which, however, are all his own work. The accentual poetry of these stories represents an uncanny sense of folkloric imitation. The first one is the traditional tale of the drowning of Stenka Razin's princess; the last one calls him away to adventure, fortune and love. They are written in four-stress lines. The middle song, in two-stress lines, shows Razin in defeat, compelled to give up a rich coat under threat of hanging. Its jerky, stabbing movements and exact repetitions appear to come straight from the mouth of some long-dead, anonymous peasant bard (known to the Russians as a *skazitel'*). It comes as a great relief to a foreigner when he learns that, as we have mentioned above, such verses have even deceived Russian experts. Lines like these are indistinguishable from the real thing:

Stal Sten'ka Razin
Dumati dumu:
'Dobro, voyevoda,
Voz'mi sebe shubu
Voz'mi sebe shubu
Da ne bylo b shumu.'

Such is Pushkin's skill at balladry that it seems as if a different quality attends and enhances each separate poem. Another successful historical ballad is set in Spain. 'Na Ispaniyu rodnuyu . . .' ('Into Spain, his own country . . .'), written as late as 1835, tells a long complex story in twenty-eight tidy quatrains. The quality of this poem is its density. It describes how Julian, for reasons of personal vengeance, invites the moors into Spain. His enemy Rodrigo is dethroned, defeated in battle and presumed dead. Actually he escapes, but, on hearing his people speak so ill of him, he retires to a cave on the seashore and becomes a hermit, replacing a dead monk. He is tempted by the devil but the dead hermit intercedes for him and he is spared. In the last stanza, recognising God's will, he returns to the people. There is, of course, more legend than history in this narrative but it is based on the real governor of Andalusia, Count Julian, the real King Rodrigo and the events of the year 711 AD. The opening two stanzas indicate the compactness of the poem. They are a model of the art of fitting masses of expositional detail, necessary for full understanding but irrelevant to the main story, into the smallest possible space but without detriment to the verse.

Into Spain, his own country,
Julian invited the Moor.
The Count had decided to take vengeance
Upon the King for a personal affront.

Rodrigo had abducted his daughter
And dishonoured his ancient family.
This was why his fatherland was betrayed
By the infuriated Julian.

The majority of Pushkin's ballads do not have historical associations. Most of them tell an exciting, usually tragic story and the same stories often appear in the literatures of different countries through borrowing and adaptation, imitation and translation. Pushkin was fond of these processes and by means of them introduced his readers to a number of good foreign stories, sometimes creating minor masterpieces as he did so. For instance, the famous Scottish ballad *The Twa Corbies*, in which two lugubrious ravens consider the fate of a dead knight, opens in Pushkin's version (1828) with a couple of lines as haunting, darkly melodic and memorable as any he wrote:

Voron k voronu letit,
Voron k voronu krichit:

The poem *Gusar* (*The Hussar*) (1833) is borrowed from the Ukrainian. After a rather wordy beginning it develops a rollicking pace as the narrator describes his adventures on a broomstick following a witch through the night sky. Again, there are some lovely sounds:

Glyazhu: gora. Na toy gore
Kipyat kotly; poyut, igrayut,

From England Pushkin took no less a work than *The Pilgrim's Progress* ... and reworked a small section of it into the poem *Strannik* (*The*

Pilgrim) (1835). Sensibly he chose the iambic hexameter for the purpose; its stately plodding suggests Pilgrim's stolid progress through great
travail. Into this solemn material, however, there darts the occasional
flash of Pushkin's genius. Perhaps the best line of the whole poem has
the utterly unremarkable 'I met a youth reading a book' the Russian for
which, 'Ya vstretil yunoshu, chitayushchego knigu', combines simplicity,
the natural cadence of an everyday sentence, with rich sounds, and does
so without any effort or strident call on our attention.

The Polish poet Mickiewicz was a rich source of material. Two splendid Pushkinian adaptations of his adaptations of stories belonging to
other nations, *Budrys i yego synov'ya* (*Budrys and his sons*) and *Voyevoda* (*The Governor*) (both in 1833) demonstrate the validity of this
complex kind of operation when it is conducted by a skilled hand.
Budrys is one of the rare ballads with a happy ending. He dispatches
his three sons into the world and, after a long interval during which he
all but despairs of them, they return successively each with a beautiful
bride. *The Governor* ends in murder but without any sense of tragedy;
a rather black joke concludes the poem. When the governor in question
returns home he discovers his wife is being unfaithful. Out he goes with
shotgun and servant, bent on vengeance. There they are! 'Shoot her!'
he commands his dithering man, 'I'll get him afterwards.' A shot rings
out, but what has happened? 'The Governor cried out, the Governor
staggered . . . The lad had obviously missed and hit *him* in the fore-
head.' Excellent entertainment is available in these two speedy stories,
the lightness of touch in both of them being a welcome change from
the sombreness necessarily encountered elsewhere in this field because
of the traditional demands of the genre.

Mickiewicz was also involved in a strange occurrence of 1834 which
resulted in a lot of work for Pushkin and a whole series of remarkable
poems — all because of a literary hoax. In 1827 the French writer Prosper
Mérimée had issued a series of Slavonic, so-called 'Illyrian', songs under
the title *La Guzla*. Mickiewicz had been persuaded of their authenticity
and Pushkin saw no reason to doubt that they were genuine. In fact
they were clever forgeries, parodies of such songs, the stories taken in
reality from an old Scottish ballad, an Italian legend, one of the idylls
of Theocritus, and other sources.[27] Pushkin translated the whole set,
producing a cycle of *Songs of the Western Slavs*, sixteen in number,
the longest extending to 119, the shortest to 23 lines. It was a serious
undertaking tackled by a great poet in his prime. The result is mirac
ulous. Despite their illegitimacy the songs are authentically Slavonic
and reach considerable artistic heights. The most succinct and apposite

assessment of these poems belongs to Henri Troyat (and it is in no way devalued by the mistranslation in the English version of his book as *Songs of the Eastern Slavs*):

> But although he was guided by Mérimée's text, Pushkin departed widely from his model and intuitively recaptured the tone of the authentic Serbian songs. He instinctively discarded everything that was false, adulterated and Western in Mérimée's text; he unconsciously altered the lines of a humorous caricature to resemble the true face and soul of a country. Learning of Pushkin's mistake, Mérimée wrote to Sobolevsky on January 18, 1835: 'Do apologise to Mr Pushkin for me. I am both proud and ashamed of having taken him in.' It was Pushkin, in fact, who 'took in' Mérimée, by transforming his parodies into real poems.[28]

This leaves us with three or four of Pushkin's very finest ballads. Significantly perhaps they sprang not from abroad but from the Russian soil. An early one dates back as far as 1819. *Rusalka* (*The Water Nymph*) was written immediately after *Domovomu* (*To my house spirit*) and has some of the same qualities. It is a genuine Russian ballad, told objectively, simply and mysteriously. A monk takes up his station above a lake, digs his own grave and waits for death, praying to God each day as he does so. One day he sees a vision: a beautiful, naked water nymph comes out of the waves and sits on the shore combing her hair. Next day she reappears and calls the monk to her. On the third day he waits for her again. By dawn he is gone. The only indication of his fate is that some little boys say they saw his beard in the water. Seven octaves may be slightly too generous for this slender story but in all other respects it is nicely told and it includes one or two lines of stunning Pushkinian simplicity.

Under another heading (Chapter Three: *Noises in the ear*) *Besy* (*The Devils*) (1830) was grouped with those poems which depend first and foremost on acoustic skill. There is no doubt that it is one of Pushkin's finest pieces of sustained sound manipulation. As was indicated earlier, however, the meaning is not only clear, it exists on two levels – an immediate one telling the story of two men caught in a snowstorm and a universal one playing on the deep fear which natural phenomena often inspire in us all. This is balladry in its most sublime form. The narrative interest is there, as is a wide range of poetic artistry. More significantly, though, the poem delivers a primitive emotional trauma by referring us back to our recent ancestors whose task it was to confront the natural world every day of their lives and who have bequeathed to us down a few centuries the ghostly memory of their fears. If we may describe this poem as a ballad – the narrative line behind it is only thinly indicated – it is probably Pushkin's very finest.

The ballad with the strongest story is *Zhenikh* (*The Bridegroom*) (1825). No amount of familiarity with other literatures will enable the reader to guess the ending of this exciting tale. Natasha disappears for three days and returns in a distressed but uncommunicative state of mind. Shortly afterwards she is visibly shaken again when a troika flies past her house driven by a young man. Soon after that a matchmaker appears, followed by the would-be groom. The marriage is arranged and at the feast Natasha surprises the company by plunging into an explanation of her recent distress. She recalls what she describes as a nightmare in which she lost her way in the forest at night and entered a hut filled with silver and gold. The bridegroom interrupts (thus increasing the tension) to suggest that this seems more like a good omen than a bad one, but she goes on with the story. A dozen lads came into the building with a girl. They were rather crude in their behaviour but they began to enjoy themselves with drinking and singing. Again the bridegroom interrupts: is this not a portent of happiness? Still she continues. The eldest lad murdered the girl and then cut off her right hand. The bridegroom, unable to pass this off as a good sign, tells her not to worry about it. Now comes the *coup de théâtre*. She looks him in the eye and asks simply, 'Where did you get that ring?' The company stands. It then takes only the final stanza to see off the bridegroom, who is arrested and executed.

The strength of this story is in its telling. Pushkin takes plenty of time, allowing himself no less than 184 lines arranged in unusual octaves rhyming aBaBccDD, but none of it is wasted in unnecessary detail. There is much to recount and the time-span is quite a long one. In no other story does the poet play more tantalisingly with the reader's curiosity. Without laying any false trails he bemuses us with apparently mysterious incidents and stirs us into a growing uneasiness as the tale progresses. The ending is abrupt and satisfying. It assuages our fears and our curiosity at a single stroke, as well as playing up our sense of justice and clearing away almost all the mystery. Anyone who cares to think back over the events of the story will be able to fit them into normal human experience. Once again the balance between the supernatural and the real world has been struck with a sensitive hand. Once again, by taking us into a dark forest at night, into a mysterious building and then, apparently, into the land of nightmare, the poet has claimed our attention by working upon the traces of primeval dread from which no one is immune.

It remains only to consider *Utoplennik* (*The Drowned Man*) (1828), a ballad in which Pushkin proceeds with the surest touch from the simple to the sinister. It begins with excited children running to say they have found something in the river — a dead body. Their father's reaction is exactly what any father's reaction would be — it cannot be true. Fathers are used to children playing tricks on them and, in any case, who wants the bad news that a corpse has arrived and needs dealing with? Nevertheless he goes down to the water, discovers the lads are not lying and gets rid of the body by heaving it back into the water and shoving it downstream with an oar. This cannot be done without a feeling of guilt. He looks round nervously as he conducts the grisly business and swears the children — with greater optimism than certainty one can only imagine — to silence. Alas for his peace of mind. That night he is awakened by a tapping at the window. There, in the moonlight, stands the naked body of his drowned man with water streaming from his beard and black crabs hanging from his swollen frame. (Gustave Doré might have made much of the scene.) Now, so the story goes, he waits for his watery visitor every year on the anniversary of the encounter, and the drowned man may be heard tapping under the window and at the gate.

The tale depends upon its beginning for the sense of actuality on which it is founded. The behaviour of the children, the reaction of the father and his urgent desire to rid himself of an awful embarrassment which he neither wanted nor deserved — these are instantly recognisable as true to human nature and thus they validate the less credible visitation scene to come. In any case, it is easy to believe that the peasant never really woke up but dreamed the whole incident. This invests the whole poem with a plausibility which may escape all too easily from the ballad and for which compensation in one form or another is usually provided. It is easy to see that this poem, like *The Ancient Mariner*, is about conscience. The peasant ought to have given the man a decent burial; he ought to have raised the opportunity of an investigation into the circumstances of his death. Moreover, he *knows* he ought to have done these things and cannot escape the punishment meted out by conscience for failing in one's duty. These ideas arise in the mind only upon mature reflection. To read this poem is to enjoy a chilling episode which begins in reality and ends with a ghost knocking at the window in the night. Its entertainment value, at the first level of perception, is high. This truth must be applied retrospectively to all the ballads which we have discussed. Pushkin may have delved into religion and history, applied himself with all the force of his intellect to a study of both foreign sources and native methods, and then beguiled us with skilfully assembled passages of sound. None of this would have availed him much, however, if he had not mastered the first technique of the minstrel which is to claim and hold attention by good story-telling.

7 THE LIMITED SUCCESS OF PUSHKIN'S DRAMA

A Distorted Reputation

Pushkin wrote five complete works for the stage, as well as several unfinished pieces. Every one of them is flawed. They have rarely ever been performed and now, in the twentieth century, they have descended to the status of texts for the armchair theatre. This does not mean, however, that they are negligible works. The five plays contain some of the poet's most famous lines which have been given to Russian children to learn for several generations already and there is no sign of this practice coming to an end. Pushkin's attitude to his own work for the theatre was serious — the plays belong to his mature period — and since his day critical opinion has paid much attention to them. Their flaws and their obvious qualities have been paraded and by now clear decisions have been reached. At some risk of oversimplification it is reasonable to assert that Pushkin's first, and major, dramatic production, *Boris Godunov*, is generally discounted as unstageable despite its considerable merits in other directions, whereas the so-called 'Little Tragedies', *Skupoy Rytsar'* (*The Miserly Knight*), *Motsart i Sal'yeri* (*Mozart and Salieri*), *Kamennyy Gost'* (*The Stone Guest*) and *Pir vo vremya chumy* (*The Feast during the Plague*) (all of which were written in a two-or-three week period in 1830), are placed among Pushkin's finest works, whatever their prospects for production on the boards themselves. Received critical opinion need not always have right on its side, however, and it is possible to argue that Pushkin's work for the theatre has been subjected to greater misjudgement than anything else he wrote. The purpose of this chapter will be to predicate that *Boris Godunov* has suffered undue depreciation, for reasons which are explicable and understandable, whereas the praise which has been showered on 'The Little Tragedies' is exaggerated and misplaced. The case must not be overstated, however, and there is no intention to disregard either the acknowledged demerits of *Boris Godunov* or the several qualities enjoyed by the 'Tragedies'.

The Story of *Boris Godunov*

Pushkin's *Boris Godunov* is a play beset by many ironies. It was carefully planned and worked out over a whole year, from November 1824

157

to November 1825 and Pushkin later referred to it as 'this tragedy which I wrote in strict isolation . . . the fruit of constant labour and conscientious study.'[1] It was deliberately directed towards an epoch-making and seminal destiny in the Russian theatre (which had yet to produce a work of true originality and indigenous quality), and it was received with stunned admiration by the friends and colleagues invited to the first reading. From then on everything went wrong. Despite its warm reception by the chosen *cognoscenti* the play fell foul of the Russian censor and had to wait years for its publication. Notwithstanding Pushkin's overt intention to create a true play rather than an unstageable long poem it waited decades for its stage premier. Although Pushkin had applied his mature poetic skills with assiduity it became clear that he had produced, unusually for him, a constrained kind of verse two and a half thousand iambic pentameters which, curiously, renounced the fluidity of the English type for the viscosity of the French. The play has never become popular, has not been widely translated and is rarely performed. On the other hand it has gained vicarious world-wide acceptance in the form of the operatic version with libretto and music by Mussorgsky. The colossal figure of the celebrated Russian bass singer, Fyodor Shalyapin, in the title role has become a legendary one in music circles. *Boris Godunov* has misfired; it has succeeded where it was not meant to succeed and has left unachieved those things that it was intended to achieve. The sad fact is that this play, which always remained a favourite work of its author, contained a range of drawbacks and deficiencies, both political and artistic, enough to debar it from success in the short term and the long. The faults are easily determined; some of them were obvious to Pushkin even as he laid down his pen. It has become customary for critics to reiterate them and look for compensatory moments of triumph, to search out what merits could be said to have survived Pushkin's mishandling of his material. Critical emphasis is all against the play. It is high time for this emphasis to be reversed. *Boris Godunov* contains some splendid poetry (some of its lines are as well known to Russians as Hamlet's meditation on suicide is to speakers of English) and magnificent moments of theatre. Its apparently loose structure has been exaggerated and is less of a drawback than many people imagine. It should be regarded as a fine play, which contains a number of deficiencies, rather than a misconceived experiment from which there have survived some residual traces of modest value and quality.

The political problem mentioned above was a major reason for the play's lack of success early on. The censor could hardly look benevolently upon a play which reviewed the relationship between a Russian tyrant and his people. The year, after all, was 1825, the one which saw the death of Alexander I, the assumption of power by Nicholas I, the brutal suppression of the Decembrist uprising, and thus the beginning of one of the darker periods of reaction and repression in modern Russian history. Pushkin was unlucky in his timing. *Boris Godunov* takes us back to an even more troubled age, to the end of the sixteenth and the beginning of the seventeenth centuries, the period of transition which followed the death of Ivan Grozny, (Ivan the Terrible). This tsar was one of those larger-than-life sanguinary monsters who crop up from time to time in Russian history to preside over a period of transition which results eventually in imperialist expansion and a strengthening of autocratic government at home, all of which is paid for by appalling bloodletting and the deaths of countless thousands of Russian citizens. Ivan's behaviour epitomises the brutality of the Russian government towards its own people. Three years before his death Ivan became involved in an argument with his own son which he settled by whacking him over the head with a great iron-tipped staff. The son died and Ivan never recovered from the remorse which immediately overwhelmed him. The moment of the onset of this anguish was captured movingly, if melodramatically, by Russia's best known painter Ilya Repin in 1885. This was more than a domestic tragedy. Ivan's other two sons were not suitable to take over as tsar when he died. Feodor, at twenty-seven, was a congenital imbecile and Dimitriy was only a small child. For a decade and a half the country was run nominally by Feodor but actually by Boris Godunov who had been a favourite counsellor of Ivan's. Pushkin's play opens a month after the death of Feodor with the country in turmoil. Feodor has left no successor and poor Dimitriy is out of the reckoning, having had his throat cut at the age of nine several years before, under mysterious circumstances. The first four scenes of the play show us the Russian people yearning for political stability and national prosperity; they implore Boris to become tsar. He refuses and then, in the manner of Shakespeare's Julius Caesar, accepts with a show of reluctance.

The scene now changes abruptly to a dark cell in a monastery where we meet an old monk, Pimen, who is busy chronicling the history of his country, and a young novice, Grigoriy, his protégé, who happens to be exactly the same age as Dimitriy would have been, had he survived. Grigoriy conceives of the idea of passing himself off as the murdered child. He escapes from Russia to Lithuania after a dramatic confrontation with border guards at an inn and proceeds to spread the rumour that Dimitriy was not, in fact, murdered at Uglich but has now returned to claim his birthright, the title of Tsar of Russia.

Dimitriy (or Grigoriy) never came into direct confrontation with Boris Godunov in real life and they do not do so in Pushkin's play. Nevertheless, suspense builds up as, on the one hand, Dimitriy rallies support, creates an army and records several military successes while, on the other, Boris becomes increasingly troubled because of his declining popularity with the Russian people and his guilty conscience. Pushkin makes it clear that he was the murderer of Dimitriy although this has never been established or refuted historically.

There are several ups-and-downs of fortune. Dimitriy is at last routed on the battle field but at that very time Boris is struck down and he dies, on stage, after reporting his crimes and entrusting the government of Russia to his son, Fyodor. It has not escaped attention that this scene is reminiscent of the death of Henry IV, as he transfers power to Prince Henry in the last scene of Act IV of *Henry IV, Part II*. The false Dimitriy recovers, advances, has little Fyodor and his sister arrested and assumes power himself. The play ends with the announcement that Fyodor has taken poison, but when the orator calls for a shout of triumph for the new tsar the crowd is unimpressed. The play has a poignant down-beat ending in the simple stage-direction: 'the people remain silent'. That alone, given the context of past and future Russian political history amounts to a taunt directed at the autocracy. It is also a sharp reminder of the political preoccupations of the play. Pushkin has studiously avoided the temptations to bring out the love element, or to develop its potential for dabbling in the supernatural — at one point Boris is said to have consulted astrologers but there are no luminous Shakespearean soothsayers or witches to direct the action. The play is actually about ethical conduct, uneasy conscience and political responsibility. Its ending reminds us of this.

Shaking off Shakespeare

Even from this short summary of the action of *Boris Godunov* it is probably clear that one of the guiding hands behind the writing of it is William Shakespeare. We need to spend a few moments considering this influence, which determines most of the qualities and shortcomings of the play. Fortunately the way has been cleared for us. One of the first English writers on this subject was C.H. Herford who wrote a 'centenary study' of *Boris Godunov* in 1925 and refers to Pushkin, in his title, as

'A Russian Shakespearean'.[2] Herford was addressing a general audience and had to spend much time speaking about Pushkin's life and telling the story of this play. Nevertheless his article shows how Pushkin learned to direct his attention to his own national past and specifically to the depiction of bloody dynastic feuds and, more importantly, how Pushkin imitated Shakespeare by creating a drama which was fundamentally *real*, a creation like life itself. Herford points out that all of Shakespeare's nine histories deal with usurpation, murder, the removal of other pretenders and often the awaiting Nemesis. Each ruler has to take account of the considerable power of his own nobles. An important innovation in the Russian theatre is Pushkin's recreation of Shakespeare's 'human truth', the mixing together of lofty personages from history with common folk, cobblers' children, fools, grave-diggers and the like. He discusses similarities between the Inn Scene in *Boris Godunov* and that in *Henry IV, Part I*.

Two decades later a second article by Henry Gifford, written for specialists, filled in a great deal of much-needed detail.[3] It was possible to compile a long list of borrowings and adaptations. The minor character Margeret is based upon Fluellen (*Henry V*). Richard III is recalled by the seizure of power after the murder of an innocent child (cf. also *King John* and *Macbeth*), while Boris's feigned reluctance recalls that of Julius Caesar and also that of Gloucester (Richard III-to-be) and his unease and foreboding put us in mind of those of Macbeth and Richard. Dimitriy's career recalls that of Bolingbroke up to his accession; Bolingbroke figures prominently in Richard II and will later become Henry IV whose cares of state will be reflected in those of Godunov. Their deaths, as we have seen, were similar; full of guilt and foreboding, they hope their sons (rightful heirs, not usurpers) will be happier and more successful. Kurbsky's joy on returning to Russia reminds us of Richard II's emotional return from Ireland. The address made by Gavrila Pushkin (no relation) to the crowd may owe something to Mark Antony's, and so on.

It is difficult to resist the temptation to add to this list. Each new reader will see his own, new borrowings. For instance, in *Richard III*, Clarence, Gloucester's brother, tells of a dream in which Gloucester knocks him down from a great height into the sea and he is drowned (Act I, scene iv). The recitation of the dream, the fall, the correct foretelling of a tragic fate (though in Pushkin's case this does not come within the play) bring to mind Dimitriy's dream in the fifth scene of *Boris Godunov* — he falls from a high tower. When Boris presses Shuysky (scene 10) for verification of the death of Dimitriy, saying: 'Didst thou recognise the murdered child?' he speaks and behaves like the anxious Richard III: 'But didst thou see them dead?' (IV, iv). At another point Richard numbers the enemy (V, iii) and his chances seem good; Dimitriy's appear to be less promising when he does the same thing in scene 18. Then there are the reflections by Boris on conscience: these remind us of many such reflections in Shakespeare, in *Henry IV*, *Richard III* (Richard and the second murder) as well as in *Macbeth* and *Hamlet*.

Such a recitation of apparent borrowings might give the impression that *Boris Godunov* is little more than Shakespeare with a Russian overcoat on. In fact it is not like that at all. Pushkin changes so much that the play is truly personalised and Russified. How is this done?

First, Pushkin localises his material firmly in Eastern Europe and overlays it richly with so many details of Russian life and history that it gathers its own authentication. The age of Godunov is illustrated by references to cathedrals and icons; the robed Patriarch, Tsar and nobles; the plan of Muscovy which little Fyodor is busy drawing; the *yurodivyy*, an idiot boy gifted with prophecy who, although in this play he may give something to Lear's fool, is nevertheless an established Russian phenomenon; traditions and practices of a particularly Slavonic character (like the habit of inverting an empty wine-glass and rapping on the bottom of it to call for service), and also by music, for the play contains a number of folk songs or laments closely related to folk music. There are geographical references not only to Russia (including several named towns) but also to Poland, the Ukraine and Lithuania. Historical references abound: Monomakh, Ivan, Feodor, right back to the Varangians, Pimen's chronicle, Boris's memories, a long speech by the Patriarch. There is certainly no danger of the reader imagining the action to be anywhere but in Eastern Europe of the sixteenth and early seventeenth centuries.

Second, Pushkin asserts his independence in an individualised style of theatrical action, at some points very different from his sources. He uses one or two scenes of very short duration, he changes locale with greater frequency than Shakespeare and he has a good number of characters who are used only once. These innovations, to which we shall refer again, sometimes worked against him.

Third, Pushkin's use of language is more sober, down-to-earth and true-to-life than Shakespeare's. He presents a broader range of differentiated manners of speech, so much so that he was much criticised at first for the shocking vulgarity of the dialogue in, for instance, the inn scene. He tends towards brevity (as always in adapting the manner of another writer) and avoids purple passages except on one or two appropriate occasions.

Fourth, he seems in some ways deliberately to assert his independence from Shakespeare. The Inn Scene, for example, is quite unShakespearean. There is no really drunken behaviour to speak of, no bawdiness or knockabout humour. Instead the scene is tight and tense, involving three confrontations and a sharp climax. (It remains unchanged on the operatic stage.) Grigoriy has escaped from the monastery and a search is out for him. He arrives with two itinerant monks, Misail and Varlaam, at an inn on the Lithuanian border. The hostess brings drinks. Grigoriy is too tense to want to drink much and he is involved in a brush with Varlaam who thinks he is being proud. Next he talks to the hostess and learns that border patrols are in the area. At that moment the guards arrive and there is no hiding place. Grigoriy first of all tries to avoid detection by being inconspicuous but then volunteers, as the only literate person, to read out the description of the wanted man. As he does so he describes not himself but Varlaam who, when he is about to be arrested, manages to decipher enough of the notice to throw suspicion back upon Grigoriy. The latter then leaps through a window and makes good his escape. As a matter of incidental interest this deliberate mistaking of identity was borrowed from Rossini's opera *La Gazza Ladra*.[4] Although nowadays only the splendid overture to this work is ever played it was performed all over Europe in the 1820s and Pushkin heard it in Odessa in 1824.

This scene is a miniature masterpiece, with a true sense of proportion and timing. It contains adventure, comedy, tension, sharp differences in characterisation, and satire of both the church and the army as represented by the self-interested, venal and slovenly monks and the ponderous guards. It is a brilliant little piece of theatre, in prose, Russian and Pushkinian rather than Shakespearean. Its very quality constitutes one of the serious shortcomings of the play as a whole. There are several scenes like this one, self-enclosed masterpieces which tend if anything to vie with each other, like excellently contrasted miniatures competing for attention, rather than to coalesce into a well-formed drama. The surprising independence and coherence of each individual scene create an impression that the play is short of overall unity. Henry Gifford has suggested that 'This gives the whole play an episodic effect . . . It is almost as though Pushkin's instinct for essentials led him to develop the concentrated single scene. What beauty the play has, lies in the contrast between these finished parts.'[5] Mirsky claims that '. . . the construction of the play is in many ways narrative rather than dramatic.'[6] Lavrin asserts that 'It is like a huge frieze full of poetry and vivid single scenes . . . Pushkin . . . achieved real intensity only in detached

episodes.'[7] Elsewhere he adds: 'And instead of the strict unity of place
and time there is a fairly loose sequence of episodes, each of them as
it were with its own climax.'[8] Seeing the danger of overstatement he
amends this comment soon afterwards by pointing out that 'To call the
play "only a series of historical scenes" or an illustration of history, as
the critic Nadezhdin did, is nonsense.'[9] There has been a lot of support
for the view that, although certain constituent scenes may resemble and
rival the achievement of the later 'Little Tragedies', this play as a whole
is ill-conceived, lacking both shape and unity.

The Five-act Structure

Such support is not misplaced; neither does it speak the whole truth.
As long as the view persists in strength the chances of restoring the
reputation of *Boris Godunov* remain poor. One cannot deny that the
individual scenes enjoy an excellence and totality which to some degree
militate against a larger unity embracing them all. It is possible, however, to demonstrate within the play a sense of large-scale, organised
purpose and also a system of interrelated references between the scenes,
both of which work to produce a centripetal force, bringing together
units which are normally considered to be destructively disparate. Much
depends on how you look at the play. John Fennell invites us to think
twice before rejecting it as a piece of theatre.

> There seems to be no symmetry of plot; no exposition, no develop-
> ment, no climax, no denouement ... Yet for all the apparent 'aim-
> lessness' of structure there *is* a unity within the play, a 'unity of
> interest', one might call it ... If ... we take the change of dynasty
> — the collapse of the old order, the end of the first phase in the
> history of Muscovy, the dramatic confrontation between East and
> West — as the *basic* theme of the drama, then what appears at first
> glance to be little more than a random collection of colourful scenes
> takes shape as a play.[10]

This is good sense and already a move in the right direction. But is
the actual structure of the play as 'aimless' as it appears to be? Let us
look more closely at this 'random collection' of scenes.
    The first, and most important point to be made is that *Boris Godu-
nov*, although it does not look like it, is actually a five-act tragedy
similar to, though rather shorter than, the Shakespearean models upon

which it was based. This is where Pushkin's obfuscation comes in. He said in an unpublished draft article on the play, 'I have not divided my tragedy into acts — and I was already thinking that the public will say "thank you very much".'[11] This interesting remark comes in the middle of a series of assertions concerning the play's originality. In all his notes and letters on the subject Pushkin is at pains to stress how revolutionary, how new, how independent of other people his play was intended to be. An even better example of his urge to be original, and one which led to failure, was his decision to avoid the stereotyped, Frenchified, inflexible, tedious Alexandrines in which serious works for the Russian stage were expected to be written. He said, with some scorn for the celebrated Gallic line, 'I have replaced the respected Alexandrine with the blank pentameter.'[12] A splendid decision, of course. Russian, with its strong word-stress, is much better suited to the English iambic pentameter than to the syllabic line favoured by the virtually unstressed French language. Except that Pushkin chose to imitate *not* the English pentameter but the French one which counts its syllables, deploys its caesura and end-stops its lines with a rigidity close to that of the Alexandrine. What reason could explain this awful amendment to a wise decision, one which hamstrung the poetry from the first scene, one which Pushkin regretted with hindsight and may well have regretted even as he wrote? (He said, looking back, 'I have retained the caesura in the second foot as in the French pentameter and, I think, was mistaken in doing so, having thus voluntarily deprived my verse of its distinctive variety.')[13] The explanation might well reside in Pushkin's over-anxious quest for originality. Having rejected the stereotyped Alexandrine, he perhaps felt that to use Shakespeare's type of iambic pentameter would put further emphasis upon his borrowing from the English dramatist. The solution would be to assert one's independence by using a non-Shakespearean kind of blank verse; the only one to hand was the undistinguished French style to which, prompted by reason more than instinct, he took recourse.

This kind of urgent need to be original, and to look original, may have directed Pushkin's similar decision not to divide his play into acts and scenes. It may not actually have been divided up into five acts, but it was apparently written in that way and shows every likelihood of having been planned in that way. To reimpose a putative five-act structure on the play is such an easy task, such a natural procedure that it seems like the acknowledgement of a true but hidden state of affairs. The twenty-three normally unnumbered scenes fall smoothly into the following grouping, which is governed by time-lapses; that is

to say each act covers a short period of time and each entr'acte a much
longer one:

	Scenes					
	i	ii	iii	iv	v	vi
ACT I	1	2	3	4		
ACT II	5	6	7	8		
ACT III	9	10	11	12	13	14
ACT IV	15	16	17	18	19	
ACT V	20	21	22	23		

Appropriately, Act I is the most clearly differentiated. Its four scenes
deal exclusively with the ascension to power of Boris Godunov in 1598.
The action takes only a few days, as is shown when Vorotynsky says,
'The other day . . .' referring in the last scene to the first one.

Five years elapse. Act II then takes place wholly in 1603, the year
indicated in the opening scene. It deals predominantly with the early
stages of the rise to significance of Grigoriy but includes a contemporaneous interpolation of Boris's present position, a report on his state of
mind after five years of rule. The action takes probably only a few days.
We do not know how much time elapses between the famous Pimen/
Grigoriy scene and the report of Grigoriy's absconding but this cannot
be long. Everything seems to suggest that the escape happened soon
after the conversation in the monk's cell. Boris confirms at least that
we are still in the same year by making a reference to the 'sixth year' of
his reign, that is any time from February 1603 to February 1604.

Act III follows after another long time-lapse, not as long as the five
years between Acts I and II but probably more than a year. Grigoriy has
by now had time to make good his escape to Lithuania, take a job as a
servant, feign illness (surely not during the first week or two), state his
new identity (that of Dimitriy, the prince murdered ten years before)
in a deathbed confession, recover and have himself taken to the king.
All this is reported as having occurred, along with the spread of the
news of it to Moscow, between Acts II and III. We are undoubtedly well
into 1604. This is confirmed by working back from the end of the act.
Kurbsky and Dimitriy arrive at the border on 16 October 1604, as is
stated at the head of the last scene (the fourteenth or Act III scene vi).
The previous scene had ended with the decision to leave for war 'at dawn'
and the lapse of time covering the earlier four scenes and this one is
clearly reckonable in days. Thus the action of Act III appears to take up

only a few days towards the end of 1604. The act develops both lines
of the story, increasing Boris's worries as well as his sense of impending
doom and precipitating Grigoriy-Dimitriy into the very limelight of the
historical stage.

Act IV follows after another fairly substantial time-lapse. The only
scene in this part of the play which was dated by Pushkin is scene ii
which occurs on 21 December 1604. The preceding scene, dealing with
Boris, may be taken to be contemporaneous; certainly the imposter has
had time by then to cross the border and make some military conquests.
Over two months, then, seem to separate Acts III and IV. The remainder
of Act IV is more difficult to date but since it treats the defeat of Dimitriy in the last scene (Act IV scene v), which we know from historical
records to have occurred in January 1605, it seems safe to state that the
Act spans the period 21 December 1604-January 1605.

Act V occurs after two or three more months, opening with the death
of Boris on 13 April 1605 and closing with the deposition of young
Fyodor on 1 June. The subject matter concerns the sudden downfall
of Boris and the unexpected, undeserved and precarious occupation of
his position by Dimitriy.

There are clear guide lines enabling us to subdivide the play like this
into five parts. Each Act is separated from its predecessor and successor
by a much more considerable time-lapse than occurs within the acts
themselves, together with a complete change of locale. The division is
at its clearest where it matters most, at the end of Act I. Besides that,
Act I is devoted exclusively to Boris. It separates so sharply and completely from Act II scene i that the reader or audience must sense a
clear step into a new direction at the end of the first part of the story.
In this way the whole constructional pattern of a five-act tragedy or
history-play suggests itself. Even then the early part of *Boris Godunov*
looks anything but a slavish imitation of Shakespeare. For one thing,
Act I, even labelled as such, does not proceed like the opening act of
a Shakespeare play; it sticks to one theme and introduces no more than
three named characters (out of an ultimately large cast) whereas Shakespeare usually favoured a longer and broader exposition.

We have suggested a reason why Pushkin might have felt it expedient
to disguise the actual construction of his play. What no-one can assess is
the extent to which its destiny might have been changed if it had been
allowed to look like what it really is, a five-act tragedy. There would
probably have been no truly substantial changes at the outset, and even
in the long run those irrefutable centrifugal forces (including the fact
that Boris and Grigoriy-Dimitriy never come into confrontation) would

still detract from the play's overall concrescence. However, the opportunity and the very temptation to stress the achievement of the parts rather than the whole would have been much reduced. Successive readers, including potential producers, would have been conditioned to think of *Boris Godunov* first of all as a Shakespearean-style history play, much amended to suit Russian history and the author's own proclivities. This concept would have established itself in their minds before they proceeded to an awareness of its demerits as a play. The whole slant of literary criticism directed at *Boris Godunov* could have turned out differently and it is possible that each generation might have extended the distance from where we now stand, as embarrassed apologists for a play which is actually less diffuse and more stageable than most people assume. Who can deny that the inheritance of canonised opinion plays a part in the raising of each successive generation of literature-lovers? It may not be too late. In some future edition *Boris Godunov* should simply be made to look more like a play than a series of poetic sketches or an unusual chronicle. No words have to be changed, not a single line or scene needs to be transposed, but it is still possible to draw out of the loose material of *Boris Godunov* a constructional basis which was already there, and to highlight it in order to show it up as a recognisable form. The following schematic representation of the play will summarise and emphasise how naturally this can be done.

Division of *Boris Godunov* into Acts and Scenes

Act	No. of scenes	Dates of Action	Time-Span
I	4	February 1598	a few days
			FIVE YEARS
II	4	1603	a few days or weeks
			OVER A YEAR
III	6	October 1604	a few days
			TWO MONTHS
IV	5	December 1604- January 1605	less than a month
			TWO OR THREE MONTHS
V	4	April-June 1605	six weeks

Unifying Cross-references

With the play divided up into a more recognisable pattern it remains
to be seen whether anything can be done about the acknowledged
tendency of its individual scenes towards artistic autonomy. To stress
the uniqueness and high finish of each scene, to point to the contrasts
between them and to compare them with the *Little Tragedies*, all this
is to suggest, unwittingly and while revealing real truths, that the scenes
do not cohere or interrelate successfully. In fact, a close examination of
the play discloses a detailed and intricate system of intermarried references, which again suggests a greater degree of overall unity than has
been recognised so far. The real trouble lies in the subtlety of the system, which depends less upon obvious, ringing echoes of earlier remarks
or events than upon unemphatic allusions and restatements all too easily
lost, especially at a first reading.

The interrelated references between scenes are of three main types:
(a) references in different scenes to the same incident outside the span
of the play; (b) predictions of future events both within and beyond
the action of the play; and (c) ordinary allusions backward and forward
to other incidents within the play. The most obvious instance of the
first type is the murder of the real prince Dimitriy and the subsequent
events at Uglich. This grisly business is referred to many times: in Act I,
scene i, when Shuysky tells Vorotynsky casually about his work as an
investigator at Uglich; in II, ii, when Pimen describes his own horrible
experiences there as a chance bystander; by inference in II, iii, when
Boris refers to 'small boys dripping blood' who assail the mind of a man
whose conscience is not clear; overtly and at length in III, ii, when the
shaken tsar makes Shuysky rehearse and emphasise what he saw and did
at Uglich; in IV, i, when the Patriarch refers to the miracles performed
at Uglich by the spirit of Dimitriy; and in IV, iii, when the fool refers
to the murder of the prince, though without specific mention of the
place itself. In the first scene of Act V there is another reference by
default to the incident when Boris tells his son not to ask how he came
to power. This is a positive admission that the subject is distasteful and
recalls the earlier, more subtle omission of any specific reference to
Uglich in a famous speech by Boris already mentioned (II, iii). In this
the tsar enumerates sourly the many crimes for which he is blamed and
of which he is innocent, famine and life, the murder of his son-in-law,
of his predecessor on the throne, Fyodor, even his sister. The only
crime he does *not* mention is the murder of Dimitriy. For that too the
people are blaming him, but, aware of his guilt, Godunov cannot bring

himself to categorise this crime with the others. It is at the point where he should have mentioned Dimitriy that he goes on to speak about conscience and the baleful vision of infants dripping blood.

There are, then, at least five varied references to Uglich and a couple more painful non-references. The whole series of allusions is carried off unemphatically but there is nevertheless a constantly recurring reminder that the whole current situation stems from a single blood incident ten years before. To that incident several characters, some of them quite disparate, relate themselves: Shuysky, Boris, Pimen, Grigoriy, the Patriarch, a number of their interlocutors and the fool, who here represents the Russian people. They themselves become thereby interrelated in a subtle but very real way. Uglich is a focal point at which they all meet outside the main theatre of action. This most important point is where the guilt of Boris is proved (for the purposes of the play if not as a historical fact) and the source of the awareness of that guilt for the eyewitnesses and those who believed their accounts. A marked reference to it in the opening scene of each Act reinforces, albeit coincidentally, such a division into Acts and scenes. There are other such extraneous reference points but none approaches Uglich in importance. Allusions to Kurbsky's father, to Ksenya's bridegroom, to the runner who took news from Cracow to Moscow, to Grigoriy's work as a servant in Lithuania, all these and others, occur in more than one scene and relate to important events outside the stage action of the play, either before it started or during one of the long intervals between acts.

The second method of interrelating references concerns prediction and its fulfilment, or otherwise, either within the play (which is normally the case) or even after it has ended (amounting to dramatic irony dependent upon the audience's knowledge of subsequent Russian history). By this we mean not the kind of vatic utterances which told Julius Caesar to beware the Ides of March, Henry IV that he would die in Jerusalem, Richard III that he would die soon after seeing Richmond, Macbeth that he would not die until several unlikely conditions were fulfilled, and so on. Despite a reference to Boris's interest in fortune-telling (II, iii) the supernatural element is not developed by Pushkin; the play is not peopled by Shakespearean witches, Irish bards or soothsayers. Nevertheless, in many scenes questions are asked openly or implied symbolically, the answers to which involve the characters in predicting the outcome of the current situation. When, later in the play, the prediction comes true, or fails noticeably to do so, the first moment is necessarily recalled. Once again as if to strengthen the proposed division into Acts and scenes an important prediction occurs in the opening

scene of each Act. The first speech of the play shows Vorotynsky asking
Shuysky how all the present trouble will end. Shuysky responds with an
accurate prediction of the course of Act I: Boris will accept the crown
after a show of great reluctance and then rule on exactly as before. Act
II begins, in the Monastery Cell scene, with Grigoriy's dream, a symbolic
prediction of his own rise to power (which we shall see) and even of his
headlong downfall which will happen a year after the end of the play.
(The dream has some similarities with that of Clarence in *Richard III*,
just before his death (I, iv).) At the end of that same scene Dimitriy
pronounces a solemn prediction that Boris's downfall is assured. The
prediction at the start of Act III, made by Shuysky and Gavrila Pushkin
between them, is that, if the news of Dimitriy's rise gets about, there is
bound to be a mighty storm and Boris will lose his crown because of it
and will deserve to do so. At the start of Act IV the tsar plans ahead
and Basmanov predicts that within three months the Pretender's name
will have been forgotten. In this case, of course, the prediction is as
wrong as could be. Act V also begins with the tsar and Basmanov planning ahead. We are now near the end of the play; there is little time to
make predictions which will be fulfilled and the situation now becomes
totally ironic as the two men make grand plans for the near and distant
future, which will be dashed suddenly for both of them with the death
of Boris which is only moments away. An unfulfilled prediction is just
as effective in calling up an echo in a later scene as one which does
come true. Poor Basmanov seems to be wrong in every forecast that
he makes: that the Pretender will be put down within three months,
that the Books of Rank will be burnt to give non-nobles an equal chance
of advancement, that the rebellious feeling of the people will come to
nothing just as a frisking horse will usually fail in the attempt to unseat
his rider. His predictions reach a peak of dramatic irony as he meditates
hopefully on the future at the very moment when Boris is being stricken
off-stage, only seconds before the news breaks:

'God grant he settle things with the accursed
Otrep'yev, and in Russia he shall make
Yet many, many benefits to come.
   . . . What a career
Shall open up before me . . .
I'll be the first adviser to the throne . . .
Perchance I'll . . .'

In only the next scene, following the tsar's death, all the predictions have crumbled to nothing and Basmanov is being tempted over to the Pretender's side; in the scene after that he addresses the people, 'truly repentant', in praise of Dimitriy.

These are the important predictions, fulfilled and unfulfilled, which are made at the beginning of each Act. This is not coincidence. Between what we have described as the five Acts there are long lapses of time. After them it is important to gather the threads together, summarising what has happened, and also to suggest the possible shape of future events. There are other predictions elsewhere. The most notable is in the brief scene in which the Abbot reports the flight of Grigoriy (II, ii). The Patriarch, in his indignation, gives Grigoriy's prediction twice: 'I shall be tsar in Moscow'.

Since the unity of the play is assisted by predictions such as these it seems justifiable to reinstate the few lines in III, iii left out by Pushkin.[14] Khrushchov plants an important seed in our minds when he tells of Boris's illness:

'But sickness plagues him. Boris scarcely drags
Himself about. 'Tis thought his final hour
Is nigh.'

The dramatic importance of this forward reference is considerable. It prepares the mind for the sudden affliction of the tsar nine scenes later. Although this has the unfortunate consequence of suggesting strongly that Boris's death occurred naturally and Pushkin may well have wanted to retain the hint of a possible poisoning, the reference does not rule out such a possibility and it is theatrically most satisfying, in so far as it knits together, casual though it may be, two disparate scenes of the drama. This is the very function of prediction in *Boris Godunov*. A prediction is made; upon its fulfilment, or even more noticeably when it is not fulfilled, it jogs the mind subconsciously into recalling an earlier scene of the play and the two scenes involved become interrelated.

Apart from references to points outside the play and predictions, there is a third network of allusion which is helpful in unifying the apparently separate scenes. This consists of multiplicity of minor references to events elsewhere in the play, forward and backward, not necessarily involving prediction or even serious comment. Frequently, for instance, one scene leads into the next by means of an actual reference. The first scene of the play ends with Shuysky referring to the people. Scenes ii and iii show the people themselves, the former scene leading into the latter when Shchelkalov announces the intention of the

Assembly to approach the tsar next day for one last attempt at persuasion. Scene iii then ends with Boris (unseen) accepting the crown and the crowd hailing him; we are well prepared by this, and all the foregoing material, for the entry of Boris in scene iv. Act I is certainly a complete unit, the scenes flowing into each other despite short time-lapses between them. The back-reference (in scene iv) by Vorotynsky to the opening scene serves well to close the ring of Act I and to prepare the mind for a new line of development. It is worth repeating that all this would be much more obvious if the Acts and Scenes were described and headed as such.

No other Act is, or need be, so obviously unified, rounded and offset from the others, but there are many more such minor cross-references. For instance, Varlaam's casual remark, '. . . ever since we slipped out of the monastery . . .' (II, iv) refers the mind back momentarily to the earlier scenes of the Abbot and the Patriarch (II, ii) and even of Pimen and Grigoriy (II, i). We are reminded subconsciously that this scene (one of those whose individuality tends to set it off from its neighbours) is still part of a growing story. Similarly, later in the play, in another highly individual scene (III, v) the Pretender will say at the outset,

'Imprisonment for life hath threatened me;
I was pursued . . .'

This is clearly a reference to the Inn scene itself (II, iv) and the pursuit which began at the end of it. Then that very garden scene (III, v) ends in turn with the words, 'At dawn we go to war', and the following one shows Kurbsky and the Pretender on their way. It is a frequently used device for Pushkin to localise and circumscribe a scene and conjoin it with another in such a way. This is a great help in the work of interlocking brilliantly independent units. The striking point about these minor references, and more so about the great range of major ones already mentioned, is − not merely that they exist − but that there are so many of them and that they have not usually been noticed.

These several swallows do not make an entire summer. There still remain strong factors which militate against the overall unity of the play. Several scenes are so short that they are here and gone before their real meaning has had time to sink in. A number of characters appear in only one scene (Pimen, Misail and Varlaam, Father Czernikowski, the fool and some other minor figures). This demerit may have been exaggerated, though it is significant that Mussorgsky decided to bind his version of the story more closely together by conflating characters who appear only once in Pushkin; this cut down the number of singing roles and established the smaller number of them with greater conviction. Another drawback in Pushkin avoided by Mussorgsky's process of simplification consists in the swift and frequent changes of locale. There are twenty different settings for only twenty-three scenes. Some of the scenes, moreover, like those in the Inn and the Sambor garden (II, iv and III, v) are so superbly constructed and timed that it is easy to lose oneself for the moment, to become involved in a miniature drama and experience difficulty in relating this to the overall movement of the larger play. That the individual scenes are not independent units is, however, a demonstrable fact. It seems arguable that the consistent undervaluing of *Boris Godunov* as a play may stem partly from its reputation as a series of disjointed scenes, which shows a lack of general awareness of what unifying features do exist. Just as Shakespeare's plays were shaped and tidied into more easily embraced forms by later editors without their tampering with the words and lines themselves (at least in the happiest instances), so it seems defensible to tidy up *Boris Godunov* in a similar way. This will involve appending a list of *dramatis personae*, at the very least numbering the scenes consecutively for ease of reference and preferably dividing them up into five Acts in the manner suggested. The play may then commend itself more directly to producers and they might see new possibilities for emphasising the unifying forces within it and minimising the centrifugal ones. The fact is that *Boris Godunov* has an overall shape beyond the sum total of its constituent scenes but this shape is not so strikingly obvious as in many other plays. Pushkin has done justice to his grand theme but that justice is not yet widely seen to have been done.

Characters, Language and Poetry

It is not proposed to look deeply into the less problematic questions surrounding *Boris Godunov*: the language, the poetry, the characterisation and that mysterious quality of *narodnost'* (popular spirit) so dear to the hearts of Soviet critics. This latter concept is neatly disposed of by Walter Vickery who deplores its current usage on several grounds. He points out that the role of the people (*narod*) in this play has been exaggerated. 'And on the evidence of the play itself the *people*, formidable force though it undoubtedly is, appears in a somewhat passive role, as something to be manipulated by the boyars and Tsars.' Pushkin's own view of *narodnost'* is a broad one more closely akin to national pride than to the cause of democracy and literary rather than political. Vickery's last word on the subject administers a rebuke to any critics who promote the cause of extraliterary considerations above those which really count in the evaluation of literature: '... *narodnost'* as a quality, while it may permeate a work, cannot be regarded as esthetically an end in itself.'[15]

The characterisation, the language and the poetry of the play, without being beyond reproach, are nevertheless positive features, and perhaps the strongest ones of all. Both the characters and their speech were invested with a complexity and variety fully intended by the author to assist their representation in terms recognisable to the audience as close to real life. Pushkin was indeed condemned by contemporary criticism for making Boris at times too ordinary for a self-respecting stage monarch. John Fennell's remarks on this subject are worthy of attention.[16] The poetic achievement of the play is surprising. In view of the self-imposed constrictions deriving from Pushkin's choice of metre the poetry ought not to work at all. Compared with the mellifluous verse of the 'Little Tragedies' it does not. However, one factor is in Pushkin's favour. Grandeur and solemnity will not be undermined by the deficiencies of a verse form which is rigidly organised. Fluency, ordinariness, conversational ease may be difficult to conjure up when every syllable must be carefully counted and marshalled so that the custodians of each line − the pauses after the second and fifth feet − be not offended, but stateliness presents itself readily under these artificial conditions. The very subject matter of *Boris Godunov* asks for a good measure of this quality and it is therefore not surprising that some of Pushkin's best known lines appear in this apparently misconceived dramatic experiment. Pimen may be the most self-effacing of monks but his task is a noble one, nothing less than charting the history of a great people. Thus his impressive soliloquy beginning 'Yeshche odno, posledneye skazan'ye/I letopis' okonchena moya ...' ('There is one record more, the last of all,/And then this chronicle of mine is finished ...') resounds with the grandeur of great and famous poetry, and is assimilated and loved by each successive generation. This single speech is the nearest equivalent to those few celebrated quotations from Shakespeare which retain familiarity even for a pragmatic English people in an unpoetic age. There are other famous soliloquies in *Boris Godunov*, such as the Patriarch's speech in scene 15 (or, as we might say, Act IV, scene i) and at least two recited by Boris himself, in scene 7 (II, iii) when he reports on six years of rule, complains of his ill-fortune and warns of the awful consequences of a guilty conscience, ('Dostig ya

vysshey vlasti . . .' ('The heights of power are mine . . .')), and in scene
20 (V, i) when he takes leave of this world and gives advice to his son
whose moment of succession has arrived. These are undisputed high
points in Russian poetry and the Russian theatre. They are magnificent
and moving; any work which contains them in such profusion deserves
the most serious consideration.

Where does the balance now come to rest? How much of *Boris
Godunov* is Pushkin, how much Shakespeare? How far have later assess-
ments of the play been misguided by political interference in Russia
and by the poet's own obfuscation? Is there any possibility of a revival
of the popularity of *Boris Godunov* as a play in its own right? Can it
ever be dissociated now from the Mussorgsky opera which has at least
preserved long tracts of Pushkin's original verse and prose? These are
not easy questions to answer. When Pushkin tackled Byron there was
no doubt about the ease with which he allowed himself at first to become an absorbed imitator and then swiftly transcended his famous
guide, particularly in *Yevgeniy Onegin* and *The Bronze Horseman.*
Shakespeare he could not assimilate and outclass with such ease. He
read the English poet, both in Letourneur's prose versions and in the
original, with a greedy fascination, especially for the history plays, and
a timorous admiration the like of which he entertained for almost no
other writer. He seems to have been unsure of his ability to override
this elementally influential power and thus to have taken unnecessary
precautions to disown and disguise his debt to it. Nevertheless the
complex achievement of *Boris Godunov* must amount not only to a
matter of literary excellence, however qualified this may be, but also
to an important contribution to the Russian theatre. Pushkin's avowed
aim was to revolutionise drama as he saw it. The method was to replace
artificiality by authenticity by flouting the rules and conventions which
existed at the time, in particular the widespread dependence on Alexandrines and the observance of the Unities. He also intended to continue
his democratisation of the Russian literary language by making his characters use real-sounding speech, differentiated according to variations
in personality and background, some of it prose, even though he was
continuing the principle of adopting verse for the more serious sections
of his drama. This infusion of 'ordinariness' applied also to his story
which introduces a strong popular element (women, babies, working
men, beggars, etc. appearing on stage) and which was directed at a wider
audience than ever before. In general terms Pushkin wished to recreate
a true historical atmosphere and, within it, to explore problems of
politics and human psychology. This is a complicated issue about which

much remains to be said. All that may be safely claimed is that Belinsky was wrong when he described this play as Pushkin's Waterloo in which 'he deployed his genius to its full breadth and depth and yet suffered a decisive defeat'.[17] In point of fact, if you strip away much of the confusing material which has entangled this subject, it is clear that Pushkin succeeded in his aims to an extent greater than he has often been given credit for.

High Praise for the 'Little Tragedies'

If *Boris Godunov* has been downgraded over the years by adverse critical opinion, more or less the opposite is true of Pushkin's 'Little Tragedies' which have been accorded extravagant praise on a very large scale. Lavrin describes them as 'amongst the most condensed things Pushkin ever wrote'.[18] Bayley's claim is that they 'show more clearly a language realising the full potential of its simplest words'.[19] Richard Hare believed that they 'rise to the high level of his best work'.[20] The encyclopaedist William Harkins limits himself to an opinion that they are merely 'superior to *Boris*'.[21] Most, though not all, critics agree that the pick of this exquisite bunch is *The Stone Guest*; several of them go so far as to suggest that this work is one of Pushkin's very finest productions. E.J. Simmons describes it as 'in every respect . . . a masterpiece in miniature';[22] G.O. Vinokur as considered by many authorities 'the most accomplished of all his works';[23] Lavrin as 'an admirable masterpiece';[24] Oliver Elton as 'a miniature masterpiece'.[25] The French school does not dissent. Charles Corbet believes it to be 'la plus intéressante, la plus vivante de ses "petites tragédies"',[26] and André Meynieux sets it down as 'une oeuvre singulière et même insolite en Russie'.[27] If anything the acclaim directed at these four works has gathered strength over the years. In recent times Bayley has expressed the view that 'the idea of the dramatic sketch . . . is elevated to the status of a master genre, culminating in *The Stone Guest*, a climax of perfection'.[28] Mirsky is so excited by the 'Little Tragedies' that even as he promotes *The Stone Guest* to the category of the most sublime of Pushkin's works, he seems reluctant to accord lower status to the other three. On one occasion he states with full confidence that '*The Stone Guest* shares with *The Bronze Horseman* the right to be regarded as Pushkin's masterpiece . . . [in certain respects] it has no equal.'[29]

Elsewhere he claims that this work is nothing less than 'admirable and perfect from whatever standpoint it be viewed', but, two pages later, suggests that *Mozart and Salieri*, 'like *The Guest*, has claims to be his masterpiece'. On the next page, however, *The Miserly Knight* is said to be 'the most *magnificent*, the most poetically saturated . . . creation of Pushkin'. On the one after that *The Feast During the Plague* has to be satisfied with the slightly lesser accolade of 'one of the greatest masterpieces of Pushkin'.[30] We have suggested that by and large previous critical opinion has been less than generous to *Boris Godunov*. It is now necessary to assert, with even greater confidence, that the 'Little Tragedies' have been misjudged and overvalued. It is not true that *The Stone Guest* may seriously take rank alongside *The Bronze Horseman* or any of Pushkin's genuine masterpieces. It is not even true that this is the most successful of the four pieces. It is wrong, and certainly misleading, to describe these experimental and by no means entirely successful works as 'a master genre', 'masterpieces in every respect', 'perfect' or existing on 'the high level of Pushkin's best work'. The enormity of this claim becomes apparent if we remind ourselves that Pushkin's real masterpieces are certainly among the finest creations in Russian literature and therefore in *world literature*. No one will blush to defend *Yevgeniy Onegin* or *The Bronze Horseman* in such elevated terms but is it really possible to present *The Stone Guest* or the other 'Little Tragedies' to an eager world audience as one of the very finest exemplars of the Russian literary genius?

The Stone Guest: Pushkin's Weakest 'Masterpiece'

The truth of the matter is that the experiments conducted in the 'Tragedies' went wrong. Not only did the pieces turn out to be unacceptable for the stage, thus admitting failure in a major part of their task; what was worse, one of Pushkin's greatest attributes, his reductive skill, his ability to epitomise, economise and compress, proved unequal to this task, or rather inappropriate for the solving of it. Too much is packed into too small a space, so that both the characters and the dialogue assume an unreality, we might even say a melodramatic simplicity, which, far from representing our poet at the height of his achievement, actually stand aside from it as atypical and unconvincing. The measure of this relative failure may be taken from what is, under other circumstances, an unreliable guide to Pushkin's genius, his translatability into English. Translations of Pushkin never succeed but, to be fair, the best ones do convey something of his spirit and intentions. They leave the bilingual reader with a sense of emptiness, an awareness of some great quality that is missing as Pushkin's simplicity turns into banality. Translations of 'The Little Tragedies' are, however, worse than this. Even the best of them sound irredeemably *absurd*. And the worst of them is *The Stone Guest*.

Here is Don Juan speaking at the very beginning of his poem:

> And so at last
> We've reached the portals of Madrid, and soon
> Along the well-known streets I shall be flitting,
> Moustache and brows concealed by coat and hat.
> What think you? Could I e'er be recognised?

In Scene Two Don Juan enters the room of his old love, Laura, interrupting a conversation between her and Don Carlos. Subsequent events could scarcely be more compressed. Within seconds the two men have argued and fought a duel, Don Carlos has been killed and Laura and Juan, now reunited after a long separation conduct a brief discussion of the murder and the circumstances of Juan's return to Madrid. Before long they embrace and the following dialogue ensues:

LAURA   You are my darling! Stop . . . not right before
                 The dead man! Oh, what *shall* we do with him?
DON JUAN   Just leave him here — before the break of day,
                 I'll take him out enfolded in my cloak,
                 And place him at the crossroads.
LAURA   Only look
                 That no one sees you . . .

The third scene shows Don Juan some days later in the cemetery where stands a monument to the Commander whom he has also killed on an earlier occasion. The Commander's widow, Doña Anna, visits the grave regularly. Don Juan disguises himself as a monk, approaches her and, against all the odds, persuades her to arrange an assignation. He throws off his first disguise and claims to be Don Diego. At the assignation itself, in the fourth and last scene, he decides to abandon even this pretence. The dialogue and action run as follows:

DON JUAN   Suppose that you should meet Don Juan?
DOÑA ANNA   I'd plunge a dagger in the villain's heart.
DON JUAN   Where is your dagger, Doña Anna? Here's
                 My breast.

DOÑA ANNA   Oh Diego! What is that you say?
DON JUAN   No Diego I — my name's Juan.
DOÑA ANNA   O God!
             No, no it cannot be, I don't believe . . .[31]

The events that follow need no rehearsal: they are, more or less, those of the traditional ending to the Don Juan legend with the Don removed sensationally to the Lower Regions by the stone statue who has been invited to the feast.

The point about the awfulness of these lines, and many others in *The Stone Guest*, is not that they have been translated with egregious insensitivity but that it is simply not possible for them ever to be rendered into English without sounding like melodramatic nonsense. This is by no means the case with translations of *Yevgeniy Onegin* or *The Bronze Horseman* which contain no such lapses.

The desire to prolong the exalted reputation of this work has led to some strange misjudgements. Two examples connected with the ending will suffice. In order to cast some amount of retrospective credibility on the work as a whole, and particularly in order to claim the status of a 'tragedy' for it, critics have looked closely at the ending and concluded that the relationship between the Don and his last 'love' transcends all his previous liaisons. Thus he is said to have perished at the very moment of his illumination and conversion. John Bayley misreads the text to such an extent that he is able to claim that 'Pushkin's is . . . the only version in which Don Juan and his final conquest are destroyed together . . .'[32] There is no evidence at all that they do; the final stage direction indicates merely that 'they disappear' and the plural pronoun clearly refers to the Commander and the Don. More widespread is the equally unfounded suggestion that Don Juan's love for Doña Anna possesses something genuine, something different from all his other affairs. How can this be so? Surely on every occasion he swore to his partner that she was different, that this was true love. The partners usually recognised the insincerity (or the infinitely repeatable sincerity) of the claim before they yielded, and in this work both Doña Anna and Laura actually state their disbelief of his easy eloquence. There is no real suggestion that the 'final love' of Don Juan has anything different about it, yet critics go on repeating the misconception. The most striking example of all occurs in Walter Vickery's sensible introduction to Pushkin's life and works. Vickery has more misgivings about this work than any of his predecessors but he will not face the truth which he has himself uncovered. Riddled with doubts about the sincerity of Don

Juan's final protestations of love he makes an observation which reveals perhaps more than was intended: 'Yet believe in Don Juan's sincerity of the moment we must . . . because, without this belief, *The Stone Guest* loses much of its point.'[33] *Quod erat demonstrandum.*

Ideas Incarnate

Are the other 'Little Tragedies' as melodramatic as *The Stone Guest* and, if so, how may we account for the munificent praise which they have attracted for so long? The crudity of characterisation and dialogue in these works is an unwanted by-product of their oversaturation. The other 'Tragedies', although shorter than *The Stone Guest*, suffer less from excessive compression because they attempt less. The characters are fewer in number and the action is limited. *The Miserly Knight* consists of three scenes. The first establishes the miserliness of the eponymous baron and the poverty of his son, the second is given over to a long soliloquy by the baron and the third culminates in his death after an overhearing scene and a verbal duel with his son. *Mozart and Salieri* has only two scenes. In the first Salieri gives voice to his profound envy of the great composer whose negligent manner stands in sharp contrast to his genius and to Salieri's dogged application to the art of music. In the second Mozart describes the mysterious events which prompted him to write his Requiem, plays extracts from it to Salieri and then leaves him, having drunk the poison which Salieri has put into his glass of wine. *The Feast During the Plague* is not an original work but a translation of John Wilson's *The City of the Plague* (1816). It has only one scene, in which a group of young people have come together defiantly to carouse in the face of death which surrounds them in the form of the plague. They are impervious to the reproaches of a priest who calls in to register a protest. The feast continues though the Master of Revels, having been reminded of his dead wife and mother, is left in a sombre, reflective mood.

It may be seen from these brief summaries that something adjacent to melodrama characterises all the 'Little Tragedies'. Eavesdropping, sudden death, poisoning, ponderous dramatic irony — these are some of the most noticeable features — though it remains true that none of them tries to compress as much material into a small format as *The Stone Guest*. Consequently none suffers to the same extent from the ludicrous oversimplification of character and action. Nevertheless, all the characters in all these 'Tragedies' are simple ones. There is neither the time nor the space to present them with subtlety or to develop them. They fare badly when compared with, for example, Onegin or the other Yevgeniy in *The Bronze Horseman* or indeed with Boris whom, according to the general opinion, they purport to surpass. The miser personifies miserliness (even if his greed is directed towards power rather than merely feeding on itself), Salieri personifies envy (even if it is of a particularly interesting kind) and Don Juan personifies amoral carnal desire (even if he is endowed with a special kind of eloquence). These 'people' are not real at all, they are ideas incarnate. At the highest level of art it should not be possible to draw such simple equations between the idea and the person as it is in the 'Little Tragedies'. Pushkin well knew this, as his famous comparison between Shakespeare and Molière indicates:

> Characters created by Shakespeare are not, as Molière's, types exemplifying some passion or vice, but living beings, compacted of many passions and many vices; and circumstances unfold to the spectators their varied, many-sided personalities.[34]

Measured by these high standards, which were set by the poet himself, the characters of the 'Little Tragedies' stand nearer to Molière than to Shakespeare. Boris, on the other hand, is undoubtedly of Shakespearean dimensions. The great drawback of the 'Tragedies' was identified unintentionally by one of their most ardent and most famous patrons, the poetess Anna Akhmatova. In her essay on *The Stone Guest*, referring to the moral complexity of the 'Tragedies' and the differing interpretations sometimes placed upon them, she suggests that they have been affected by Pushkin's 'golovokruzhitel'nyy lakonizm'.[35] This is itself a nicely condensed phrase which means 'style so concentrated as to make the reader dizzy'. It was meant as a compliment but need not necessarily be construed as such.

Abstracting the Poetry

The shortcomings of the 'Little Tragedies' are thus clearly identifiable. It cannot be reasonable to say that any of them is 'perfect from whatever standpoint it be viewed' or a 'masterpiece in every respect'. Nevertheless we are faced with the problem that many critics and fellow artists have spoken about these works with great enthusiasm. If the characters, the action and the dialogue of these playlets are so unsatisfactory what great quality do they possess which can have beguiled so many serious minds? The answer is not far to seek; it is in the poetry. All of the foregoing negative criticism applies to the 'Little Tragedies' *as complete literary works.* Each of them, as it happens, includes at least one section of utterly memorable poetry, some of the most fluent and captivating lines ever penned by the poet, certainly his finest iambic pentameters. He has now abandoned the formalities of the French pentameter and his phrases soar unconstrained across the gaps that were observed before. Now it becomes possible for him to pen a line like the seventeenth one of *The Feast*: 'Khotya krasnorechiveyshiy yazyk . . .' which has cast the unwanted caesura into oblivion. With the shackles off the verse runs free. Salieri's soliloquies which open and close *Mozart and Salieri* are impressive outpourings of emotion with which it is only too easy to sympathise. The two original insertions into the otherwise drab playlet *The Feast During the Plague* are songs sung by Mary and the Master of the Revels. The second of these has become well known and now stands as an independent creation, outclassing the modest lines which surround it. It can well do without the rest of the work. The whole spirit of *The Feast* is infused into these six sestets which are filled with good sounds and ringing defiance in the face of death. The poem needs to be read in its entirety but some of its provocative excitement may be sampled in stanzas four and six.

> There is an ecstasy in battle
> And on the brink of the dark abyss
> And in the infuriated ocean,
> Amid the threatening waves and the stormy darkness,
> And in the hurricanes of Arabia
> And the foul breath of the Plague . . .
>
> Praise be to you, then, O Plague,
> We do not fear the darkness of the grave
> We do not fear your summons!
> We raise our foaming glasses in friendly spirit
> And drink in the rosy fragrance of a maiden's breath,
> Filled, for all we know, with the Plague!

The penultimate line, 'I devy-rozy p'yem dykhan'ye' is particularly difficult to translate. It is so saturated with meaning and sensual, almost necrophilic overtones that it belongs really with the Decadents at the other end of the nineteenth century.

The memorable lines in *The Stone Guest* are fewer in number but they are genuinely outstanding. They all appear in the earlier parts of the poem before the action speeds up and endeavours to take over most of the interest. Don Juan falls easily into a lyrical tenderness in Scene One when remembering past loves for the benefit of Leporello. The ill-starred Don Carlos, as pathetic a semi-participant in Pushkin as he is in Mozart/Da Ponte, has one strikingly original speech in Scene Two. It is no more than a dozen lines long yet it achieves unequalled heights of gentleness and philosophical admonition, pointed but couched in the most tactful terms:

> You are young . . . and you will stay young
> For five or six years yet. Around you
> Men will flock for another six years or so,
> Bringing you gifts, tender caresses and soft words.
> They will soothe you with serenades in the evening
> And they will fight to death over you
> At the crossroads by night. But when
> Your hour is over, when your eyes
> Sink deep, when your eyelids darken and wrinkle,
> When your braids are silvered with grey
> And they begin to call you an old woman —
> What will you have to say then?

Laura's reaction is natural and sensible. She ignores the warning and takes Carlos out on to the balcony where she pronounces the best known soliloquy in the whole work, a brief but heady recitation of the charms enjoyable on such a quiet evening from a Spanish balcony.

> How still the sky is.
> The warm air knows no movement, the night is scented
> With lemon and laurel, the radiant moon
> Shines out against the dark, dense blue of the sky
> And the night-watch calls out his slow: 'All is well!'

These magical lines are worthy of Shakespeare. Their secret depends upon a brief and beguiling concatenation of beautiful sights, sounds and scents; their head-spinning onslaught on every sense simultaneously, once experienced in the original language, is quite unforgettable. This is an example of Pushkin's 'golovokruzhitel'nyy lakonizm' at its most effective.

The Miserly Knight contains perhaps the most generous apportion-
ment of poetry which is instantly and permanently memorable. The
whole of the second scene is given over to the Baron who pronounces
a famous monologue, 118 lines of sustained magnificence. This hymn
to avarice, and the potential authority over men which great wealth
may bring, is among Pushkin's finest creations. The miser and the poet
search their minds together for the richest metaphors available to express their solitary excitement. (Mirsky's claim that Pushkin achieves
excellence in this poem without any recourse to metaphor and imagery
is incomprehensible.[36]) The baron sees himself successively as an ardent
young rake, a great prince supervising the construction of a vast moun-
tain, a dark brooding demon, a masochistic murderer, a ruling monarch.
Flitting in and out of these highly coloured images are everyday expressions of surprising simplicity. A good example is in line sixteen of the
soliloquy:

I more, gde bezhali korabli.
And the sea where ships were running.

This line has become a celebrity. It was picked out long ago as typical
of Pushkin at his simplest and most effective in an essay by Maurice
Baring.[37] Without a single epithet, Baring points out, Pushkin evokes a
whole picture. Walter Vickery suggests that the success of this particular
line is inexplicable: '. . . it cannot be explained why a sensitive reader
like Maurice Baring was so struck and so deeply moved by this simple
enough line.'[38] Mirsky recapitulates Baring's enthusiastic response but
without any adequate elucidation.[39] The whole of the secret might
be difficult to get at but it is at least clear that the real impact of this
powerful line depends upon its rich context. The poet-baron tells of a
wealthy tsar who commanded (*velel*) his warriors (*voinam*) to bring
handfuls of earth until a proud hill (*gordyy kholm*) arose (*vozvysilsya*)
from which the tsar could take delight in scanning the vale dotted with
white tents (*dol, pokrytyy belymi shatrami*) and . . . Now, the reader's
expectations, urged on by these grand words, must have risen with the
hill. Surely something of utter magnificence must be visible from its
summit, distant isles, marauding vessels, beguiling mists, approaching
galleons . . .? The utter simplicity of the now-famous line, consisting
of three of the most ordinary words in the Russian lexicon, the sea,
ships and the verb 'to run' carries a tremendous impact because of its
surprise. It was the stroke of a poetic genius to resist the temptation to
complete the crescendo of his extended metaphor with a grand chord

in a major key. The whole passage depends for its undoubted success upon such judicious decisions. The baron wavers between the meta-phorical visions which are his only means of expressing ecstasy and the incursion into them of day-to-day reality. Memory reminds him of the vile means by which he acquired his latest doubloon, apprehension visits him when he thinks of his own death and the inevitable dissipa-tion of his treasure. The poetry of this section is put together with such good taste that it may truly be said to be admirable, perfect, rising to the heights of Pushkin's best achievement.

Commenting on this scene, Prince Mirsky makes a revealing observa-tion. 'It is one of the most famous and familiar passages in the whole of Russian poetry', he states. 'We all learned it by heart in the lower forms . . .'[40] This tells us a good deal. Mirsky's judgement is highly reliable. If he has a weak spot other than his excusable excesses of enthusiasm it is related to the poetry which made a particular impact upon him in childhood. Elsewhere, for instance, he makes the following outrageous claim. 'The longer one lives, the more one is inclined to regard *King Saltan* as the masterpiece of Russian poetry.'[41] This piece of silliness arising in the mind of a brilliant man is explicable only in terms of his having heard that fairy-tale repeatedly in childhood. He can no more assess it objectively in his maturity than Tatyana in hers could recall dispassionately her past encounter with Onegin. Both occurrences are encrusted with so many bitter-sweet memories that sensible judgement is out of the question. But there is a second con-clusion to be drawn from Mirsky's observation. The baron's monologue was *abstracted* from its surrounding poem and given to the children for learning by heart and public declamation. It is significant that the out-standing sections of the 'Little Tragedies' — the baron's monologue, Salieri's first soliloquy, certain short speeches by Don Juan, Don Carlos and Laura, and, most noticeably of all, the two interpolated poems in *The Feast* — are, without exception, detachable units. Some of them are not only detachable, they are actually enhanced by being separated from less effective material that surrounds them. They stand up as individual lyrics better than as parts of a whole and, when they do so, they achieve an undisputed excellence which accounts for all the praise which has come their way. The mistake has been to spread the magnifi-cence of such isolated passages over the whole of the works in which they appear. For all the brilliance which irradiates some of their sec-tions, the 'Little Tragedies', viewed either as playlets or even as dramatic poems, in other words viewed as complete works of literature, must count as experiments that ended in failure.

8 YEVGENIY ONEGIN

Champagne in Sunshine

Pushkin's *Yevgeniy Onegin* is a long poem in eight cantos which run to three hundred and sixty-odd stanzas of fourteen lines each, in all five and a half thousand lines of verse. It has a rather thin story and consists mainly of discursive and digressive remarks interpolated by the author. It is a desultory work which, if it throws out useful ideas, does so in passing and unclearly. Written over a long period throughout most of the second decade of the nineteenth century, it avails itself of the newly evolved Romantic concept of freedom in matters of literary form. Its hero belongs to the tradition of the alienated young man afflicted with what was known in Europe as the 'mal du siècle'. The poem spends much of its time discussing literature almost as if this was as important as any other aspect of human experience. It is accepted as a thoroughly Russian product and has been considered even an 'encyclopaedia of Russian life'. It is a negative work which uncovers dark truths about human nature and leads us to pessimistic conclusions.

This is one way of looking at *Yevgeniy Onegin*. It is possible, however, to describe the work in terms which appear quite different. It is not a poem, or not merely a poem, but a *novel* and it consists of eight *chapters*. There may appear to be little enough action in it but what there is includes a fatal duel, an unhappy love story with an ironical twist at the end and a relationship between the hero and heroine of such compelling interest that it was taken up, later in the century, by a whole series of important Russian writers. The digressive manner is intentional and the desultory air illusory. In fact, the digressions are never allowed to extend into garrulity, the ideas are linked into the overall scheme with remarkable subtlety and the construction of this apparently amorphous work is one of its strongest features. The association with Romanticism is superficial; what rules *Yevgeniy Onegin* is a spirit of harmony, elegance and forebearance which speaks of an author who must be described as Classical by both inclination and training. The hero is not depicted in the hyperbolical terms which make Werther, René and Childe Harold so remote from everyday human experience; for all his unhappiness Yevgeniy belongs to a world that is recognisable as real. This quality of realism pervades the whole work, despite the frequent references to literature which might suggest either a flight from reality or a bookish narrative manner. Russian it may be, but it is neither representative of Russia *in extenso* nor is it limited to that country in the applicability of its ideas. Whatever dark truths and pessimistic conclusions are arrived at, this work is ultimately an affirmation of human happiness and a life-enhancing experience for anyone who has the good fortune to come across it.

Thus we arrive at a set of antithetical principles relating to *Yevgeniy Onegin*. They are not to be resolved by setting them at variance with each other in the hope of deciding once and for all whether the work is a poem or a novel, disorganised or carefully structured, Romantic or Classical, Romantic or Realistic, pessimistic or optimistic. Pushkin's universe is directed by paradox and nowhere more so than in regard to this work. In order to illustrate, and then resolve, the central paradox it will be useful, as a first step, to draw up a balance sheet indicating what various critics have said about *Yevgeniy Onegin* and what constitutes the actual subject matter of the work.

Pushkin himself describes the work, in his prefatory statement, as 'the careless fruit of my amusements', but this seems too modest. A standard Russian critical work of the Soviet period claims more generously that in *Yevgeniy Onegin* '. . . every facet of the "all-embracing" genius of Pushkin sparkles with an iridescent, diamond-like brilliance.'[1] The same writer goes on to say that 'Laughter and "gaiety" are intrinsic elements in Pushkin's love of life and in his optimism, in the vital and invigorating strength which is to be found in the work of the author of *Yevgeniy Onegin*.'[2] An earlier Russian writer described the work as 'a brilliant original creation'.[3] Prince Mirsky informs us that it contains 'an abundance of beautiful and perfect poetry . . .', it is 'genial and hospitable'.[4] Recent Soviet criticism still leans in the same direction. To take an example almost at random from one of the numerous studies devoted to this work alone: G. Magonenko refers to the 'liberating, ennobling moral strength which comprises the inexhaustible and mighty energy of *Yevgeniy Onegin*'.[5] So much for the Russians. In the West enthusiasm for this novel has been equally unconfined. Recently translators of the work have referred to 'the *brio* of the Russian text'[6] or used a series of words like '. . . beguilingly . . . psychologically plausible . . . charm; . . . a poetic output of astonishing and sustained perfection'.[7] Bayley asserts that this novel is 'a triumphant hybrid . . . the most glitteringly poetic of poems'.[8] Freeborn begins his chapter on Pushkin with the words: 'No work in Russian literature solicits our attention more charmingly than *Eugene Onegin*'.[9] He will go on to claim that 'a dance rhythm is perceptible in every stanza of *Eugene Onegin*'[10] and that what this unique stanza achieves 'is never sombre'.[11] The prettiest statement of all, perhaps, belongs to Lavrin who tells us that the novel 'sparkles like champagne in sunshine'.[12] Can there, then, be any doubt of the positive qualities in *Yevgeniy Onegin*? From descriptions like these it emerges as one of the most agreeable and inspiring works of the world's literature.

The reader who did not know the novel might be led astray by a string of such epithets which could, of course, be prolonged indefinitely. How can they be squared with the banal, sometimes squalid and even revolting subject matter of *Yevgeniy Onegin*? Here is a short plot summary, taken from a reliable encyclopaedia of world literature, which seems at variance with the descriptions so far advanced.

> The novel relates the experiences of its Byronic hero, Eugene. Bored with the social life in St Petersburg, he visits his country estate and meets Tatyana, a young girl who falls in love with him and naively offers herself to him. The bored Eugene is not interested and rather bluntly tells Tatyana this. For lack of any other amusement, he then provokes a duel with Lenski, a young romantic poet who has become his friend. Lenski is killed, and Onegin goes back to the world of society. After his departure, Tatyana visits Eugene's country manor, browses through his library, and begins to realize how hollow and artificial he is. A few years later when Eugene meets Tatyana, who is now the wife of a prince and a prominent member of St Petersburg society, her beauty and charm, and perhaps her eminence in society, turn his head. He announces his love to her in a letter, as Tatyana had to him in years before. Tatyana admits she still loves him, but refuses him because of her duty to her husband.[13]

The story evidently concerns characters who are bored, naive or romantic. Alienation and immaturity seem to be the mainsprings of its action. Yevgeniy (Eugene) acts 'for lack of any other amusement' and in such a way as actually to kill someone who has 'become his friend'. The love affair is a double non-event. What could be more unsatisfying, more negative? Can this be the work that has been variously described as sparkling, iridescent, diamond-like, brilliant, optimistic, invigorating, strong, brilliantly original, beautiful and perfect, genial, hospitable, liberating, ennobling, inexhaustibly energetic, beguiling, charming, glitteringly poetic, dancing, never sombre and even sparkling like champagne in sunshine? The discrepancy that yawns between the bare story and the manner of telling it measures the span traversed by Pushkin's artistic achievement. He has a way of transforming experience, without ignoring or running away from its darker aspects, so that the maximum amount of affirmative energy may be generated. A twentieth-century balladist has referred to this attitude as 'accentuating the positive'. Wholesome and regenerating, it is a sure antidote to depression and it characterises Pushkin's work as a whole. We need to look now at *Yevgeniy Onegin* and see how unpleasantness is neutralised, so that, even as he confronts it, the reader forms an impression that things must be better than they appear according to the surface evidence. By what means does the poet convert boredom into something fascinating, death into something acceptable, non-events into something exemplary and a naughty world into a place fit to live in?

A Phenomenon of Style

The overall tone of *Yevgeniy Onegin* is determined ultimately by its characters and the ideas associated with them. But it is established initially by the narrative manner. The novel is a prodigy without direct comparison and its originality rests more upon artistic inventiveness than the force of intellect. Structures and sounds account for much of the quality; imagination holds sway over intelligence. This is what Vladimir Nabokov has in mind when he says that 'Pushkin's composition is first of all and above all a phenomenon of style'.[14] At all times in this novel one is affected by the sheer enjoyment of its style. The reader cannot fail to be impressed and moved by the power of art *even as he contemplates unpleasantness*. The death of Vladimir Lensky in Chapter 6 serves as a good example. In terms of day-to-day reality this must represent the nadir, and the most serious moment, in the whole novel. If ever blackness and evil threaten to descend upon the story it is now. Yevgeniy's shortcomings lead him frequently into behaviour which seems reproachable but here we are speaking of the wanton destruction of a fellow creature. He has engineered a duel out of almost nothing, by flirting outrageously with Olga, to whom Lensky is betrothed, and by taking no steps to mollify his old friend as circumstances develop following the insult. The pressure builds up so that an unnecessary skirmish becomes an inevitable fight to the death and Lensky is killed. Everyone is guilty; Yevgeniy most of all as the instigator, Lensky because of foolish pride, the seconds for not having taken a moral stand against senseless destruction, society in general for permitting, encouraging and even imposing such barbarous procedures and, by implication, human nature itself which makes all these things possible. The moment ought to be bleak indeed but it is rescued by sheer artistry. Pushkin recounts it in one or two simple stanzas; the key ones are XXXI and XXXII describing the immediate aftermath of the fatal shot, Lensky's fall, Onegin's examination of the fresh corpse and the poet's reaction to events. Nabokov has defined for us the artistic excellence of this moment.

> The torrent of unrelated images with which XXXI closes − young bard, untimely end, the storm has blown, the bloom has withered, the flame upon the altar has gone out − is a deliberate accumulation of conventional poetical formulas by means of which Pushkin mimics poor Lenski's own style . . . but the rich and original metaphor of the deserted house, closed inner shutters, whitened window-panes, departed female owner (the soul being feminine in Russian), with which XXXII ends, is Pushkin's own contribution, a sample as it were of what *he* can do.[15]

Thus the inventive imagination of a great poet sees him through a crisis. Starkness, brutality, prurience, sentimentality have all been avoided and the result, ironically, is a moment of artistic triumph. At the very time when the reader ought to be in despair, contemplating the unacceptable face of human nature, he is forced to yield to a sense of *magnificence*. Here we have a dramatic example of the poet's transforming skills at work. Less obtrusively the same force animates the whole of the novel, and indeed the bulk of Pushkin's work.

The Onegin Stanza

Momentary splendour exists plentifully in *Yevgeniy Onegin* but does not account for its stylistic success. This rests upon one inspired, happy choice − the decision to create a new stanza form especially for this story. What has now become known as the 'Onegin stanza' is the clearest singly identifiable device of style which underwrites the quality of the novel from start to finish. This stanza is a paradox in itself, being both fixed and flexible. Its fixity is demonstrated by a rigid adherence to a single rhyme scheme, AbAbCCddEffEgg (capital letters indicating feminine (two-syllable) rhymes and small letters masculine (single-syllable) ones). The self-sufficiency of this stanza is illustrated by its employment in studied isolation. The first two chapters, containing almost one hundred stanzas, introduce not a single example of interstrophic en-jambement; every stanza ends in a full-stop or its equivalent. In Chapter 3 and subsequently, the device is used sparingly, though sometimes with a devastating impact, all the more forceful because of its rarity. Thus, at first sight, the Onegin stanza looks like a rather stern task-master; it never changes and it rarely condescends to link hands with its fellows.

On the other hand, it is possible to describe this same stanza (in terms which are often applied to Pushkin himself) as plastic, protean, mercurial, infinitely expressive, malleable, adaptable to suit any occa-sion. Since it has fourteen lines it belongs in some degree to the family of the sonnet. Although it tries to disguise its kinship by adopting a four-foot rather than a five-foot line the blood ties are undeniable. (Even Shakespeare broke the rule occasionally: his Sonnet No. 145 is written in tetrameters, beginning: 'Those lips that Love's own hand did make/Breathed forth the sound that said 'I hate . . .') To which of the main branches of the Sonnet Family Tree does it owe allegiance? There are two main stems. To the first, the Italian, belong the sonnets of Dante and Petrarch. These divide sharply into two slightly unequal halves, an octave followed by a sestet, and the commonest rhyme scheme for the whole stanza is abbaabba/cdecde. This form is both ele-gant and melodic. It is more stylised than its successor, the second stem, the English Sonnet (sometimes so called though it is neither strictly in-digenous nor universally used by English poets, among whom Milton in particular preferred to revert to the Italian model). What is particular about the English Sonnet, especially as used by Shakespeare, is that it plays down and, indeed, usually does away with the break after line eight. The sense is allowed to flow on beyond this point and, although there are several possible dispositions of rhyme, the commonest form for the whole sonnet is three quatrains plus a terminal couplet. This is a sturdier creation and it carries a great capacity for emphasis, wit, irony or other such telling effects in the detached final couplet. Italian and English sonnets are distinct forms, not interchangeable, and their various sub-divisions or permutations (to which the English side is especially prone) are seldom sufficient to suggest a tendency to revert to the type characterised by the other stem. Italian is Italian, English is English, and most sonnet rhyme-schemes belong recognisably to the one clan or the other. Where does the Onegin 'sonnet form' belong?

Seen in the abstract it may not be assigned definitely one way or the other. It may break up the Italian way into 8 + 6 lines: ababccdd + effegg. Or it may go English: ababccddeffe + gg (basically 12 + 2 lines).

This must apply, of course, to any sonnet, or pseudo-sonnet, which has the imagination to incorporate an envelope quatrain (effe) in lines nine to twelve. There are not many sonnets which do this, however, and those that do share some of the plasticity of the Onegin form. But the Onegin stanza has another unusual property. It begins in the most orthodox way imaginable, with an alternating quatrain (with feminine rhymes leading: AbAb). It seems about to repeat this formula when a new feminine rhyme is introduced in line five. Line six clearly calls for a different rhyme, and a masculine one; instead it destroys the illusion of orthodoxy by brusquely ushering in a repetition of the new rhyme and forming an unexpected couplet. Anything could now follow. In fact, another couplet ensues (with masculine endings), almost apologetically completing a rather spurious quatrain (CCdd) which is ready at the drop of a hat to fall apart into two halves, but thus giving some appearance of respectable regularity to the first eight lines, enough for them to hold up their collective head as a true octave if that is what the reader cares to construe, according, of course, to the actual sense of the lines concerned. Really he cannot be sure whether he has read two quatrains or a quatrain and two couplets; the impression will differ from stanza to stanza. The real villain is line six. His subversive behaviour, although to some extent mitigated by the brave line eight, can never be quite undone. With these rather unsettling experiences behind him in the 'octave' the reader now moves into the equally uncertain regions of the last six lines which are only too ready to present themselves ambiguously, either as a sestet (Eff+Egg) or as a quatrain plus couplet (EffE+gg). On occasions it is even possible for the whole 'sonnet' to become inverted, beginning with a sestet and ending with an octave (ababcc+ddeffegg). Chapter 1 Stanza X is a good example. The first quatrain here is perfectly normal and so is the following couplet. But line six is so sharply end-stopped that a break after it is inevitable. The next six lines fall palpably into two tercets and they are succeeded by the final couplet. The sense of this stanza so disposes the lines that the strongest break, at the end of the first long sentence, comes after line six, and the remaining ones group together with the unavoidable appearance of an octave.

From all of this it is apparent that in the Onegin stanza there is no inborn predisposition towards one or the other of the orthodox sonnet forms. It has its own inbuilt flexibility. Everything depends on the layout of the sentences within any particular stanza. At the point where they break off or pause, automatically and without any sense of strain, they shape the stanza to themselves. Both the Italian and the English sonnets set themselves with greater rigidity against this kind of disruptive intrusion. The Onegin form, by contrast, is a pliable instrument bending itself this way and that as may be necessary. It is, in fact, pregnant with so many possibilities that it seems almost to embrace every one at once. It is a skeleton key among sonnet forms, unlocking them all.

Hence the infinite variability of the basic building block of *Yevgeniy Onegin*. There is no repetitiveness, no predictability. One stanza reads like a pure Italian sonnet, the next like a Shakespearean one. More frequently the stanzas hover between the two with only a ghostly tendency one way or the other, or else they look like neither because of a string of irregularities. The only rule is that the mind has to wait until the final couplet before daring to place a retrospective construction on the stanza just read. And who is going to bother to do so when such a beguiling narrator is telling the story? The effectiveness of the stanza is confined to a level of awareness below that of the reader's conscious attention. Its sinuous movements draw no attention to themselves but they provide a guarantee of constant change and thus an insurance against monotony.

For the record it is instructive to consider what actually happens at least to the opening stanzas of the novel. The celebrated first stanza is clearly Italian. The first two quatrains are (in this context) orthodox ones. The only suggestion of enjambement which they bear occurs between lines six and seven, with no great pressure but persuasively enough to tie together the two quatrains comprising the second quatrain. (In future stanzas this will be a weak point; the two couplets, each insisting on autonomy, will prove disruptive.) Thus the novel begins with an indisputable quatrain followed by another one, slightly less united but still quite strong. The two fit together to form a neat octave rounded off not merely by a full-stop, but by an exclamation mark. This will be echoed by the final exclamatory rhetorical question which ends the sestet and thus the whole stanza. That sestet, in this instance, resists any possible tendency to collapse into a quatrain-plus-couplet formation (and thus the danger of changing the whole appearance of the stanza from Italian to English) by flowing on from line 12 to line 13, without sensational enjambement but nevertheless quite palpably, by adding two more infinitives to the three which have just gone and thus detaching only the last line (not the last two) from the earlier meaning. In this way the dangerous crack between quatrain and couplet is successfully papered over and the last six lines emerge with every appearance of an integrated sestet. Thus the retrospective eye construes a near-perfect Italian sonnet in the first stanza.

If that eye now looks forward in anticipation of a whole series of similar stanzas it is in for a disappointment. Even the second stanza is felt to be less strongly Italian. The last two lines want to cleave together as a couplet and thereby push the preceding four into envelope-quatrain form. This tends towards a reshaping of the whole stanza but, fortunately and for the moment, the break between lines eight and nine remains strong, and, in any case, the 'couplet' is not entirely detached. Stanza VII is the first one really to cut across the Italianate form. It contains a fairly sharp enjambement between lines eight and nine which removes any sense of distribution into octave and sestet. Moreover, the terminal couplet is, for the first time, a detached, offset and self-enclosed sentence. This stanza immediately assumes a strong 12+2 appearance and thus aligns itself with the English form. Stanza VIII is predominantly Italianate because of the change of direction at line nine and the strong enjambement between lines twelve and thirteen. Stanza IX does not exist and stanza X is, as we have already seen, entirely unorthodox, refusing to subordinate itself to the Italians or the English and seemingly eager to stand the sonnet on its head in a sestet-plus-octave formation.

And so it goes on throughout *Yevgeniy Onegin*. The long vehicle of the Onegin stanza has such variable articulation in its fat middle section that, rather like the jointed double buses which now ply the streets of what was St Petersburg, it can surprise the incredulous onlooker by nipping in and out and negotiating, when necessary, the tightest of corners.

One final word on this stanza and its surprising flexibility. An even fuller appreciation of its quality is accessible to us by comparing it with Byron's favourite form, *Ottava Rima*. Pushkin began *Yevgeniy Onegin* with Byron's *Don Juan* in mind, though, as many a critic has pointed out, the conciseness and control of the one makes comparison with the garrulity of the other an unprofitable exercise. The two stanza forms merely accentuate these differences. The *Ottava Rima* stanza, rhyming abababcc (with any disposition of masculine and feminine rhymes), sets up a normative scheme from which there will be no deviations of any palpable significance. One is aware of this at the end of the first stanza if only because the form has become traditional. So firm is the normative run that it is easily accepted and completely assimilated by the reading eye. To be sure, enjambement and unusual sentence breaks will occur but they are sensed as moments of tension. If, for example, a sentence finishes at the end of line three a slight shock is imparted to the reader who expected a run-on at least for another line. But there is no tendency at all for the stanza to reshape itself into something new, perhaps quite at variance with the established norm. The stanza is so rigidly cemented into one intractable form, and locked there by the triple rhymes, that there can be no question of pulling it out of shape. It is what it appears to be and no one can make it any different. The Onegin stanza on the contrary, invites the reader to pull it out like plasticine into any new form. It is worth pointing out also that whereas *Don Juan* treats us to over two thousand stereotyped *Ottava Rima* stanzas *Yevgeniy Onegin* regales us with a mere three hundred and sixty modulated 'sonnets'.

The power of the Onegin stanza to distract and bedazzle is something to be reckoned with. Nabokov describes it in some detail, emphasising the clarity of its rhyme scheme at the beginning and the end, and its unfocused middle section. In a metaphor worthy of the occasion he compares it to a painted ball, or top, with its pattern visible at the start and finish of its movement but blurred in mid-spin.[16] John Bayley cites Nabokov and is himself at pains to stress the paradox of regularity and flexibility in this stanza; he refers to its 'endless permutations of tone, stress and flow' and suggests that we are led 'with each verse to a new contemplation of what it achieves'.[17] Richard Freeborn in his turn cites John Bayley and adds this telling remark. 'It suggests a sprightliness and inherent vivacity even at those moments, particularly at the time of the duel and Lensky's death, when the words and images are specifically intended to invoke solemnity. It is a rhythm primarily of the dance . . .'[18]

This brings us back to our starting point and begins to explain the apparent inconsistency between the dross of Pushkin's subject matter and the gold which is spun out during its presentation.

The Technical Skills of a Novelist-poet

The well chosen stanza is not everything. Using this as his basis Pushkin builds a grand edifice of style and elegant structure, peopling it with interesting characters as he proceeds. We must look briefly at one or two further devices which Pushkin found useful, at some of the constructional details and at the characterisation of *Yevgeniy Onegin*. This is not virgin territory. During the centenary of Pushkin's death in 1937 Edmund Wilson wrote a special essay on the poet apologising for the fact that 'We have always left him out of account' and drawing particular attention to this novel. The Russians had always accepted *Hamlet* as real for their own nation. 'Let us', Wilson enjoined the American public, 'receive *Evgeny Onegin* as a creation equally real for us'.[19] He even had to tell the story of the novel in some detail. In that year no less than three new verse translations of the novel appeared, together with a host of celebratory articles of mixed quality. In mid-1938 the translations were reviewed by E.J. Simmons in *The Slavonic Review*. They did not 'reveal the full glory of Pushkin's language' and Simmons came to a sad conclusion. 'Until we have several generations of cultural English-speaking people brought up in the knowledge of Russian, as they are in French and German, the true genius of and full stature of Pushkin as a great poet will never be fully appreciated among us.'[20] Since then much has happened that would have pleased these pioneers. The nasty necessity of military preparedness forced governments to spend money on the training of Russian interpreters and translators. Many of these people, with national service behind them, penetrated universities all over the English-speaking world and small departments of Russian began to proliferate. The teaching of Russian expanded as never before and relatively large numbers of undergraduates began to encounter Pushkin. In recent years three more translations of *Yevgeniy Onegin* have appeared, one literal, the other two in verse, and numerous articles and even books have begun to explain Pushkin to a broader public. His name is now widely known in the West. By a large margin *Yevgeniy Onegin* outstrips all Pushkin's other works in popularity and a serious body of critical comment on this work is now available in English. The structures and the characters of this novel have received much attention. Thus there is some justification for treating some of these subjects scantily and passing on to other areas which have either had less generous treatment or where, apparently, mistakes have been made.

The sheer fluency of *Yevgeniy Onegin* has often been remarked upon. This is, in fact, one of the several qualities which underwrites its claim for status as nothing less than a novel. Poetic artistry is minimised by the author so that the characters and the ideas may hold the foreground. When dialogue becomes desirable, from the third chapter onwards, it fulfils the demands of rhyme and rhythm with a naturalness which enables the reader to take it, like everything else, in his stride. Anyone looking closely at Pushkin's use of language will receive the impression time after time that he has found a happy and extended formulation which is just what would have been needed by a story told in prose yet which happens to fit the iambic metre and supply rhymes exactly as required. To take a single example: at the climax of Tatyana's dream in Chapter 5 it becomes necessary for the narrator to say 'Onegin gently draws Tatyana into a corner and sets her down on a rickety seat and leans his head on her shoulder. Suddenly Olga enters, followed by Lensky . . . etc.' And that is precisely what he does say, without bending or twisting his phraseology, and yet somehow it all comes out in perfectly rhymed lines of poetry. Perhaps the finest stanza in the whole *Yevgeniy Onegin*, as far as this kind of prose-poetry is concerned, is Chapter 8, stanza XX, in which fifty-nine words build up into a single continuous sentence, one long rhetorical question, exactly in the manner of a narrator in the medium of prose fiction, though admittedly during an emotional crisis. This is the moment when Yevgeniy recognises Tatyana at the high-society party. It is an impressive achievement for Pushkin to have kept his poetry under such strict control at such a sensational turn of events. Observance of the exigencies of the complex stanza is total, the sense of effort is nil and thus the intense balance between poetic form and narrative ease has been struck once again to a nicety. The same is true of Pushkin's scientifically precise description of the preparations for the duel in Chapter 6 of which no critic worth his salt dare omit mention.

These are only some of the outstanding examples of what is, with Pushkin, a basic and instinctive poetic skill. It reappears in *Yevgeniy Onegin* also in other manifestations. For instance, after her nightmare Tatyana consults Martin Zadeck's guide to the interpretation of dreams. Naturally she turns to the index and there she sees the words '*bor, burya, ved'ma, yel', yezh, mrak, mostok, medved', metel'*, etc.', various subjects likely to figure in dreams. The substantives are so arranged by Pushkin that they proceed broadly in the order of the Russian alphabet, two beginning with 'b', one with 'v', two with 'ye' and then four with 'm'. Under each letter it is true that there are minor deviations from strict alphabetical order: these serve merely to suggest that, although Tatyana proceeded properly through the index, she did so with a slightly disordered impatience exactly in accordance with her mood. Needless to say the whole calculated catalogue exactly fits all poetic demands. Martin Zadeck, Pushkin and Tatyana work together in effortless co-operation. The 'catalogue' device, employed now with distinction, now with mechanical monotony to provide padding, is a favourite of Pushkin's and has had its fair share of attention.[21]

Another example of his easy poetic manner is the happy device of fitting long words comfortably into the iambic tetrameter. Some two or three dozen lines in *Yevgeniy Onegin* consist, for example, of no more than two words. The least interesting of these have two exactly matching halves: e.g. *udivlena, porazhena* (8, XVIII), *umen'sheny, prodolzheny* (4, XXVIII). Not much more striking are those lines which possess syntactical, if not metrical parallelism: *uyedinen'e, tishinu* (2, XXII), *kosmopolitom, patriotom* (8, VIII). A better effect is produced, even if the division of the line occurs half-way through, when the two halves differ in syntax: *razveselit' voobrazhen'ye* (4, XXIV). Adjective plus noun is a successful formulation for this kind of line; its very ordinariness gives rise to a sweet shock of surprise when it slips into a perfect tetrameter: *inoplemennyye slova* (3, XXX), *blagoslovennoye vino* (4, XLV), *odnoobraznaya sem'ya* (5, XXXV), *oligarkhicheskikh besed* (8, VII), *samolyubivuyu nichtozhnost'* (8, IX), *perekrakhma-lennyy nakhal* (8, XXVI). As may be seen from these examples the nicest effect of all is produced by a simple grammatical form in an asymmetrical line. The more natural the phrase, the greater the impact and the sunnier the impression. *V Akademicheskiy Slovar'* (1, XXVI) is an inspiration; (true, it adds a third one-letter word, but this has no independent vowel sound). However, the most striking example of this device, so winsomely effective that Pushkin used it twice in *Yevgeniy Onegin*, is the simple phrase 'she stopped', which, because Russian is an inflected language permitting infringements of normal word order, sounds just as natural when subject pronoun and verb are inverted: *ostanovilasya ona.* (3, XLI and 5, XI). This unassuming statement is magic in the hands of Pushkin. The Russians, as it happens, do not have a good word for stopping; this usually sharp movement has to be rendered by a long word, a reflexive verb of at least five syllables. (Nowadays they use the transliterated English STOP for urgent purposes like traffic signs.) Pushkin takes this long word and actually lengthens it by using the full reflexive pronoun 'sya' instead of the customary abbreviation which amounts to no more than a letter 's' when following a vowel. Thus he fills the whole line with his six-syllable verb, except for the last two syllables into which the personal pronoun fits. By a happy chance also seven of the eight vowels enjoy the same open sound 'a' (since in Russian the unstressed 'o' is not given its full value). The net result of all this is that the necessarily abrupt movement of Tatyana — who in the first example experiences the sudden shock of encountering Yevgeniy at last — is deliciously spread over eight syllables, a whole line. The line *says* merely that she stopped but it manages to suggest that she staggered, wound down haltingly and came to rest in open-mouthed astonishment. That is actually the end of Chapter 3, in which, for the first time, we have witnessed some real events.

After the devastation of this simple verb plus subject pronoun Pushkin himself stops, with the offhand remark that he needs a rest and a stroll to recover his strength. The narrative technique of breaking off just when the reader is eager for more, although an obvious one, imparts an irritating flavour of suspense at this point. We can only imagine that, with such a fine achievement behind him in the whole of the exciting third chapter and especially in its clever last stanza, Pushkin must have enjoyed a very satisfying stroll in the grounds of the Mikhaylovskoye estate. When he came to repeat the line *ostanovilasya ona* in Chapter 5 he did so almost as sensationally. It occurs at the end of the first stanza of Tatyana's dream, it provides the last line of the stanza and, uniquely, it is preceded by another two-word line, *nedoumeniya polna*. 'Full of perplexity, she stopped' is stretched out over a couplet of sixteen syllables, retarding the action after a series of vigorous impressions in a way that amazes the sensitive reader in much the same way as the events themselves amazed the heroine. Even the amazement is muffled, however. All the effects produced by this simple device − the shaping of two words to fit a four-foot iambic line − are unsensational. They have no obvious capacity for devastation; their actual impact exceeds the apparent modesty of their means. All the poetry in *Yevgeniy Onegin* is, in point of fact, understated. If you are looking for striking examples of poetic technique you may well find the most colourful ones elsewhere.

Dmitri Čiževsky refers to Pushkin's 'comparatively infrequent use of euphonic devices, especially alliteration'.[22] In Chapter 3 above we have attempted to show that this is wrong (and that Bryusov, whom Čiževsky rejects, is right) as far as very many of the lyrics are concerned. Čiževsky's observation does apply, however, to *Yevgeniy Onegin*. The utter impossibility of translating this kind of direct and natural poetry into any other language while retaining both the simplicity and the sophisticated overtones of the original Russian has been the undoing of all the brave people who have attempted a verse rendering of *Yevgeniy Onegin* (including, let it be said, the present writer who is full of sympathy for those who have completed the task). 'Restraint' is a term frequently used with regard to Pushkin. It marks the difference between an adolescent and an adult in literary terms. It is the quality that rescues *Gavriiliada* (*The Gabrieliad*) from smuttiness and many another work from excess. Without going into too much detail in relation to *Yevgeniy Onegin* it is possible to exemplify the quality merely by considering a single device, the running on of the sense of the story from one stanza to another − interstrophic enjambement. This device is used sparingly, and always to good effect, throughout *Yevgeniy Onegin*. Its shocking potential is obvious to all and what surprises us more than any particular use of the device is Pushkin's ability to withhold from it. Let it be stated plainly that every single one of the ninety-four stanzas used in Chapters One and Two ends in a full stop or its exclamatory or interrogative equivalent. Not once does the sense run on. The third chapter strikes a new note. Not only does it begin with direct speech, the first since the opening stanza (which, despite the quotation marks, was unvoiced) but this is, for the first time, dialogue. There, between the second and third stanzas of Chapter Three, we meet the first example of interstrophic enjambement; '. . . they'll be glad to see us (end of stanza II). Let's go . . .' (beginning of stanza III and end of conversation). This is somewhat shocking after such a prodigious run of end-stopped stanzas but it is small beer when set beside later examples supplied by Tatyana. The first one comes along very soon, between stanzas VII and VIII. Stanza VII is the first one in the novel to end with a comma: 'Her soul had been waiting . . . for someone,', while the next stanza begins with an untranslatable expression meaning, in this context, 'And here he was'. This example of the device is surpassed, however, by the one between stanzas XXXVIII and XXXIX. What happens here is that Tatyana, having sent her love-letter to Yevgeniy and received no response, suddenly sees him arrive at the front door. She flies away, panicking, in one of the speediest, most breathless stanzas in the whole novel. By the end of it, after she has traversed hall, steps, ornamental garden and all intervening obstacles, her head is spinning from both shock and physical effort. She might well have run into a tree or fallen into a brook; instead what she does is tumble over, by one word only, into the next stanza. This may be illustrated even in translation:

XXXVIII

. . . Down steps, across the yard she flies,
Flies down the garden — and her eyes
Dare not look back. She flashes, rushes
By borders, bridges — never stops —
Down the lake path and through the copse,
Past flower-beds, lilacs — snapping bushes —
Towards the brook on flying feet.
She gasps and on a garden seat

XXXIX

Collapses.

The artistic impact of this important moment depends equally on what Pushkin achieves now and what he has *not* done before. The restraint of Chapters 1 and 2 pays full dividend. Interstrophic enjambement will be used again (another good example occurring between stanzas XXXIX and XL in Chapter 8), always to maximum effect if only because the poet refuses to yield lazily to the appeal of such a striking device and go for easy effects whenever he might feel like it. This is merely one example of the artistic restraint which is widely encountered in various forms throughout Pushkin's work.

There are many other properties of style, form and structure which distinguish this novel but they may be given no more than a passing mention here. Under the general heading of Pushkin's 'realism' the poet is credited with an eye for the detail of everyday life and the desire to include it, whenever appropriate, in order to democratise poetry itself and provide a background of verisimilitude against which his characters and his ideas will be able to move with absolute credibility. Henry Gifford called this 'the poet's spontaneous pleasure in human variety, in the local and the characteristic.'[23] John Bayley refers to his 'disordered *density*' as if belonging to the 'Flemish School'.[24] Richard Freeborn gives a number of examples of what he calls Pushkin's 'vigour and concreteness' and his 'remarkable sense of factuality'.[25] Undoubtedly the most eloquent description of this quality comes, however, not from a critic but from a fellow poet, Yuriy Zhivago, working from within another fellow poet, Boris Pasternak. Here is an extract from Zhivago's diary written towards the end of winter at Varykino:

> We go on endlessly reading *Eugene Onegin* and the poems . . . We go on discussing Pushkin . . . It's as if the air, the light, the noise of life, of real substantial things burst into his poetry from the street as through an open window. Concrete things — things in the outside world, things in current use, names of things, common nouns — crowd in and take possession of his verse, driving out the vaguer parts of speech. Things and more things, lined up in rhymed columns on the page.[26]

Some of these 'things', such as Istomina's lovely little feet (1, XX), Onegin's curved nail scissors (1, XXIV), the flies squashed year in, year out by his uncle (2, III), the flying corks and foaming bottles (5, XXXIII and 1, XVI) have acquired familiarity through constant reference and thus passed into legend. The fat, red-footed goose who makes such an undignified guest appearance at the end of Chapter 4 (stanza XLII), intending to stride manfully across the ice and then skidding into a collapse, has become one of the world's most celebrated fictional animals, known personally to many a million Russian-speakers. These 'concrete things' constantly reassure every reader that Pushkin has lived in the real world, *his* world, and that there is nothing pretentious, abstract, academic or insubstantial about that world or its portrayal in literature.

The playful tone of *Yevgeniy Onegin* and most of Pushkin's other works has received much attention, as we have seen (at the end of Chapter 2) from references made by Nadezhdin and Richard Freeborn. Part of this generalised sense of humour depends upon the poet's irrepressible taste for parody. This, again, has been considered in some detail by other critics. Viktor Shklovsky sees *Yevgeniy Onegin* primarily as a parody of the novel as a literary form. His ideas were taken up by John Bayley.[27] The whole question of the 'written, literary nature' of the novel is considered by John Fennell.[28] Both these critics make much of Pushkin's use of literary clichés, which, at first sight, might strike the uninitiated as stereotyped and unnecessary but which are actually deposited in the narrative with the highest degree of assurance and good taste.[29] The question of defining the work – is it a poem or is it a novel? – has been much discussed and decided unanimously in favour of the latter description. The decision is based upon the narrative fluency, to which we have alluded, the confident employment of dialogue in poetry and, more importantly still, by the establishment in the work of a set of characters, a situation and a series of moral questions which bear a direct relationship to similar ones in the work of several subsequent Russian prose writers. The relationship is almost that which exists between the work of a Messiah and his disciples and there can be no doubt that it has added stature retrospectively to *Yevgeniy Onegin*, removing any last doubts that the term 'novel in verse' has been too generously bestowed.

The construction of the novel has been described and discussed enough to dispel any misgivings which might trouble the inattentive reader. It certainly looks like a ragbag of ideas and an excuse for amiable chatter. Do the digressions detract from or add to its achievement? Is there any sense of organic growth within and between the eight chapters? How can such a diffuse piece of work lay serious claim to unity?

Are there any real differences between this novel and Byron's rambling *Don Juan* on which it was initially modelled? These questions, some of which may have called for direct attention in the days of Edmund Wilson, have now been settled beyond dispute. As to the question of unity Vladimir Nabokov has written a long, convincing essay entitled 'The Structure of *Eugene Onegin*' which he describes as 'original, intricate and marvellously harmonious'. The novel is, he states, nothing less than 'a model of unity' and its eight chapters 'form an elegant colonnade'.[30] The same question, which comes down to an assessment of the many digressions and their relationship to the work as a whole, has been tackled by others, including – to name but one or two – Cizevsky,[31] Freeborn[32] and Fennell.[33] The special chronology and the use of set scenes and dramatic episodes are discussed by Freeborn.[34] The differences between the chapters and the organic growth of the novel as a whole are described by Nabokov and Čiževsky at length. Gifford also gives this question serious consideration.[35] Here we might add merely that the first chapter which was written without any clear concept of future development is distinctly offset from the succeeding seven. Devoted exclusively to Onegin himself (yet also to the author himself in both his *personae*, as narrator and participant) and characterised by a sparkle of wit and insouciance, despite the obligation to portray Yevgeniy's boredom, Chapter 1 is a unified entity. To this extent it is actually detachable from the rest of the novel if there be good reason for detaching it. Thus the various examination boards which have used this chapter as a set text are justified artistically, though the misgivings expressed by a critic on this subject recently remain justified in terms of the difficulty of the text for anyone below undergraduate level.[36]

So much for the form, the style and structure of *Yevgeniy Onegin*. They are its first claim to fame. Despite their superficial air which suggests they arose by some spontaneous process out of nothing and that they are easily assimilated and rather unimportant these basic features of the work were put together with an unremitting attention to detail. They are both intricately organised and profoundly significant, in the individual devices and in their combined effect upon the reader's conscious and subconscious sensibilities. They account for the immediate appeal of the novel if not entirely for its enduring success.

Lucent Sorrow

Yevgeniy Onegin may well dawn upon us as a phenomenon of style. It is, however, also full of ideas. These ideas are complex and open-ended. Perhaps it would be truer to say that they are presented to us so dismissively — Pushkin being a diligent student of the offhand manner — that at first there appear to be no ideas at all and then the ones which emerge after a moment's reflection seem to be anything but serious. They are, in point of fact, both cogent and consistent.

The problem with Pushkin is that people learn from him without effort and almost without knowing it. Rather than dealing with pointed problems and simple solutions, or even the lack of them, he prefers to communicate a spirit and an attitude. His thoughts are not scrupulously formulated in a way that makes them easy to summarise, accept or repudiate. This does not mean that he is without any thoughts. The impact and value of his work as a whole, and *Yevgeniy Onegin* in particular, are surprisingly far-reaching; they amount to much more than any adding together of the constituent parts of his works might lead us to believe. Countless numbers of his later compatriots have had their spirits sustained in disastrously adverse circumstances, particularly in emigration and the prison-houses by their intimate knowledge of his works. When this occurs — and it still continues today — these poor people are drawing sustenance not merely from the agreeably adaptable Onegin stanza or the fluent narrative manner. They are learning from and drawing on Pushkin's *very attitude to life as expressed in his works*.

The great danger of expressing an attitude to life in oblique terms, as the ostensibly unphilosophical Pushkin insisted on doing, is that the studied lack of definition will leave the field open to all comers. Sure enough, all have come subsequently into his territory and left it with the certainty of having found there precisely what they had hoped, or intended, to find. Both sides of this problem were neatly summarised by Vladimir Solovyov. He reminds us that 'the polychromatic nature of Pushkin's poetry is obvious to everyone, but an external, superficial glance notices only a lack of content, a paucity of ideas and an absence of backbone . . .'[37] Earlier he has issued this warning: 'In Pushkin we meet no preconceived, conscious and premeditated tendency and no affectation, provided only that we ourselves approach him free of any preconceived tendency and any unjustified determination to discover in the poet that which we especially like and to take from him, not what he offers . . . but what we need from him . . .'[38] The danger is a very clear one: 'Given a strong desire and using extracts and snippets from his whole corpus, one may of course ascribe to Pushkin every conceivable tendency, some of which are even diametrically opposed to each other.'[39] We have already referred to Roman Jakobson's description of the 'eternal variability of the myth about Pushkin'; the same critic reminds us that 'Every perceptive reader comes to a standstill before the multitude of heterogeneous images that inhabit Pushkin's world *with equal right* . . . Ambiguity, or more precisely multiplicity of meanings, is a basic component of Pushkin's poetic works.'[40] Boris Tomashevsky is aware of the same problem: 'It is quite natural that those who have analysed Pushkin in depth have always found in him, to their great satisfaction, a complete correspondence with their own philosophy.'[41]

A good example of Pushkin being forced into a mould which does not fit him is the attempt mounted from time to time by Soviet critics to equate him, as a man and a writer, with the Decembrist movement. Only recently a substantial volume (422 pages) entitled *Pushkin and the Decembrists* culminates in the statement 'Without the Decembrists there would have been no Pushkin' and looks forward to a series of works which will examine the same question.[42] Even the slender relationship between *Yevgeniy Onegin* and the Decembrist movement becomes exaggerated in the hands of Soviet editors. D. Blagoy admits that 'there is no directly political theme to the novel' but follows this immediately with a qualification. The novel is nevertheless 'covered all over with the breath of contemporary life' which, being translated, means sympathetic to the revolutionary cause. A manuscript reference to the possibility that Lensky 'might have been hanged like Ryleyev' is referred to as 'a shaft of light shining directly upon the theme of the Decembrists', and Pushkin's attempt to direct us towards the same theme via the personality of Yevgeniy himself is said to be 'even more significant'.[43] To anyone outside the USSR this line of enquiry is of only peripheral interest. Nabokov has no time for it in biography or literary criticism: 'It is quite clear that our poet was not a member of any Decembrist organisation, and the attempts of certain Soviet commentators to force him into it retrospectively are, to say the least, ridiculous.'[44]

Many other critics, in and out of Russia, have made their own attempts to appropriate Pushkin's genius in support of their own cause. Solovyov reminds us that this poet has been persuaded by various Procrustean methods to assume a position construable in retrospect as 'ultra-progressive and ultra-reactionary, religious and free-thinking westernist and slavophile, ascetic and epicurean'.[45] Tomashevsky refers to a recent attempt to enrol Pushkin as a proto-anarchist.[45] Thus it behoves us to look carefully at what previous commentators may have said about Pushkin's ideas, particularly as expressed in his most influential work, *Yevgeniy Onegin*, and to reflect at length before prolonging the series of subjective interpretations. Tomashevsky holds back his coldest douche until the end of his essay. 'Pushkin', he says, 'should be read without any intricate philosophising.'[47]

On the other hand, the novel clearly is replete with ideas and some ordering of them seems advisable if the uncommitted are ever to be persuaded of its enhanced value. Much has been made of the moral content of *Yevgeniy Onegin*. Here, perhaps, we have the secret of its success and significance? Is this where readers, as well as being entertained, can learn to be better people? This view has a noble and enduring pedigree, established by Belinsky and prolonged by Dostoyevsky. It centres, of course, around Tatyana, whose rejection of Yevgeniy in Chapter 8 amounts to what Dostoyevsky calls 'the idea of the poem' and 'the truth of the work'.[48] He saw her as someone who refused to base her own happiness on another person's unhappiness and who thus achieved nobility of soul through the suffering of her heart. It is a fine idea, one which still has wide currency. Richard Freeborn completes his essay on this novel with this suggestion: 'What Tatyana asserts . . . is the privacy of conscience, the singularity of all moral awareness . . ., the discovery of the single, unique moral self . . .'[49] A more recent commentator, Joe Andrew, asserts something similar. Pushkin's 'primary concern is with moral values. (How to live better? What is the truth?).'[50]

This is a serious proposition not to be refuted entirely or out of hand. Elsewhere in his work Pushkin does show an interest in ethical conduct and the consequences of ignoring it. The idea circulates freely in *Boris Godunov*, the 'Little Tragedies', *Andzhelo*, *The Queen of Spades* and elsewhere. It has relevance also to *Yevgeniy Onegin*, but not so precisely as has been intimated. The trouble with the expression of ethical principle in this work is that Pushkin presents us with situations and characters which are too lifelike to stand as abstract embodiments of unadulterated moral truth. Of course Yevgeniy was to blame for what amounted virtually to the murder of Lensky, but Pushkin is at pains to avoid heaping reproaches on him and he even allows us to believe that the surrounding characters, together with society itself and its rigid, inhuman codes, must bear some of the blame. Pushkin actually makes Yevgeniy appear less guilty than he really is – a remarkable intention and a remarkable achievement. Of course Tatyana is to be applauded for her upright conduct. In an ideal world all dutiful wives would send would-be seducers packing with a few sharp words such as 'I shall always be faithful to him'. Nevertheless, if one looks closely at her decision it seems not to have been a clear-cut distinction between reluctant probity and illegal happiness. Even Dostoyevsky makes the interesting point that, had she been freed from her obligation by, say, widowhood, the chances are that Tatyana would still have rejected Yevgeniy. The evidence seems to endorse this. As things stood, she had an enviable position in society and was well respected all round. Her husband was certainly not the old buffer that some critics (Dostoyevsky notoriously included) took him for and there must have been many compensations in living with him. The idea of throwing all this up for the feckless Yevgeniy, who, as she herself remarked, might well have based his atypical onrush of affection partly at least on her sheer un-attainability, can scarcely have presented itself as a serious proposition.

Nabokov has an interesting comment or two on this situation. With some acuity he draws our attention to Tatyana's unmistakable agitation, as expressed in a run of 'anguished, poignant, palpitating, enchanting, almost voluptuous, almost alluring enjambements' in Chapter 8 stanza XLVII.[51] He takes this, however, to be a genuine outpouring of requited love. Has Pushkin achieved his purpose in communicating the finality of Tatyana's decision? Would not any eager lover recognise her uncertainty and press his case even more strongly? On the other hand, the genuine nature of her 'love' itself may be questioned. We know that Tatyana was not happy with her transfer to the city. Yevgeniy has reawakened the lovely dream of returning her to her rural origins, to the village where her dear nanny lies buried as well as to her unspoilt innocence and passion of some years before, which were preferable, in hindsight, to the sophisticated pleasure provided by the *haut monde*. This dream alone, together with the emotional memories reawakened with it, would be enough to cause anyone a few palpitating enjambements. The idea of her falling in love with Yevgeniy wholeheartedly enough to contem-plate abandoning everything for him − an illicit union would have been even more improbable − looks less and less likely the more one contem-plates it. Thus the moral issues, although they exist in *Yevgeniy Onegin*, are not so clear cut as has been suggested. The 'idea' and the 'truth' of the work, those qualities which might impart spiritual strength in dire adversity, and have been known to do so, lie somewhere else.

Before we consider where this may be it is necessary to take issue with certain ideas which extend the concept of morality as the basis of *Yevgeniy Onegin*. Mirsky suggests that the spirit of the poem is 'domi-nated by the stern moral law of the Fates'. He bases this judgement on the fact that 'Onegin's irresponsible self-indulgence and fidelity to self . . . undo him'. Moreover the stern moral law of the Fates operates here 'As in all the mature works of Pushkin'.[52] Elsewhere Mirsky states this point with even greater clarity when referring to the workings of Nemesis in *The Stone Guest*. 'It is Pushkin's highest achievement on the subject of

Nemesis — his greatest subject.'[53] Is Nemesis really Pushkin's greatest subject and may this term really be applied to the outcome of *Yevgeniy Onegin*? Nemesis is retributive justice and it is obvious that something approximating to this is meted out to Yevgeniy himself at the end of the novel. Surely however, the surrounding circumstances scarcely justify the use of this term with all its connotations of divine intervention, stark tragedy and the real, deserved undoing of a base character. We have seen that Pushkin softens Yevgeniy's baseness as much as he can. He thinks of him as a friend and describes him at worst as a 'strange eccentric'. His downfall is in any case not all that noticeably *tragic*. If Tatyana's hunch is right he may well soon recover from his malaise and continue to live on at least as contentedly as before. Evil, retribution, justice and tragedy ought to attend the scene if we are to use a term like 'Nemesis'. Here there is only a sense of justice and that applies only to one character. The really unfortunate characters in *Yevgeniy Onegin* are Lensky and Tatyana, and they are also the most innocent ones. Shall the innocent suffer more than the guilty when Nemesis is the ruling spirit?

A similar misconception arises with another serious Pushkin critic, Max Hayward. Reviewing Sinyavsky's *Strolling with Pushkin* in 1976 he makes the following claim: 'Pushkin . . . regarded the world as something to be ordered, believing that chaos could be contained by harmony, as surely as Peter had tamed the treacherous waters of the Neva with his granite embankments.'[54] This is sadly and ironically wrong. Just as Peter's granite embankments, for all their apparent security, were drowned by the elements in short order so Pushkin's work suggests that the ordering of chaos by harmony, however agreeable the idea may be, is both temporary and illusory. Both of the ideas put forward by Mirsky and Hayward are too neat and too optimistic. They attempt to persuade us that Pushkin's essential idea indicates an ordered universe governed by laws like that of Nemesis. This may have been Dante's view of cosmic affairs but it was not Pushkin's. There is really no evidence of such satisfactory schematism in his work. The city of St Petersburg, so precisely and elegantly laid out by the hand of man, is destroyed. The characters perishing with it are among the most innocent representatives of mankind. The strong men at the head of human society are powerless to defend their underlings. Impermanence, disappointment, a sense of impending disaster, uncertainty and a guarantee only of unhappiness — these are the forces which directed Pushkin's own life and they are clearly represented in his work. *Yevgeniy Onegin*, for all its smiling manner, gives clear token of their existence and their haphazard effects.

What is so strange about *Yevgeniy Onegin* — and this is surely what has misled many people — is that matters do not, after all, seem so tragic. This is no accident. It is the essence of Pushkin's achievement that he shows us how best to become reconciled to adversity. His works, individually and collectively, time after time, remind us that in the last analysis, there is no happiness, no freedom, no peace, no permanence, no order and no moral law protecting the good. Yet they do not *seem to do so* because their overall spirit is so wholesome, beautiful and joyful. There is no flight into escapism. There is no suggestion of the arduous, though ultimately restorative, processes of catharsis. The poet shows us the universe in all its beauty but without ignoring the horrifically finite and unsatisfactory nature of human life. At the same time he shows us how to avoid despair. The secret is in reconciliation, distraction and creativity. It is necessary, natural and, when all is said and done, easy enough to become reconciled to the human condition, to go on living without any great hope of its improvement and yet with real enjoyment of its short-lived pleasures. Distraction is within the grasp of us all. Again this means not the panicking rush of escapist extremism but a steady devotion to whatever aspects of human life offer the relief of absorbing interest or gratification, to the natural world, the bodily pleasures, art, music and humour. Reconciliation and distraction are easily available. Creativity is more difficult to achieve though Pushkin's example is a great encouragement whereby lesser men might be impelled to put things together in new ways, to explore new ideas, to develop the imagination, to think and act constructively.

The most serious problem arising from this system of ideas and attitudes is not the possibility of misunderstanding it, treacherous though that has often proved, but the danger of undervaluing it because of its ordinariness. Reconciliation, distraction and such creativity as may be achieved — these not only add up to a coherent philosophy of life as presented by Alexander Pushkin, they actually amount to the very philosophy which most of us do actually adopt, consciously or otherwise, during our few short decades of existence. Hence the basic attractiveness of what Pushkin has to tell us. To that attractiveness there are two qualities which need to be added in order to raise it above banality: an inordinately high level of artistic achievement in Pushkin's presentation of his ideas and an irrepressible affection for his fellow humans. The latter spirit bathes the whole of his work in that atmosphere of agreeable, sympathetic warmth for which it is famous. Sheer good will is one of Pushkin's most noticeable and most attractive features. Fellow-feeling is his hallmark. When Sinyavsky says 'Pushkin is so kind that it brings tears to your eyes' he is referring specifically to the

poem 'Bog pomoch' vam, druz'ya moi . . .' and yet applying the thought
to Pushkin's work as a whole. 'Let the soldier fight', he tells us 'the tsar
rule, the woman love, the monk fast, and Pushkin, let Pushkin watch all
of this and write about it all, caring for all and heartening everyone.'[55]
Sinyavsky speaks from personal experience of six years' forced labour
for a non-existent crime, six years during which he drew strength from
his memory of Pushkin, learning to face his adversity without bitterness or despair, to distract himself from the awfulness of his situation
by rehearsing the captivating lines of his literary idol, to think and act
dynamically and to increase rather than diminish his store of good will.

The contradiction presented by *Yevgeniy Onegin* — the difference
between what people have really read and the way they react to it — is
now reconcilable. A succinct description of what occurs in this novel
is provided by S.L. Frank, (though he is writing here about Pushkin in
general):

Aldous Huxley . . . has rightly observed that although Mozart's music
seems gay, it is in fact sad. The same can be said about the poetry of
Pushkin . . . the explanation is the same in both cases. The artistic
expression of sorrow, grief and the tragic is so filled with the light
from some quiet, unearthly and angelic sense of reconciliation and
enlightenment that the content appears joyful.[56]

The essay from which this paragraph is taken, 'Svetlaya Pechal''
(*Lucent Sorrow*), was described by its author as 'a modest contribution
to the comprehension of Pushkin's sprititual world', quite inadequate
and nowhere near exhaustive. It is, in fact, one of the most brilliantly
perceptive essays ever written on the poet and should be thrust into the
hands of anyone who still believes that Pushkin's work is banal, shallow
or insignificant. Frank is at times as guilty as others of claiming Pushkin
for his own — exaggerating Pushkin's positive qualities by means of
phrases like 'spiritual radiance' and 'an enlightening religious experience'. Nevertheless his analysis of the poet's apparent insouciance and
triviality, his tragic vision of the cosmos and his transmutation of this
into a force of positive inspiration and love amounts to a lucid statement of what Dostoyevsky called 'the idea' or 'the truth' of Pushkin's
thinking, the like of which is rare in the torrential flow of Pushkiniana.

Perhaps the last word should be left to the poet himself. At the conclusion of Chapter 6 of *Yevgeniy Onegin* he writes a stanza of valediction. He is actually bidding farewell to his youth as he approaches the
age of thirty but his words, as on many other occasions, are of broader

applicability. They might be addressed by the reader to the author as he comes to the end of the novel, or by the author to the work itself, or by anyone departing even from his earthly life. Like the poem *Vospo-minaniye* (*Remembrance*), which was written at the same time, they seem to place all the emphasis on anguish, toil and trouble and yet show quite clearly that it has all been worth while. Here the poet begins and ends by saying thank you for the enjoyable experience. On this occasion all we need is a simple prose translation.

> Let's part as friends . . . Thank you for the delights: for the sadness, the dear torments, the hubbub, the storms, the feasting, for every-one of your gifts I thank you. Amid the turmoil and in stillness you have brought me delight . . . and in full measure. That is enough! With a clear spirit I set off now down a new road to find rest from my former life.

9 PROSE

An Illusion of Simplicity

There is more to the subject of Pushkin's prose than meets the eye. This area of his work is famous for its simplicity and exactitude. The stories are readily comprehensible and translatable. They have been subjected to close scrutiny and generous comment. Nevertheless, what appears to be straightforward is really beset with difficulties and complications. The first surprise is to discover that Russia's foremost poet not only turned increasingly to prose in the years preceding his death but actually wrote much more prose than poetry over his whole career. A good deal of this may be dismissed as irrelevant to literary criticism since it took the form of letters, articles and historical researches, but even when these are discarded there is still more prose than many people realise. According to diligent scholars who have added up all of his lines, words and even printed signs, 'Pushkin's works divide equally between prose and verse.' To be precise his legacy consists of almost exactly a million printed signs in either medium.[1]

This does not mean that his prose must be taken as seriously as his poetry. The latter is, all in all, a sublime achievement unsurpassed by any successor. As to the former, although it is sometimes described in undiscriminating terms of effusive praise, it is, in general, a disappointment. Here, however, the first complication arises. When we speak of Pushkin's 'prose' we must distinguish with care between the language he used (which is anything but disappointing) and the literary works he produced. Even that distinction is inadequate. On the artistic side intrinsic literary merit needs to be set apart from historical significance. Sometimes Pushkin's prose works have had an influence on subsequent writers of prose which is so well attested and of such obvious importance that glory is reflected backwards on to Pushkin himself so that his original story assumes an exaggerated degree of overall literary merit. We must therefore look with some scepticism at many recorded judgements and strive for the greater degree of objectivity when assessing the linguistic, literary and literary-historical virtues of this poet's prose. The subject is worth a study on its own; for the purpose of this chapter we shall discuss only the three major works — *The Tales of Belkin* (1830), *The Queen of Spades* (1833) and *The Captain's Daughter* (1833-6).

The Linguistic and Literary-historical Achievement

When Prince Mirsky expresses the opinion that 'Pushkin's prose has never been equalled by any subsequent Russian writer'[2] it is clear that he does not mean to indicate the superiority of *The Captain's Daughter* and *The Queen of Spades* over, let us say, *War and Peace* and *Crime and Punishment*. He is speaking about a unique quality of *language*, specifically a neatness and exactness of expression which had never been seen before and remain unsurpassed. Pushkin's role in the development of the Russian literary language, which he forged single-handed by bringing together all the available materials and beating them into new forms of startling modernity, has been acknowledged with the generosity which it deserves. The best-known tribute came from the novelist, Ivan Turgenev, an irrepressible enthusiast both for this writer and for the merits of their common native language. These enthusiasms came together in his speech written for the celebrations arranged to mark the dedication of a monument to Pushkin in Moscow in June 1880. He referred to his celebrated predecessor as one who 'gave a final form to our language, which in richness, strength, logic and beauty is acknowledged even by foreign philologists to be inferior only perhaps to that of ancient Greece.'[3]

Foreign readers of Pushkin have had no difficulty in accepting his linguistic importance. Here, for instance, is an assessment by Henry Gifford:

> There can be no doubt that Puskin blended his genius with that of the Russian language; he set upon it a character and a style which have lasted and are still to be sensed wherever good Russian is written. His candour, mobility, daring, restraint — these personal qualities provide the gold standard of Russian feeling. And it was he who so far as any one man could do this, made Russian the vehicle for a great literature.[4]

Such tributes are not limited to literary minds. The eminent Russian linguist, G.O. Vinokur accords Pushkin pride of place in his book *The Russian Language: a brief history*, particularly in its penultimate chapter 'The creation of the national standard language.' 'What is usually implied by Pushkin's role in the history of the language', writes Vinokur, 'is that he was responsible for the new and final act of combining together the bookish and everyday elements of our language.'[5] Details and examples follow this remark, together with a clear description of what Pushkin actually did. In a word or two, he brought together the elegant new language bequeathed to him by Karamzin and enriched it with vulgarisms, colloquialisms and the actual speech of the most ordinary of Russian citizens. He did so on the basis of an intimate knowledge of the Russian people, their history, mode of life, and psychology, and he emerged ultimately as the 'liberator of Russian speech from the multitudinous trammels of convention.'[6] The achievement is summarised in two paragraphs at the end of the chapter:

> Simplicity, naturalness, a feeling for moderation and complete internal freedom in the selection of means of expression are the characteristics of Pushkin's language, from the point of view both of vocabulary and also of compositional structure . . .
>
> Thus it was in Pushkin that the national language achieved the standard towards which all the complex development taking place in the language from the end of the 17th century had tended.[7]

Comments such as these refer, of course, to Pushkin's overall linguistic achievement. It is to his enduring credit that they are directed as much at his use of the apparently unspontaneous medium of poetry as to his prose. On the other hand, the prose is certainly included. It may be taken as proven to the general satisfaction that the language of Pushkin's prose works is original, exemplary, inimitable and epoch-making. Its very quality is enough to beguile even the sober-minded into a belief that the works themselves must possess a literary excellence of similar magnitude.

This suggestion is further promoted by knowledge of the impact that Pushkin's prose clearly made on his great successors. It is impossible to read that 'Tolstoy's *War and Peace* would not have seen the light of day if Pushkin had not written *The Captain's Daughter*'[8] without feeling onself pulled through the facts of literary history into an artistic association of the two works. And what are we to make of the established fact that Tolstoy sat down to write *Anna Karenina* under the immediate influence of Pushkin's prose? Tolstoy wrote to a friend that 'it came upon me in spite of myself, thanks to the divine Pushkin, who fell into my hands quite by accident . . .'[9] He had come across a volume belonging to his son which included *The Tales of Belkin* and also the beginning of an unfinished Pushkin story which opened with a particularly striking series of words. In this instance it is clear that we are speaking once again of a linguistic rather than a literary phenomenon. The short sentence which astonished Tolstoy consisted of only four

Russian words: 'Gosti s'yezzhalis' na dachu ***'. This is a remarkably
expressive statement informing us that guests were still in the process of
arriving in their vehicles at a country residence. Most of the details are
packed into the single word *s'yezzhalis'*, a product of the sophisticated
verb system in Russian which, although it is meagre in tenses, allows for
delicate refinements by permutating aspects, prefixes and reflexive
particles. The concepts of driving down and coming together are thus
made explicit in a single verb and its imperfective aspect tells us the
process is still incomplete. Needless to say all the English translators of
this short sentence use two or three times the number of words and still
omit some of the details. There is nothing particularly exciting about
guests arriving at a house; Tolstoy must surely have been excited by a
flash of awareness suddenly illuminating the rich expressiveness of his
native language. Ironically this is, in any case, an attraction of
opposites. Tolstoy lacked any sense of poetry – he genuinely preferred
Pushkin's prose – and he is famous for writing not the world's most
laconic literary works but one of the world's longest. Nevertheless the
connections between Pushkin's prose and Tolstoy's two famous novels
have come to be accepted as nothing less than umbilical, which somewhat distorts our vision of the former.

Nor is Tolstoy the only case in point. Without going into detail it is
worth indicating that associations have been drawn up linking *The
Queen of Spades* with *Crime and Punishment*; Pushkin's urban stories
(*The Station Master* and, again, *The Queen of Spades*) with
Dostoyevsky's *Poor Folk* and *A Raw Youth*; *The Station Master* also
with Gogol's *The Overcoat* and with Chekhov; *Dubrovsky* with
Turgenev's *Sportman's Sketches*; and *A History of the Village of
Goryukhino* with Saltykov-Shchedrin's *The History of a Town*, and
Aksakov's *Family Chronicle*. Some of these connections are tenuous
but they do exist. The emphasis placed on them seems to corroborate
Pushkin's title as the initiator of the modern Russian prose tradition.
There is no inconsistency in accepting this claim while at the same
time regretting one of its effects – the sweeping together of linguistic,
historical and artistic attributes which has resulted in an exaggeration of
the literary merits of Pushkin's stories.

Infectious Hyperbole

Some of the more hyperbolical evaluations of Pushkin's stories give rise
to doubts that their authors can have thought through the full implica-

tions of what they are saying. Henri Troyat, for instance, writes that
'*The Captain's Daughter* is a masterpiece of both psychology and
expression . . . Future generations hailed this novel as Pushkin's finest
work.'[10] Two of these three claims are false; only in terms of its
'expression' does this story earn the right to call itself a masterpiece.
Lavrin, too, oversteps the mark. It is one thing to assert that 'its disciplined style and language are uniformly superb', but quite another to
suggest that 'not only the characters but also history and manners are
perfectly adjusted.'[11] N. Chernyaev goes further still: '*The Captain's
Daughter* is an historical novel in the full sense of the word . . . an ideal
for the historical novel – an ideal to which Walter Scott aspired, but
which only Pushkin managed to achieve.'[12] When his compatriot N.L.
Stepanov accepts this judgement it causes no surprise in view of his own
earlier statement that the same work 'occupies a prime position in
world literature.'[13] Anna Semeonoff thinks in similar terms: '*The
Captain's Daughter*, in respect of its historical interest, as well as of its
literary quality, is one of the finest short novels of its kind.'[14] It may
seem improbable that a serious literary commentator should express the
opinion that Stendhal's *The Red and the Black* is 'much overrated',
dismiss Balzac in a passing remark as 'essentially mediocre' and then in
the same work go on to describe *The Captain's Daughter* as 'a charming
short novel' and 'an admirable novella'. This was achieved, however, by
the admittedly idiosyncratic Vladimir Nabokov.[15] Judgements like
these seem unduly biased in Pushkin's favour and they are likely to
puzzle outsiders approaching his work through translation.

The five slender stories which comprise *The Tales of Belkin*, without
ever appearing so high on the international scale, have also had their
share of generous praise. 'As pure narrative . . .' writes Mirsky, they are
'unsurpassed in Russian literature' and 'acknowledged as masterpieces.'[16] According to Lavrin they are 'commonly regarded as masterpieces'[17] and Richard Hare sets them down also as 'masterpieces . . .
alive with penetrating character sketches.'[18] Slonim goes further: for
him they are 'perfect specimens of the short story'.[19] As for Troyat,
he will settle for nothing less than the idea that they are 'the fore-
runners of the whole of Russian literature to come.'[20] Anyone who
had not read them would be led by such comments to expect more
from *The Tales of Belkin* than they are able to give.

Similar noises have been made about *The Queen of Spades*. It is 'an
amazing example of Pushkin's prose . . . worked out with incredible
economy and detachment'[21], 'pure art'[22], 'a masterpiece . . . the best
of his stories'[23], even 'a classic in the short story genre'.[24] Mirsky's

evaluation is particularly generous: '*The Queen of Spades* is to the modern mind one of the most attractive of Pushkin's works' and it is 'beyond doubt Pushkin's masterpiece in prose'.[25] Here everyone is on safer ground. No one has attempted to take over the literary world in the name of this story; at the same time, it does have a genuine claim to pre-eminence as Pushkin's prose masterpiece.

The case of Pushkin's prose recalls that of his drama and particularly that of *The Stone Guest*. Once again a kind of infectious hyperbole has overtaken certain critics, inherited opinion may have played its part and a distortion of the poet's reputation has occurred as a result. His stories in prose, for all their linguistic excellence, are not the equal of his poetry, not the best works he ever wrote, not unalloyed masterpieces and none of them occupies a prime position in world literature. They ask for a more sober assessment.

Parody and Beyond

The Tales of Belkin and *The Queen of Spades* invite comparison because of the trappings of Romanticism with which they are so strikingly decorated. Each of the five *Tales* contains a plot, characters, situations or attitudes which are outlandish; they are oversimplified or exaggerated to accord with the contemporary taste for the fantastic and the sentimental. For instance, the main character of *The Shot*, Silvio, is presented in these terms:

> His sombre pallor, the sparkle in his eyes and the thick smoke issuing from his mouth gave him a truly diabolical air.

Two other tales *The Snowstorm* and *Mistress into Maid* are rather silly love stories based upon disguise, misunderstanding and coincidence. The one story which possesses some subtlety of character and situation, and the only one with an ending in which sadness predominates, is *The Station Master*, and even this tale contains a good deal of raw sentimentality, including an abduction, a pathetic parent left behind, his rejection and subsequent death followed by valedictory visits to the cemetery by his daughter and then the narrator. As for *The Coffin-Maker*, it contains a passage which begins,

> The room was full of corpses. Moonlight, shining in through the windows, lit up their faces all yellow and blue, their sunken mouths,

their dim, half-closed eyes and protruding noses . . . Adam was horrified to recognise them as people who had been buried by his own efforts . . .

But what of *The Queen of Spades*? This story, too, deals with the supernatural; magic joins forces with murder and the outcome of it all is madness. Both works are well stocked with Romantic preoccupations and methods; is there really any difference between them?

The difference, which is substantial, hides ironically within another shared similarity — the intention of both works to neutralise by parody the excesses of literature in the Romantic period. This purpose is, in both cases, overtly expressed. *The Snowstorm*, for instance, includes a now celebrated assertion that, 'Mariya Gavrilovna had been raised on French novels and was therefore in love'; later on she is referred to as 'a veritable heroine of a novel'. Similarly, a well known exchange near the beginning of *The Queen of Spades* reminds us of the awfulness of recent popular literature. The Countess is speaking to her grandson:

' Paul . . . send me some sort of new novel but, please, not one of those that are being written nowadays.'

'How do you mean, grand'maman?'

'I mean a novel that doesn't have the hero strangling his father or his mother and doesn't have any drowned bodies. Drowned bodies terrify me!'

These amount to clear statements — though the point is obvious enough without them — that the writer is not wholly serious. Part of his purpose is to ridicule people who take literature too seriously, people with execrable literary taste and the writers who pander to them. This is a common practice for Pushkin who is at his best when toying with the literary illusion while simultaneously exploiting it to the full. A great deal of his work hovers tantalisingly between virtuosic fulfilment of chosen literary possibilities and a genial mockery of them. We saw this in Chapter 2, but the best example of all is provided by *Yevgeniy Onegin* which develops its story and examines the process doing so at one and the same time, in a light-hearted and offhand manner worthy of its distinguished predecessor *Tristram Shandy*. Ever since the Russian Formalist critic, Viktor Shklovsky, exposed this method more than half a century ago,[26] it has become increasingly clear that the attitude extends well beyond that novel. It is now possible for John Bayley to state without risk of exaggeration, 'The question and quality of parody is never far away in Pushkin . . .'[27]

The question is, what lies beyond the parody? This is where *The Tales of Belkin* and *The Queen of Spades* part company. In the former the parody seems to have got out of hand. Again it is Bayley who expresses this cogently when he says that these stories 'escape into a dramatic limbo in which elements of parody appear and vanish without the apparent consent or intention of the compiler.[28] As they do so they cannot avoid acquiring a resemblance to their despised targets which is too close for comfort. Furthermore, with the possible exception of *The Station Master* they exclude extraneous material which might be held to possess greater value than mere parody, itself an excellent art-form but not one by means of which an artist can rise to the greatest heights. *The Tales of Belkin* are slender pieces. There is no denying their neatness. Perhaps for their style alone they even deserve to be called 'compact novels'[29] or 'the first stories of permanent artistic value in the Russian language'[30] though there is in such statements a sense of straining literary charity as far as it will go and of doing so in the knowledge that their author produced masterpieces on other occasions. The original readers and reviewers did not have that advantage since the stories were not published under Pushkin's name. If one tries to imagine the now impossible task of reading and criticising these stories *ab ovo*, with no knowledge of the author's identity, it is hard to be too harsh on the contemporary critic who wrote of them,

> There is not the slightest point to any of these stories. You read them: they are nice, they run along harmoniously, but when you have finished nothing remains in your memory but a vague notion of the plot.[31]

Attempts to read more into *The Tales of Belkin* are fraught with danger, though they have been made. Mirsky dismissed them by accepting *The Tales* as masterpieces though 'not because of the deep hidden meanings which imaginative criticism has of late discovered in them.'[32] He would have been unimpressed by the most recent attempt which, setting aside literary considerations, sees this work as an elaborate code, furnished with reverberating clues and used by Pushkin to give voice to otherwise inexpressible political ideas.[33]

The Queen of Spades is different. The story does have a mischievous inclination towards parody. Germann hears of a magic three-card formula certain to win a fortune and sets his heart on learning it from an old countess. Working on the susceptibilities of her downtrodden ward, Liza, he gains entry to the house but when he confronts the old lady she drops dead before him from terror. Later her spirit appears to visit him at night and he is told the secret. Alas, when he plays he wins twice only to lose all his fortune, 47,000 roubles, on the third card in the playing of which he mistakes the Queen of Spades for an ace. The shock of his loss turns his mind. The story is full of interest, suspense and mystery. It is hard to understand why John Bayley should have described it as 'both flat and confusing'.[34] Pushkin uses this material to satirise what one critic lists succinctly as 'the popular romantic themes of ghosts, the superman, madness and genius, unrequited love, demonic interference, the triumph of virtue, the midnight tryst, and so forth.'[35] Nevertheless all of this is played down. The accompanying explanations preserve verisimilitude until the very end. Complex ideas provide the story with sophisticated meanings beyond the scope of *The Tales of Belkin* — the illusory concept of human freedom, the contrary awareness of our rough-hewn ends being shaped by an outside destiny, the hidden power of human sexuality. This latter energy, which, as we have seen elsewhere, was one of Pushkin's urgent preoccupations, runs throught *The Queen of Spades* in a curious course of negative eroticism. There are two levels to the amorous theme, the courtship of Liza, which is only slightly improper, and the hidden sexuality surrounding the countess. Although Liza's main aim in encouraging Germann is to liberate herself from the countess, physical attraction nevertheless plays its part in forming her attitude. Finally she does invite the young man into her room in the middle of the night and the wandering mind cannot resist a rapid contemplation of what might have occurred between them if Germann had had a real interest in her as a woman, which she thought he had.

In fact his attitude towards her was utterly cynical, as is demonstrated by his heartless copying out of love letters from a German novel — another reminder of the haunting presence of parody. The sexual motif relating to the countess is more overt; it may verge upon the grotesque but it is recurrent and therefore not to be ignored. First of all we hear of her as an all-conquering young beauty, known to everyone as the Muscovite Venus. There is no mention of her promiscuity but, given her physical charms, high living, headstrong manner and contempt for her husband we can take this for granted. Almost every time we meet this woman she is in the process of dressing or undressing. For the first showdown with her husband she chose a moment when she was peeling off beauty-spots and removing the hoops of her dress; Pushkin will continue to present her *en toilette*, even as an ugly old woman. He will show her receiving guests as she finishes dressing and, later on, even disrobing for bed while a young man watches the whole grisly business from behind a screen. The voyeuristic undertones here, if safely removed from actuality by her advanced age, are nevertheless obvious to all, and are emphasised by Germann's own thoughts. Did he not at one time even consider the possibility of becoming her lover if that should prove necessary (Chapter 2)? Was he not haunted by the spirit of a long-dead seducer of the countess who, sixty years before, had used the same secret staircase (4)? The theme of her sexuality and promiscuity accompanies the countess even to the grave. In a passage rich in all kind of irony the bishop pronounces a funeral oration in which he selects as an image her awaiting, of all things, the midnight bridegroom. Her apparent gesture from the coffin was not a smile, nor a whisper, nor a nod, but a wink, that intimate form of communication which, if it is not merely playful, is often taken to be a sign of amorous encouragement. Finally, a bit of gossip to the effect that the young officer who fainted at the funeral is her illegitimate son ensures that as her body passes from our general consciousness we are reminded again of its promiscuous misuse. From all of this it is clear that the constant hints at sexuality in *Pikovaya dama* amount to an important sub-theme. We must emphasise that it is delicately done. There is no suggestion of actual or impending sexual activity; equally, however, there is no escaping the regular reminders of the importance of sexual matters.

Meanwhile, a sense of the passage of time remains strong as the action alternates between two distinct ages, the mid-eighteenth and early nineteenth centuries, and a sense of place is secured by the most judicious arrangement of detail. Time and place are together brought into sharp focus in the remarkable, and often quoted, third chapter. Germann waits like an impatient tiger outside the countess's home, enters it at the appointed hour, takes up his station in her boudoir and waits again until she returns. Time is on our minds and his throughout the long sequence. He consults his watch repeatedly, urging the minutes along before entering the house; once in he is shocked by the striking of clocks all over the house shattering the silence every hour. Meanwhile he is forced to gaze on an array of decorations and personal possessions which take his mind back more than half a century. They are listed in the text in Pushkin's neatest cataloguing manner — a sanctuary lamp and icon-stand, faded brocade, outdated Chinese wall-paper, portraits of people who had been young several decades before, china shepherdesses, Leroy clocks, boxes, roulettes, fans and ladies trinkets. The room is summed up by the arrangement of its furniture 'in sad symmetry'. Pushkin has chosen his words well; the symmetry belongs to the eighteenth century, the sadness to the outworn countess.

Symmetry attends another of the famous scenes in this story, the ghostly visitation in Chapter 5. All absurdity has been removed from this by making it into a dream rather than a transcendental experience. Germann has been drinking — something he rarely did — and seems to wake up in the middle of the night. A face glances in through his window, the outer door is heard opening, a shuffling figure approaches onomatopoeically (*tikho sharkaya tuflyami*), his own door opens and there she is before him — the countess. When her message has been delivered she departs as she came, going through the exact sequence of events in reverse order, closing the door, shuffling away (*sharkaya tuflyami*), banging the outer door and glancing in again through Germann's window. This exquisite moment shows Pushkin's literary style and elegant constructional sense at its finest. Not the least of its qualities is that it is followed by a gentle thrust of bathos as Germann tries to awaken his orderly but fails to do so because he is roaring drunk.

The characterisation of *The Queen of Spades* is likewise of a high order. It is sketchily dealt with, in Pushkin's usual manner, but nevertheless persuasively conducted in a series of differentiated portraits. Each character has just enough time and space to become established not as a simple entity useful for the plot, which is often the case elsewhere in Pushkin's stories — not excluding *The Captain's Daughter* — but as a complex and sympathetic personality. Even Germann has much of his obvious guilt mitigated by other details — his moral superiority over licentious colleagues, the pressures of modern society, Liza's co-operation, the temptations and opportunities arranged for him by his destiny. Henry Gifford stands in no danger of exaggeration when he suggests that '*The Queen of Spades* can be said to reveal much psychological finesse.'[36]

All the time the tension rises and falls according to a carefully arranged sequence of events which open up possibilities and expectations, only to reduce them, close them off and then reopen them or create new ones, in a rhythmic sequence guaranteed to retain the reader's attention. Profound ironies, based particularly on a series of non-events or failures to achieve close objectives, work upon his consciousness with a wry humour. Furthermore, the qualities of this story are accessible to foreign readers. Its poetic language may be untranslatable, but its elegant structures, narrative interest and teasing questions

of morality and psychology are all transmutable into other media.[37]
At the end of it all, and only on mature reflection, an awareness is
gained of the delicacy of this operation. Pushkin has brushed against
the grotesque, sailed near to melodrama, approached sensationalism,
dallied with prurience and sentimentality, but at no time has he been
guilty of an indiscretion. If *The Queen of Spades* has parodied the
cheap tale of the supernatural it has done so in the most effective
way, by demonstrating how a good one should be written.

Misapplied Brevity

We must not be tempted to look for parody in every corner of the
poet's work. Parody could not rescue *The Black Shawl*, *The Fountain
of Bakhchisaray*, *The Stone Guest* or *Boris Godunov* from whatever
faults they possess. Nor has it any determining presence in Pushkin's
historical story *The Captain's Daughter*. Despite Chernyaev's bold claim
and Stepanov's endorsement of it this work does not even claim to be a
'historical novel' proper. It describes itself accurately as a *povest'*, or
novella, a title which should lead us to expect rather sketchier material
than, for instance, Scott's *Waverley* (1814), Stendhal's *The Red and the
Black* (1830) or that outright masterpiece of historical fiction in the
first third of the nineteenth century, Manzoni's *The Betrothed* (1827).
For literary rather than historiographical reasons Pushkin's modest
story ought to be excluded from comparison with these more substantial works, let alone with Tolstoy's. The deficiency which makes this
so is precisely the opposite of the shortcoming identified as detracting
from the merits of *The Stone Guest*. Whereas the latter is too densely
packed with a surfeit of material, *The Captain's Daughter*, on the
contrary, supports too rarified an atmosphere. Pushkin has applied to
it his famous formula, 'Precision and brevity — these are the two
virtues of prose',[38] as if it were appropriate to all forms of prose at all
times, which is not the case. It is no accident that all the best known
and most successful historical novels (as well as most of the lesser
known and less successful ones) are long. Length and leisure are fundamental requirements of this genre in order to build up convincing
historical pictures as well as rounded literary characters. Scott, Manzoni
and Stendhal spread themselves — sometimes too luxuriantly — over
two or three hundred thousand words; Pushkin restricted himself to
less than thirty thousand. Length itself is not sacrosanct but it was
mistaken for Pushkin to have believed that, because precision and

brevity had served him well on so many occasions before, in verse as in prose, these same qualities were needed to produce a good historical romance. From this mistake arise both the minor irritations and the larger shortcomings of *The Captain's Daughter*. The minor irritations may not matter a great deal though one or two examples are worth citing.

First the plot and the action. These fail to give satisfaction not so much because they are intrinsically unconvincing — we can accept the several coincidental encounters — as because they take laconism too far by omitting background material which is, if not essential, at least comforting and persuasive. A young nobleman, Pyotr Grinyov, is sent east on military service to a remote and ramshackle little fortress. He falls foul of a fellow officer, Shvabrin, and falls in love with his Commandant's daughter, Masha. The fortress is captured by an insurgent group headed by Emelyan Pugachov. Shvabrin goes over to the enemy. Grinyov, who refuses to, is spared execution because he is recognised by Pugachov himself. Grinyov had earlier helped the rebel out, without knowing his identity, and even given him a warm coat. He is now allowed to leave. Eventually the rebels are defeated and Grinyov comes under suspicion through his association with Pugachov. Finally his name is cleared by Masha, now his fiancée, who travels to St Petersburg and puts his case to the Empress Catherine II herself. Grinyov, naturally enough, proceeds to marry the captain's daughter. This story is an ambitious undertaking. For the first time Pushkin introduced into Russian literature a historical work dealing with a vast range of personages from the top of the social scale to the bottom, including both real people and invented characters. He made a genuine, and not unsuccessful, attempt to recapture the flavour of a past age. What is lacking is that which he deliberately eschewed, complexity. It would have been reassuring for us to have had more details of the process by which young Grinyov fell in love with Masha; when this occurs and a proposal is made in Chapter V, it seems premature and scarcely justified by the thinly described previous encounters. In the same way we thirst for details of the agony Grinyov must have experienced on the eve of his duel (Chapter IV), of the tactical thinking behind the apparently foolish sortie from the fortress which led to its easy capture (Chapter VII) and of the surprising decision (in Chapter XII) by Pugachov to spare the grovelling Shvabrin, caught out in his infamous treatment of Masha, which was expressed in the unconvincing sentence, 'I shall spare you this once, but don't you forget that the next time you commit any offence this one will also be remembered against you.' Most historical novels, if anything, lay on the detail too thickly, but in *The Captain's Daughter* we have a right to complain of short measure. The same deficiency amounts to a major flaw when applied to Pushkin's depiction of character. It is true that, by some mysterious process worked by a fine artist, the major characters Grinyov, Savelich and Pugachov manage to appropriate sufficient detailed attention to establish themselves with conviction, even though the rebel leader has been portrayed rather too sympathetically, according to popular image rather than historical truth. The trouble occurs with the two characters who play parts of real significance but who do not appear often enough, or stay long enough in the forefront of our consciousness, to create the appearance of anything more than a simple personality presented to us in a single dimension and thus divorced from our general impression of what human nature is like. Masha and Shvabrin are characters from melodrama, the one a vulnerable and swooning heroine, the other a villain in everything he does. Not that everyone would agree with this statement. John Bayley, for instance, anticipates such criticism by stating the very opposite. According to this critic not only has Masha 'none of the artificial detachment of a Scott heroine' but 'Shvabrin's fictional villainy is convincingly established', and 'Certainly there is nothing of the stage villain in Pushkin's economical sketch of Shvabrin's nature.'[39] If the certainty implied in this last sentence (which forms part of a footnote) is well grounded one wonders why the contrary suspicion need be denied at all. In any case it is hard to see how such a charitable estimation of these two characters is to be justified. On almost every appearance Masha can be relied upon to blush, weep, swoon or hide away and we are not told of much else that she does. Pushkin, in any case, ought not to have named this story after one of its minor characters but to have left her so thinly sketched compounds the mistake.

Similarly, almost all Shvabrin's actions resound with caddishness; they tend to be qualified by expressions such as 'with sincere malice and feigned mockery' (IX), 'in his bitterness' (XI), 'His face . . . expressive of sombre malice' (XII), 'vile' (XIII), 'with a malign smile' (XIV) and (in the omitted chapter) 'his face expressing malice and pain.' In the character of Shvabrin, Pushkin stands condemned by his own high standards. In an often-quoted comparison drawn between the characters of Shakespeare, who enjoy a rich complexity which is recognisably human, and those of Molière, who are so over-simplified that they carry over their monomaniacal characteristics into the simplest of everyday actions, Pushkin accuses the latter as follows:

> Molière's Miser is miserly — and that is all . . . Molière's Hypocrite trails after his patron's wife — hypocritically; takes on the care of an estate — hypocritically; asks for a glass of water — hypocritically.[40]

It may be that Shvabrin is not so bad as he seems. Perhaps he performs ordinary functions not like a villain but like an ordinary person; but if he does Pushkin has not seen fit to fill out this part of his personality. These two characters do have an air of oversimplification. They contradict the claim made by Avraham Yarmolinsky that to this story belongs 'the best character drawing that Pushkin ever did'.[41] Masha and Shvabrin lend weight to the general feeling of discomfort which builds up throughout *The Captain's Daughter*, a feeling that we are being hustled too rapidly through complex events and are allowed only cursory glances at important issues and characters. Pushkin is in error; precision and brevity are not the two virtues of prose if you wish to create a masterpiece in the genre of historical fiction.

The difference between Pushkin's poetry and his prose is that between spontaneity and conscious effort. It is best summed up in these remarks by Mirsky:

> Pushkin's literary prose (as distinct from that of his letters) has not that appearance of ease and freedom which his verse has . . . It is obviously canalized. It produces the effect of being premeditated, of following an external rule, in short, of being . . . 'stylized' . . ., drawn to a foreign pattern. In reading Pushkin's prose one always feels its form . . . and . . . the higher level is never reached (as it always is in Pushkin's verse) where all awareness of effort and resistance disappears and perfection seems to be the result of a natural, unpremeditated growth.[42]

It is a matter for regret that at the very point where Pushkin is accessible to foreigners, by means of translation, which distorts his prose stories far less than his verses, he is not at the peak of his artistic achievement.

10 READING PUSHKIN

In the preceding chapters we have looked at the breadth and depth of Pushkin's achievement. An attempt has been made to establish the excellence of a number of his poems when judged by the most rigorous of standards. One or two works, including some which have attracted a good deal of praise, do not seem to have met these standards. There are areas of Pushkin's work — notably his voluminous correspondence, minor prose works and historical researches — into which we have not even glanced, believing that Pushkin's poetry is his singular claim on our attention. It remains to summarise the more important conclusions that have been drawn in passing, to assist those who may be approaching Pushkin for the first time with a proposed minimum reading schedule which will guarantee a comprehensive grasp of the poet's accomplishment, and then to search for a definition of that special quality which at once defines this writer, universalises his appeal and substantiates his claim to greatness.

A Pushkin Profile

Pushkin's first quality is the spirit of enjoyment which runs through his work. No one should approach this poet with a sense of obligation or reluctance, merely because he is a literary celebrity. There is no 'classic' writer who will impart more direct pleasure. A great deal of his work, as we have seen repeatedly in the preceding pages, is written with humour. The literary illusion is continually undermined by levity and parody working together. It must never be forgotten, however, that the levity disguises both personal unhappiness and seriousness of purpose, while the parody places the thinnest of veils over the highest degree of literary skill. False appearances and paradox attend much of his work and perhaps the most noticeable of all Pushkin's qualities is his dismissive manner. He writes deathless poems and, as he does so, pretends to be no more than an idle chatterer. As one friendly Russian critic put it, 'If he was writing poetry with his right hand he would be picking his nose with his left.'[1]

The literary skill of Alexander Pushkin is founded upon an instinctive mastery of all the basic mechanical requirements of a poet. With a

228

sure knowledge he selects his metre and arranges his stanzas, if there are to be any. He has no interest in revolutionary innovation yet his work provides many examples of remarkable inventiveness, notably in the Onegin stanza. His rhyming generally has an unspectacular air, yet, especially in the narrative poems, it plays a doubly important role as the guarantor of diversity and the creator of special effects. He has a remarkable eye for design which imparts an overall shapeliness to his individual works and shows itself also in an intricate series of finely wrought structures hidden within them. All the other poetical devices are under his command — assonance, alliteration, onomatopoeia, enjambement, simile, symbol, metaphor and a range of other tropes. What is remarkable about this array of natural skills is its negative implementation. Pushkin's manner keeps him so down-to-earth and close to everyday experience that he has no regular or urgent need of impressive language or figurative speech. Thus he uses his overt poetical devices with reluctance and has earned for himself epithets like 're-strained', 'economic' and 'laconic'. When he does employ them the impact is consequently all the more forceful, particularly since there is no poet more adept at turning them off as soon as they have begun. Perhaps *The Bronze Horseman* provides the best examples of this complex attribute.

Pushkin's propensity for compression and diversification is accompanied by a quality which normally works against the former: a communicative fluency which makes life easy for the reader. The ordinary rhythms of Russian speech seem to fit Pushkin's lines with such ease that every one of them has the air of a happy coincidence. Sinyavsky gives us a description of what it feels like for a native speaker of Russian to read his national poet:

> There is something providential about Pushkin's harmonies: his speech rushes off helter-skelter in every direction without a second glance only to discover with astonishment that it has been caught in a ring and locked up — fate and freedom having come to an understanding.[2]

Another description of this elusive quality comes from an unusual source. Ezra Pound noticed it in Robert Browning's *Sordello* (1840), a narrative poem which in other respects must be thoroughly unPushkinian since Tennyson claimed to have understood only the first and last lines, and they were both untrue. Be that as it may Pound's eloquent explanation of the effect produced on him by Browning's use of the English language states more or less exactly what Puskin does with Russian all the time.

> There is a certain lucidity of sound that I think you will find with difficulty elsewhere in English and you very well might have to retire as far as the *Divina Commedia* for continued narrative having such clarity of outline without clog and verbal impediment . . . the reader must read it as prose, pausing for the sense and not hammering the line-terminations.[3]

If only the last remark could have reached the ears of those Russian actors who have recorded so much Pushkin over the years. Only in very recent times have recordings begun to emerge from the USSR which allow Pushkin's liquid verses to flow as they were meant to. Traditionally the readers have been schooled to stop at the line-end, whatever degree of enjambement might be waiting there. The listener can only grind his teeth and try to ignore the deficiency, though the experience is like driving a fast vehicle while intermittently applying the handbrake. The occasions when Pushkin himself departs from his normally fluent style are rare and all the more noticeable for being so. *Boris Godunov* provides the standard example of his voluntary relinquishing of flexibility; even here he seems to have made another lucky choice since the stilted character of his iambic pentameters appears to suit the formality of historical drama as a genre and to throw into greater relief his relaxed scenes in prose.

Among Pushkin's recurrent preoccupations are the following: women, sex, literature, country life, morality, nemesis, the imposition of order upon chaos, the concept of destiny, magic and superstition, and, perhaps above all, the idea of freedom and all the personal, moral and political problems arising from it, together with the questions of individual responsibility and conscience. Each of these aspects of human experience is considered repeatedly in his work and there is much to be learned by what Pushkin describes and contemplates. We must re-emphasise that no attention is to be paid to the dismissive manner adopted by the poet on most occasions. His poetry is crammed with interesting, challenging and useful ideas. Many mistakes have been made by hasty judgements passed in the light of only a superficial assessment of what appears to have been written. Pushkin's attitudes are more complicated and sophisticated than they seem to be. His attitude to women is a case in point. At first sight this seems to be self-seeking. Are we not looking at the case-notes of a practising Don Juan, moving from woman to woman and interested only in gratifying one of the more urgent of human desires? It turns out on closer inspection that Pushkin's erotic poetry is less male-directed and selfish than one might think. A wide range of tender emotion is expressed and with much emphasis on the reciprocal pleasures available in love and sex. Togetherness, shared excitement and mutual satisfaction predominate over one-way personal indulgence. Nowhere is this more apparent than in the so-called 'obscene' verses which, far from degrading or exploiting femininity, approach sexual matters with a vindicating touch of humour and leave the women most satisfied of all. Tsar Nikita's forty daughters, Mary (in *The Gabrieliad*), Istomina (in the Orlov epigram), Natalya Pavlovna (in *Count Nulin*) Parasha (in *The Little House in Kolomna*) and many another Pushkin heroine emerges from a sexual encounter, and often from a series of them, with smiling face and twinkling eye. The poet knows well that if he is to enjoy himself his female partners must do so as well. Thus his whole attitude towards women and sex is broad, generous and refined. The same breadth, generosity and refinement extend also to many of his other preoccupations listed here and discussed in earlier chapters.

A Learner's Guide to Pushkin

It is worth learning Russian simply in order to read Pushkin. Vladimir Nabokov had this possibility in mind when he wrote his translation of *Yevgeniy Onegin* and the accompanying voluminous commentary. 'It is hoped', he says in his Introduction, 'that my readers will be moved to learn Pushkin's language and go through *Eugene Onegin* again without this crib.'[4] Ironically his work is more useful to the specialist than the amateur, but the idea is sound enough. Pushkin can only be properly appreciated by being read in Russian, and that language, in any case, brings great rewards in the learning of it. Even unliterary souls who are going to have dealings with the Soviet Union need both the language and the poet. The mere mention of Pushkin's name, or better still a snappy quotation from his work, (there being one for every occasion) will give access to good will and mutual understanding with the Russians in a way that outsiders can scarcely begin to appreciate. Students in school and at university will, in any case, approach Pushkin with imperfect Russian; it is important that the student, the poet and the language should avoid being bruised unnecessarily by the experience.

With all these people in mind it might be useful to indicate where to

begin reading Pushkin, how to continue and at what point the reader
might consider himself thoroughly familiar with this writer. Very
early in his career the learner might be encouraged, with due caution,
to work his way through a short and simple poem such as 'Ya vas lyubil.
Lyubov' yeshche byt' mozhet . . . ('I loved you. Perhaps love still . . .').
Even at this stage reading and translation will not suffice alone. The
poem should be committed to memory. Later on some of the Pushkin
showpieces should also be learned by heart. Some examples are:
Pimen's speech in *Boris Godunov* beginning 'Yeshche odno, posledneye
skazan'ye . . .' ('There is one record more, the last of all . . .'), the
address to St Petersburg in *The Bronze Horseman* beginning 'Lyublyu
tebya, Petra tvoren'ye . . .' ('I love you, city of Peter's making . . .'), the
miser's monologue in *The Miserly Knight* beginning 'Kak molodoy
povesa zhdet svidan'ya . . .' ('Like a young rake waiting for his meeting
. . .'), almost any of the best known lyrics which appear in all the
anthologies and any of the famous extracts from *Yevgeniy Onegin* a
single example of which might reasonably be the second stanza of
Chapter 5 beginning 'Zima . . . Krest'yanin, torzhestvuya, . . .' ('Winter
. . . the peasant, celebrating, . . .'). The benefits of learning poetry by
heart, which is now sadly out of fashion, are considerable. The only
disadvantage to this practice is the undoubted effort, discipline and
stamina which it requires. Against that, in the case of Pushkin, the
learner can set a number of gains: the consolidation of language skills,
a psychological boost of confidence in his own abilities, a deeper
intimacy with the poet's work which brings rich aesthetic rewards, and
the acquisition of materials guaranteed to impress the Russians on
whom he will want to use his language. This latter intention should be
based not on a cynical desire for manipulation but on genuine fellow-
feeling worthy of Pushkin himself.

Pushkin's prose may also be tackled at an early stage. For the
reasons given in the preceding chapter *Pikovaya Dama*, (*The Queen of
Spades*) is much the best starting point. *The Tales of Belkin*, although a
relatively easy read, will make Pushkin seem unduly insubstantial,
whereas *The Captain's Daughter* may be considered too long for
beginners.

Except, perhaps, for a few exemplary stanzas, Pushkin's novel
Yevgeniy Onegin ought to be left to the intermediate or advanced
stage. When it is tackled it must be done properly. This will involve a
very close reading, at least of certain sections, some learning by heart
and listening to a good recording or a reading by a fluent speaker. There
is nothing wrong, we must reluctantly suppose, with reading the

perfidious translations, provided that task does not end at this level of hypocritical pretence that the student knows much about Pushkin or his novel. A translation should be read rapidly, at a sitting or two, in order merely to acquire a knowledge of the story and the characters. This is similar to reading up on the plot of a lesser known Shakespeare play or an unfamiliar opera before going to a performance. In all these cases nothing can replace familiarity with the work itself and, in order to be properly appreciated, Pushkin's actual words must be read, understood, fitted together, repeated and preferably learned. Nothing less will do. This is the road not only to intellectual success but also to genuine enjoyment. Enjoyment should be retained as a main aim when working through Pushkin. For this reason *Count Nulin* is much the most suitable of the narrative poems written before *The Bronze Horseman*, a ballad like *Utoplennik* (*The Drowned Man*) suggests itself as an exciting story and a glance at the bawdy verse, particularly *Tsar Nikita*, will maintain interest as familiarity begins to grow.

Two poems may be recommended as incorporating more than average Pushkin quality. One of these, 'Zima . . .' ('Winter . . .') has been analysed above (Chapter 2) and presented as perhaps the nearest thing to an epitome of Pushkin's art. The other is the little known poem 'Kakaya noch'! Moroz treskuchiy . . .' ('What a wonderful night! The crackling frost . . .'), also discussed above (Chapter 3), which demonstrates Pushkin's originality, forbearance and secret insinuation of serious ideas. The selection of a representative group of lyrics beyond these two examples is largely a matter of personal preference, though there is a small number of poems which are regularly available and, by general agreement, indispensable. Proudly at their head stand *Anchar* (*The Upas Tree*) and *Prorok* (*The Prophet*). Not far behind are *Besy* (*The Devils*), *Vospominaniye* (*Remembrance*), *Exegi Monumentum* and *Osen'* (*Autumn*). Great popularity is also enjoyed by 'Pora, moy drug, pora! Pokoya serdtse prosit . . .' ('It's time, my friend, it's time. My heart seeks peace . . .') because of its longing for better times and other places which, although manifestly an expression of Pushkin's personal problems, speaks with a universal spirit about difficulties and desires familiar to us all. A small selection of love poems must be added to the list; as good as any are the following: *K* *** (To A.P. Kern), 'Dlya beregov otchizny dal'noy . . .' ('For the shores of a far-off land . . .'), 'Net, ya ne dorozhu myatezhnym naslazhden'yem . . .' ('No, I do not value stormy pleasures . . .') and the two Talisman poems mentioned in Chapter 3. Love on a broader scale of meaning is expressed nowhere better than in the short lyric 'Bog pomoch' vam, druz'ya moi . . .' ('God help you, my friends . . .').

From then on the Pushkin-lover will build according to taste. At some stage, preferably a late one, he will work through *Boris Godunov* and the *skazki*. The remaining narrative poems should be taken in something like the following order: *The Gipsies, The Captive of the Caucasus, The Little House in Kolomna* and *The Robber Brothers* to begin with and *Poltava* and *Andzhelo* delayed for some time. *The Gabrieliad* should precede all of these works because of its irreverant sense of fun. There are several ballads, such as *Zhenikh (The Bridegroom)* which could well be taken early. The 'Little Tragedies' contain such lovely poetry that all of them must be considered strong competitors for priority of attention though, as we have seen, *The Stone Guest* deserves probably the last rather than the first recommendation.

In a word or two, the aspiring reader of Pushkin would be well advised to acquire a close knowledge of *Yevgeniy Onegin, The Bronze Horseman, Count Nulin, Boris Godunov*, one of the 'Little Tragedies', *The Gipsies, The Queen of Spades* and at least twenty or thirty of the shorter poems according to preference. By the time he has done so he will have done wonders for his knowledge of Russian and gained an intimate familiarity with one of the greatest of writers in that language. Without a doubt he will have begun to sense that extra quality of spiritual enrichment which Pushkin imparts to his faithful readers and which it is our final task to pin down by definition.

The Final Question

We are left with a final question, the crucial one. On the scale of ultimate values where are we to place Alexander Pushkin? More specifically, do we set him down as a virtuoso entertainer or does he have a claim to some greater quality? Is it proper to place him alongside the great national literary masters, Dante, Cervantes, Shakespeare and Goethe? For this to be so there must be in his work a new, individual and meaningful contribution to human experience. Minstrelsy alone is insufficient for his inclusion among the absolute masters of modern literature.

At first the decision seems likely to go against Pushkin. We have to take account of his signal failure to overwhelm foreign audiences. He is burdened with a reputation for having tried and failed. From Flaubert's famous 'Il est plat, votre poète' to Donald Davie's 'Is it all, perhaps, a confidence trick?' the air is thick with noises of disappointment issued by intelligent, artistic people who have not seen any special magic in the poet. These include responsible critics who must have been looking for it. Moreover, as time goes by their number is increasing rather than the reverse. An encyclopaedia of World Literature published in 1955 concludes a three-page article on Pushkin with these words, amongst others:

> *Estimate.* Pushkin is regarded as a great poet not for the depth or nobility of his ideas nor for the grandeur of the personality which his poetry mirrors . . . He is primarily a national bard rather than a universal one . . .[5]

Encyclopaedists have a lot of reading to do and it is possible for them to overlook even important matters, but worse is to come. One of the few books in English devoted wholly to Alexander Pushkin ends on a similar note. 'It is not unusual', writes Walter Vickery in 1971, '. . . to find Pushkin hailed as a brilliant and profound thinker. This approach is misleading and inaccurate. There is nothing radically original in the view of life which emerges from Pushkin's poetry. The originality lies in the poems themselves.'[6] It looks bad for the poet when an author who must have spent many long hours amongst his work can find nothing original in his view of life. Equally unpromising conclusions emerge from the editors and translators of no less than twenty-six critical articles written over the years on Pushkin by the Russians themselves. In their introduction to this invaluable volume David Richards and Christopher Cockrell express the view that 'Pushkin's response to the world was primarily an aesthetic one . . . What Pushkin appears to lack in comparison with Homer, Dante, Shakespeare and Goethe is the weight and the obvious originality of the greatest minds.'[7] All of these people are in good company. Boris Pasternak, alias Yuriy Zhivago, writes in his Varykino diary:

> What I have come to like best in the whole of Russian literature is the childlike Russian quality of Pushkin and Chekhov, their shy unconcern with such high-sounding matters as the ultimate purpose of mankind or their own salvation. While Gogol, Tolstoy and Dostoyevsky worried and looked for the meaning of life . . . these two were distracted . . . by the current, individual tasks imposed on them by their vocation as writers . . .[8]

We appear to be faced with a definition of Pushkin as a childlike, rather lightweight and unoriginal mind, one who leaves the thinking to more serious philosophers. This is precisely what one would have liked to avoid in the prosecution of his claim to international, indeed universal standing. Where is the magic in his magic crystal? While it is true that Pushkin does not glow with the luminosity of a great metaphysician this is by no means the end of the argument. Once again we must conjure up the spirit of paradox, for, without entirely overturning the preceding judgements, we may state with every confidence that Pushkin does have an original view of human affairs and that, in all its innocence, it is anything but childlike. To argue thus is not to indulge in sophistries; the matter is genuinely elusive as well as being of the first importance. The case for Pushkin's originality and transcendent value was advanced in outline at the end of Chapter 8. It must now be restated and brought to its conclusion.

The most striking aspect of Pushkin's reputation is its amplitude and depth. It reaches out elementally, the only force that could possibly unite into one vast brotherhood all Russians, Tsarist and Soviet, home-bound and émigré, along with so many outsiders fortunate enough to have come under the benign influence of this genius. Every member of this multi-million fraternity —with exceptions that are ludicrous and negligible – regards its figurehead with a curious blend of affection and reverence, almost as if Pushkin was, at one and the same time, a personal friend, a blood relation and a demi-god. It is nonsense to write this phenomenon off as mere emotion, something of an exaggeration, or a confidence trick. Nearly all these people have emerged from their acquaintance with Pushkin as improved individuals, or at least with an adjusted and more indulgent outlook on humanity and its condition – not that many of them are fully conscious of the transformation or able to give it proper articulation. Most literate people, in any case, nowadays live out their lives without coming face-to-face with personal disaster over a protracted period of the kind which will test their spirits and cause them to consider what it is that they truly value. Thus the influence on their spiritual constitution of one particular writer never comes up for assessment. On the other hand, if we may be permitted a historical generalisation, the Russian people have had a close kinship with adversity of various kinds. Yevgeniy Yevtushenko says laconically in his autobiography, 'The Russian people have had it hard . . . For the Russians suffering has become a kind of habit.'[9] Verifiable historical truth seems to suggest that this is more than an encrusted myth. Hence there are in the history of Russian culture many examples of men and women really up against it, facing unhappiness, uncertainty, deprivation and tragedy. Under these circumstances thinking people tend to revert to basic truths and search for sustenance from outside. By no means everyone is soulful enough to include in this ultimate experience anything as otherworldly as poetry, but, in the Russian context, Alexander Pushkin is remarkable for his intrusion into the very centre of so many lives subjected to suffering and dire threats. Here is a statement made by Lev Kopelev which will sound like an exaggeration to those unfamiliar with Russia and her problems, but which is indisputably genuine and accurate.

In the most terrible days and hours of the war, when death was really near, in the days of cruellest misfortune and most severe sickness, the marvellous power of the word invariably helped me. Memory called friends − both living and dead − to my aid − good men, good books, and always Pushkin.[10]

Examples of this kind of preternaturally close association with a long dead poet are not rare. Nadezhda Mandelstam, widow of another celebrated poet, indicates a similar bond between her husband, Osip, and his distinguished predecessor. Tired, ill and agitated, Osip travels with his wife by steamer from Perm *en route* for Voronezh. 'These days were a turning point for M,' Nadezhda records, 'I was quite astonished at how little he needed to get over his illness − only three days of peace and quiet. He calmed down, read Pushkin and began to talk in a completely normal way.'[11] It is scarcely surprising that Pushkin should have been summoned to assistance in this crisis. Earlier on Nadezhda has reminded her readers that her husband 'always had very little to say about things and people dear to him − his mother, for instance, or Pushkin. In other words there was an area which he thought it was almost sacrilegious to touch on . . .'[12] Such is the measure of Pushkin's value to two Russian citizens − and they stand for countless others. He is there when the need is greatest, radiating a strange kind of benevolent assistance, comparable only with one's most intimate relations and emerging from a region into which outside intrusion is described as sacrilege. These people are clearly under an influence which offers protection, the like of which is not merely original, it is unique, and for which the epithet 'childlike' seems inadequate. Whatever the doubts of our literary critics the magnitude of this force has been widely attested. Our last task is to define it and discover whether it extends beyond the Russians into universality.

The mysterious power which belongs to Alexander Pushkin is

definable in a single word — goodness. In its pure form this is a rare quality. Most of us have difficulty in sustaining a belief in its very existence. Let it be made clear that we are speaking neither of maudlin sentimentality nor of childlike innocence. Pushkin's goodness takes two forms, both of which have been described in the previous pages. The first, and less significant, is a deep sense of fellow-feeling, a genuine desire for the wellbeing of others which radiates from Pushkin's poetry to such an extent that, in Sinyavsky's words, it 'brings tears to your eyes'.[13] This is only the surface of the matter. Pushkin's goodness extends beyond an empathetic bond with his fellow sufferers to the arrangement of an attitude to life itself. He makes no attempt to postulate a philosophical system. There is simply no need for this to be done. Each of us knows the nature of his existence — it is this consciousness which distinguishes our species from the lower animals. The awareness is both dark and frightening. Our lives are finite, indeed they are painfully brief, and the immediate evidence suggests that our nature is irredeemably brutish. Every individual must in his own way come to terms with these sombre truths and find a means of living with them. It is here that Pushkin makes his mark. Through the spirit of his work he scours out malevolence and disappointment. He provides an antidote to the poisons of our general condition and our disagreeable modern world. Reading Pushkin is a sure way of coming round to view the universe from a different, better angle. He delivers purification without the agony of catharsis.

A degree of sophistication is essential even to understand this process. Pushkin's goodness has nothing to do with whistling in the dark or running away from trouble. His work is filled with sadness, disappointment, failure and tragedy as well as with entertainment, sensual pleasure and good jokes. No one was more aware of, or more prepared to acknowledge, the cruelty of human life. Pushkin instructs us, gently but unambiguously, in the art of dealing with this cruelty. The process is one that we know of in any case by animal instinct; it begins with acknowledgement and, as we have indicated at an earlier stage, proceeds through reconciliation and distraction to creativity. Primitive man, it is clear to us, knew of this process and all the evidence we can gather suggests that he followed it himself assisted along by two other forces through which Pushkin's work is also readily identifiable — humour and music. Without ignoring any unpleasant truths Pushkin finds that rare thing a positive message for his fellow creatures. Vladimir Solovyov spells it out for us when he says 'The light and fire of Pushkin's poetry did not emanate from a rotting marsh.

Its genuine beauty was inseparable from goodness and truth . . . We
cherish him without reservation not because his works are *intelligent*
but because they are *inspired*. Faced with inspiration the mind is
silent.'[14] Lev Shestov also captures the spirit of Pushkin in these words.
'Dangers, disasters and misfortunes, far from undermining the Russian
writer's creative spirit, strengthen it. He emerges from each new trial
with renewed faith.'[15] Earlier this same writer describes with some
eloquence the very quality which we are attempting to define.

> The greatest European writers have not been able to find those
> elements of life which would reconcile the manifest injustices of
> reality with those invisible but universally esteemed ideals which
> each person, even the most insignificant, preserves for ever in his
> innermost being. Proudly we can say that this question has been
> resolved by Russian literature and we can point to Pushkin with a
> sense of astonishment and awe: for he was the first to stand his
> ground when confronted by the terrible sphinx who had already
> devoured more than one great standard-bearer for humanity. The
> sphinx asked him: How is it possible to look at life and still believe
> in truth and goodness? Pushkin replied: Yes, it is indeed possible,
> and the mocking and terrible monster disappeared.[16]

Such grandiloquence will appear suspect to the cynically minded.
Shestov himself admits that 'These words might seem exaggerated to
some people', and proceeds to justify them by direct reference to the
poet's work. The other means of vindication is by reminding ourselves
of the documented impact of Pushkin on men and women in the real
world. This is clearly in accord with a force of the spirit which cannot
be expressed in anything less than terms approaching hyperbole, such is
its uniqueness and immensity. In view of what we know of him Osip
Mandelstam may well have declined towards his very death in a Soviet
transit camp with three people in his mind, Alexander Pushkin moving in
alongside his mother and his wife. All three would have sustained him as
he faced extinction. Whether this bitter-sweet speculation is true or not
no-one will ever know, though the idea seems feasible. Alongside it we
might care to set a curiously instructive piece of information. Another
writer informs us that, 'On his way to Siberia the soldiers guarding the
persecuted poet were, ironically, reading Pushkin.'[17]

NOTES

Chapter 1: The Problem of Pushkin

1. P.J. and A.I. Wreath, 'Alexander Pushkin: a Bibliography of Criticism in English, 1920-1975', *Canadian-American Slavic Studies, Special Edition, Pushkin (1)* (Summer 1976), pp. 279-304.

2. Donald Davie, a review of 'The Letters of Alexander Pushkin, translated by J.T. Shaw', *Guardian*, 21 August 1964, p. 7.

3. Ibid.

4. Donald Davie, a review of 'Pushkin: Selected Verse, ed. J. Fennell', *Guardian*, 20 March 1964.

5. Walter Vickery, *Alexander Pushkin*, (Twayne Publishers Inc., New York, 1970), 211pp.

6. John Bayley, *Pushkin: a Comparative Commentary* (Cambridge University Press, Cambridge, 1971).

7. D.J. Richards and C.R.S. Cockrell (eds. and trs.), *Russian Views of Pushkin* (Meeuws, Oxford, 1976), pp. xx-xxi.

8. Prince D.S. Mirsky, *Pushkin* (Routledge, London, 1926), pp. 206-7.

9. Bayley, *Pushkin*, p. 309.

10. Mirsky, *Pushkin*, p. 78.

11. R. Jakobson, 'Marginal notes on Pushkin's lyric poetry' in *Pushkin and his Sculptural Myth*, tr. J. Burbank (Mouton, The Hague, 1975), p. 50.

12. Ibid., p. 47.

13. Janko Lavrin, *Pushkin and Russian Literature* (Hodder and Stoughton, London, 1947), 226pp.

14. J. Fennell (ed.), *Pushkin* (Penguin, Harmondsworth, 1964), p. xvi.

15. Vladimir Nabokov, *Eugene Onegin: a Novel in Verse* by Alexander Pushkin, translation and commentary in four volumes (Routledge, London, 1964), vol. 1, p. 8.

Chapter 2: An Approach to Pushkin Through One Poem

1. A. Kvyatkovsky, *Poeticheskiy slovar'* (Sovetskaya Entsiklopediya, Moscow, 1966), pp. 15-16.

2. A. Tertz (Sinyavsky), *Progulki s Pushkinym* (Overseas Publications Interchange in association with Collins, London, 1975), p. 41.

3. Alexander Pope, *Essay on Criticism*, lines 357-8.

4. Draft version of *Domik v Kolomne* (1830), A.S. Pushkin, *Sobraniye Sochineniy v desyati tomakh* (Gosudarstvennoye Izdatel'stvo Khudozhestvennoy Literatury, Moscow, 1959-62), vol. 3, pp. 455-6.

5. This is recounted in A. Slonimsky, *Masterstvo Pushkina* (Gosudarstvennoy Izdatel'stvo Khudozhestvennoy Literatury, Moscow, 1963), p. 100.

6. Slonimsky, *Masterstvo Pushkina*, p. 100 and p. 131; M. Pursglove, 'Pushkin's "Zima. Chto delat' nam v derevne?"', *Journal of Russian Studies*, 20 (1970), pp. 24-5; Pursglove also points out that Belinsky located this line within the family of Russian poetry by demonstrating its similarity to a line by Batyushkov — see V.G. Belinsky, *Polnoye Sobraniye Sochineniy* (Gosudarstvennoy

Izdatel'stvo Khudozhestvennoy Literatury, Moscow, 1953-9), VII, p. 226.
  7. R. Freeborn, *The Rise of the Russian Novel* (Cambridge University Press, Cambridge, 1973), pp. 13-16.
  8. Slonimsky, *Masterstvo Pushkina*, p. 99.
  9. The story is told in A. Gessen, *Rifma, zvuchnaya podruga: etyudy o Pushkine* (Nauka, Moscow, 1973), p. 208.
  10. Freeborn, *Russian Novel*, p. 11.
  11. D.D. Blagoy, 'Pushkin's Laughter' (1968) in Richards and Cockrell, *Russian Views of Pushkin* p. 246.

Chapter 3: The Shorter Poems

  1. 'Poetry Please', BBC Bristol, Radio 4, February 1981.
  2. C.M. Bowra, *The Romantic Imagination* (Oxford University Press, Oxford, 1961), p. 278.
  3. Ibid., p. 277.
  4. Mirsky, *Pushkin*, p. 96.
  5. Ibid., p. 66.
  6. Valeriy Bryusov, 'Zvukopis' Pushkina' in *Sobraniye Sochineniy* (Khudozhestvennaya Literatura, Moscow, 1975), vol. 7, p. 128.
  7. Ibid., p. 129
  8. Ibid., p. 147
  9. Ibid.
  10. Nabokov, *Eugene Onegin*, vol. 3, pp. 148-9.
  11. A.S. Pushkin, *Sobraniye Sochineniy v desyati tomakh* (Gosudarstvennoye Izdatel'stvo Khudozhestvennoy Literatury, Moscow, 1959-62), vol. 2, p. 667.
  12. E.J. Simmons, *Pushkin* (Vintage Books, a division of Random House, Alfred A. Knopf Inc., New York, 1964), p. 219.
  13. Henri Troyat, *Pushkin*, tr. N. Amphoux (1974), p. 78.
  14. Simmons, *Pushkin*, p. 172.
  15. Bayley, *Pushkin*, p. 300.
  16. Ibid., p. 301.
  17. Maurice Baring, *Oxford Book of Russian Verse* (Oxford University Press, Oxford, 1953), Introduction, xxx.
  18. Bayley, *Pushkin*, p. 304.
  19. Tertz (Sinyavsky), *Progulki s Pushkinym*, p. 27.
  20. *Slovar' yazyka Pushkina* (Gosudarstvennoye Izdatel'stvo Inostrannykh i Natsional'nykh Slovarey, Moscow, 1956-61), vol. IV, pp. 58-62, vol. II, p. 348, p. 346.
  21. See Pushkin, *Sobraniye Sochineniy*, vol. 2, p. 672.
  22. Bayley, *Pushkin*, p. 141.
  23. Tertz (Sinyavsky), *Progulki s Pushkinym*, p. 61.
  24. Sir Cecil Kisch, KCIE, CB, *The Waggon of Life, and Other Lyrics by Russian Poets of the Nineteenth Century* (The Cresset Press, London, 1947).

Chapter 4: Nine Narrative Poems

  1. Tatiana Wolff, *Pushkin on Literature* (Methuen, London, 1971), p. 82.
  2. These estimates are taken from totals given in N.V. Lapshina,

I.K. Romanovich and B.I. Yarkho, *Metricheskiy spravochnik k stikhotvoreniyam Pushkina* (Academia, Moscow-Leningrad, 1934).
3. John D. Jump, *Byron* (Routledge and Kegan Paul, London, 1972), p. 166.
4. Ibid., p. 74.
5. Mirsky, *Pushkin*, p. 114.
6. Vickery, *Alexander Pushkin*, p. 78.
7. B. Unbegaun, *Russian Versification* (Oxford University Press, Oxford, 1956), pp. 24-5.
8. P. Henry, introduction to *Tsygany* (Bradda Books, London, 1962), xxix.
9. Bayley, *Pushkin*, p. 42.
10. Ibid., p. 68.
11. Ibid., p. 47.
12. Mirsky, *Pushkin*, pp. 39-40.
13. The quotations from *Count Nulin* are from my verse translation: *Slavic Review* (vol. XXVI, No. 2, June 1967), pp. 286-94.
14. Wolff, *Pushkin*, pp. 272-3.
15. Vickery, *Alexander Pushkin*, p. 74.
16. Bayley, *Pushkin*, p. 118.
17. Mirsky, *Pushkin*, pp. 135-6.
18. Bayley, *Pushkin*, p. 285.
19. Mirsky, *Pushkin*, p. 207.
20. Bayley, *Pushkin*, p. 186.
21. Vickery, *Alexander Pushkin*, p. 141.
22. Wolff, *Pushkin*, p. 197.
23. John Wain, *The Living World of Shakespeare* (Macmillan, London, 1978), p. 92.
24. W. Vickery, 'Pushkin's Andzhelo: a Problem Piece', *Mnemozina studia litteraria in honorem V. Setchkarev* (Fink Verlag, Munich, 1974), p. 336.

Chapter 5: *The Bronze Horseman*

1. Bayley, *Pushkin*, p. 164.
2. W. Arndt, *Pushkin Threefold* (E.P. Dutton, New York, 1972), p. 128.
3. See W. Lednicki, *Pushkin's Bronze Horseman: the Story of a Masterpiece* (University of California Press, Berkeley, 1955). This well researched study of background material has an obvious importance for Pushkin scholars but its importance has been exaggerated. The more one dwells upon localised influences of this nature the more restricted and inward-looking becomes one's appreciation of a poem which depends upon universality for its true significance.
4. Charles Corbet, 'Le symbolisme du *Cavalier de Bronze* (Revue des Etudes Slaves, 45, Paris, 1966), pp. 129-44.
5. Edmund Wilson, 'In Honour of Pushkin, II *The Bronze Horseman*' in *The Triple Thinkers* (Penguin, Harmondsworth, 1962), p. 62.
6. Confirmation of this is provided in C.R. Proffer, 'The similes of Pushkin and Lermontov', *Russian Literature Triquarterly* (3, Spring 1972), p. 153, where the table of Simile Frequency indicates that *The Bronze Horseman* is well ahead of all Pushkin's other narratives in the number of similes used in proportion to the length of the poem.
7. The Academy Edition of Pushkin, A.S. Pushkin, *Polnoye Sobraniye Sochineniy* (16 vols., Akademiya Nauk USSR, Moscow-Leningrad, 1937-59), includes photographs of a number of Pushkin's manuscripts. By a happy chance the section beginning 'But my poor, poor Yevgeny . . .' appears in vol. 5, p. 472.

It looks unusually agitated and hastily written even for Pushkin's much amended manuscripts, which confirms the suspicion that, far from there being any cold calculation of an unusual effect, this was a moment when a turbulent flow of inspiration dictated the course of events.

8. Bayley, *Pushkin*, p. 159, describes this passage as 'So good . . . that many editions . . . ignore the MS cancellations and retain it.'

Chapter 6: Story-poems in the Popular Tradition

1. Mirsky, *Pushkin*, p. 77.
2. Tertz (Sinyavsky), *Progulki s Pushkinym* p. 8.
3. Anthony Cross, 'Pushkin's Bawdy; or Notes from the Literary Underground', *Russian Literature Triquarterly* (No. 10, Autumn, 1974), p. 222.
4. *A.S. Pushkin bez Tsenzury* (Flegon Press, London, 1972).
5. The quotation is from my translation 'The Godyssey: or The Deviliad', *Russian Literature Triquarterly*, No. 3 (Spring, 1972).
6. Quoted by D. Magarshack, *Pushkin: a Biography* (Chapman and Hall, London, 1967), p. 134.
7. Bayley, *Pushkin*, p. 69.
8. Simmons, *Pushkin*, p. 146.
9. Quoted by Magarshack, *Pushkin*.
10. From the only English translation, by Arndt, 'Tsar Nikita and his Forty Daughters' in *Pushkin Threefold*, pp. 52-8.
11. Cross, 'Pushkin's Bawdy', pp. 225-6.
12. Mirsky, *Pushkin*, p. 206.
13. S. Bondi, 'Skazki Pushkina' in Pushkin, *Sobraniye Sochineniy*, vol. 3, p. 523.
14. From the English translation by Oliver Elton, *Verses from Pushkin and Others* (Edward Arnold, London, 1935), pp. 109-26.
15. From the prose translation by John Fennell, *The Penguin Book of Russian Verse* (Penguin, Harmondsworth, 1962), pp. 18-19.
16. *The Song of Igor's Campaign: an Epic of the Twelfth Century*, tr. V. Nabokov (Vintage Books, a division of Random House, Alfred A. Knopf, New York, 1960), pp. 8-11.
17. Mirsky, *Pushkin*, pp. 205-6 and *A History of Russian Literature*, pp. 93-4.
18. Bayley, *Pushkin*, pp. 53-5.
19. Elton, *Verses from Pushkin and Others*, p. 17.
20. Bayley, *Pushkin*, pp. 53-4.
21. Magarshack, *Pushkin: a Biography*, p. 107.
22. See, for instance, Henri Troyat, *Pushkin*, p. 326.
23. Details of musical versions are given in N. Vinokur and R.A. Kagan, *Pushkin v muzyke: spravochnik* (Sovietskiy Kompozitor, Moscow, 1974), p. 160.
24. Mirsky, *Pushkin*, p. 75.
25. Nabokov, *Eugene Onegin*, vol. 3, p. 155.
26. Bayley, *Pushkin*, p. 87.
27. This is attested by Henri Troyat, *Pushkin*, tr. Nancy Amphoux (Allen and Unwin, London) who credits an unnamed Serbian critic with the back-up research. See *Pushkin*, p. 641, Note to Part VII, Chapter 5, p. 23.
28. Troyat, *Pushkin*, p. 453.

Chapter 7: The Limited Success of Pushkin's Drama

1. Draft preface to *Boris Godunov* (1830). See Wolff, *Pushkin on Literature*, p. 247.

2. C.H. Herford, 'A Russian Shakespearean: a Centenary Study', *Bulletin of the John Rylands Library*, vol. 9, no. 2 (July 1925), pp. 1-30.

3. Henry Gifford, 'Shakespearean Elements in *Boris Godunov*', *Slavonic and East European Review*, vol. XXVI, no. 66 (1947), pp. 152-60.

4. This was spotted first by B. Tomashevsky, 'Pushkin i ital'yanskaya opera', *Pushkin i yego sovremenniki*, vol. VIII, 31-2 (1927), p. 50, and the discovery is referred to in Nabokov, *Eugene Onegin*, vol. 2, p. 247.

5. Gifford, *Boris Godunov*, p. 158.

6. Mirsky, *A History of Russian Literature*, p. 95.

7. J. Lavrin, *Russian Literature* (Benn's Sixpenny Library, London, 1927), p. 21.

8. Lavrin, *Pushkin*, p. 152.

9. Ibid., p. 153.

10. Fennell, *Pushkin*, p. 58.

11. Draft article on *Boris Godunov* (1828); see Wolff, *Pushkin*, p. 221.

12. Ibid.

13. Draft preface to *Boris Godunov* (1830); Wolff, *Pushkin*, p. 248.

14. This is the only excluded variant worthy of reinstatement. Two complete scenes were discarded by Pushkin: *Beside a Monastery Wall* (originally intended to follow the present Act II, scene i) and *Castle of Governor Mniszech in Sambor* (after III, iii). Without mentioning the other shortcomings of these scenes, one need only recall the absurd metrical pyrotechnics within them (trochaic octameters which lollop along like a padded piece of *Hiawatha* and then fancifully rhymed combinations of iambic hexameters and tetrameters) in order to be amazed that Pushkin could ever have been insensitive enough to write them and relieved that he saw the need for their excision.

15. Vickery, *Alexander Pushkin*, pp. 67-8.

16. Fennell, *Pushkin*, pp. 59-64.

17. V.G. Belinsky, *Polnoye sobraniye sochineniy* (1935-59, vol. VII), p. 505.

18. Lavrin, *Pushkin*, p. 161.

19. Bayley, *Pushkin*, p. 206.

20. Richard Hare, *Russian Literature from Pushkin to the Present Day* (Methuen, London, 1947), p. 37.

21. W.E. Harkins, *Dictionary of Russian Literature* (Littlefield, Adams & Co., Paterson, New Jersey, 1959), p. 319.

22. Simmons, *Pushkin*, p. 328.

23. G.O. Vinokur, 'Pushkin as a Playwright' in Richards and Cockrell, *Russian Views of Pushkin*, p. 203.

24. Lavrin, *Pushkin*, p. 174.

25. Elton, *Verse from Pushkin and Others*, p. 11.

26. C. Corbet, 'L'Originalité du *Convive de Pierre* de Pouchkine', *Revue de la littérature comparée*, vol. XXIX (1955), p. 49.

27. A. Meyneiux, 'Pouchkine et Don Juan', *La Table Ronde* (November 1957), p. 99.

28. Bayley, *Pushkin*, p. 208.

29. Mirsky, *A History of Russian Literature*, p. 97.

30. Mirsky, *Pushkin*, pp. 164-8.

31. The translation used here, which is as good as any, is by A.F.B. Clark in A. Yarmolinsky, *The Poems, Prose and Plays of Alexander Pushkin* (The Modern Library, Random House, New York, 1936), pp. 438-63.

32. Bayley, *Pushkin*, p. 199 (footnote).
33. Vickery, *Alexander Pushkin*, p. 97.
34. Pushkin, 'Table Talk', published posthumously in *Sovremennik* (1837); see Wolff, *Pushkin*, p. 464.
35. Anna Akhmatova, *Sochineniya* (Inter-language Associates, 1968, vol. II), p. 259.
36. Mirsky, *Pushkin*, p. 167.
37. Maurice Baring, 'Russian Poetry', *Landmarks in Russian Literature* (1960), p. 210. This essay appeared as the introduction to *The Oxford Book of Russian Verse* first published in 1925.
38. Vickery, *Alexander Pushkin*, p. 192.
39. Mirsky, *Pushkin*, p. 167.
40. Ibid., p. 166.
41. Mirsky, *A History of Russian Literature*, p. 93.

Chapter 8: *Yevgeniy Onegin*

1. Blagoy, 'Pushkin's Laughter' in Richards and Cockrell, *Russian Views of Pushkin*, p. 245.
2. Ibid., p. 254.
3. P. Kropotkin, *Russian Literature: Ideals and Realities* (Duckworth, London, 1916), p. 47.
4. Mirsky, *Pushkin*, p. 137.
5. G. Magonenko, *Roman Pushkina 'Yevgeniy Onegin'* (Gosdarstvennoye Izdatel'stvo Khudozhestvennoy Literatury, Moscow, 1963), p. 143.
6. Pushkin, *Eugene Onegin*, tr. Charles Johnston, 1977, Translator's Note, p. 6.
7. Pushkin, *Eugene Onegin*, tr. Walter Arndt (Dutton, New York, 1963), v.
8. Bayley, *Pushkin*, p. 236.
9. Freeborn, *Russian Novel*, p. 10.
10. Ibid., p. 14.
11. Ibid., p. 12.
12. J. Lavrin, *From Pushkin to Mayakovsky* (Sylvan Press, London, 1948), p. 23.
13. W.R. Benet (ed.), *The Reader's Encyclopedia* (A. and C. Black, London, 1965), p. 325.
14. Nabokov, *Eugene Onegin*, vol. 1, p. 7.
15. Ibid., vol. 3, pp. 52-3.
16. Ibid., vol. 1, p. 10.
17. Bayley, *Pushkin*, p. 238.
18. Freeborn, *Russian Novel*, pp. 12-13.
19. Edmund Wilson, 'In Honour of Pushkin' in *The Triple Thinkers* (Penguin, Harmondsworth, 1962), p. 40.
20. E.J. Simmons, 'English Translations of *Eugene Onegin*', *Slavonic and East European Review*, XVII, no. 49 (July 1938), p. 208.
21. See, for example, Nabokov, *Eugene Onegin*, vol. 1, p. 13 and Fennell, *Pushkin*, p. 50.
22. D. Čiževsky, *Evgeny Onegin: a novel in verse*, text, introduction and commentary (Harvard University Press, Cambridge, Mass., 1953), xiv.
23. H. Gifford, *The Novel in Russia* (Hutchinson, London, 1964), pp. 17-18.
24. Bayley, *Pushkin*, p. 282.

246   *Notes*

25. Freeborn, *Russian Novel*, pp. 15-18.
26. Boris Pasternak, *Dr. Zhivago*, tr. M. Hayward and M. Harari, (Collins and Harvill Press, London, 1958), p. 256, pp. 257-8.
27. Bayley, *Pushkin*, p. 245 and p. 267.
28. Fennell, *Pushkin*, p. 45.
29. Bayley, *Pushkin*, pp. 277-9; Fennell, *Pushkin*, pp. 46-50.
30. Nabokov, *Eugene Onegin*, vol. 1, p. 16.
31. Čiževsky, *Evgeny Onegin*, xv.
32. Freeborn, *Russian Novel*, p. 20.
33. Fennell, *Pushkin*, p. 39.
34. Freeborn, *Russian Novel*, p. 19, p. 21.
35. Gifford, *The Novel in Russia*, pp. 16-19.
36. E. Little, 'Onegin at School and University', *Journal of Russian Studies*, no. 41 (1981), pp. 33-41.
37. V. Solovyov, *The Significance of Poetry in Pushkin's Verse* in Richards and Cockrell, *Russian Views of Pushkin*, p. 103.
38. Ibid., p. 102.
39. Ibid.
40. R. Jakobson, *Pushkin and his Sculptural Myth*, tr. J. Burbank (Mouton, The Hague, 1975), p. 49.
41. B. Tomashevsky, 'Interpreting Pushkin' in Richards and Cockrell, *Russian Views of Pushkin*, p. 154.
42. N. Eydel'man, *Pushkin i Dekabristy* (Khudozhestvennaya Literatura, Moscow, 1979), p. 404.
43. Pushkin, *Sobraniye Sochineniy*, vol. 4, pp. 527-8.
44. Nabokov, *Eugene Onegin*, vol. 3, pp. 348-9.
45. V. Solovyov in Richards and Cockrell, *Russian Views of Pushkin*, p. 102.
46. B. Tomashevsky, ibid., p. 155.
47. Ibid., p. 161.
48. F. Dostoyevsky, ibid., p. 78 and p. 79.
49. Freeborn, *Russian Novel*, p. 37.
50. J. Andrew, *Writers and Society During the Rise of Russian Realism* (Macmillan, London, 1980), p. 39.
51. Nabokov, *Eugene Onegin*, vol. 3, p. 241.
52. Mirsky, *A History of Russian Literature*, p. 89.
53. Ibid., p. 97.
54. Max Hayward, 'Pushkin, Gogol and the Devil', *Times Literary Supplement*, No. 3872, 28 May 1976, p. 630.
55. A. Tertz (Sinyavsky), *Progulki s Pushkinym*, p. 61.
56. S.L. Frank, 'Svetlaya pechal'' in *Etyudy o Pushkine*, reprinted from the first edn (Munich, 1957) by Prideaux Press, Letchworth, Herts, pp. 125-6. This translation is taken from Richards and Cockrell, *Russian Views of Pushkin*, p. 223.

Chapter 9: Prose

1. Lapshina, Romanovich, Yarkho, *Metricheskiy spravochnik k stikhotvoreniyam Pushkina*, p. 21.
2. Mirsky, *Pushkin*, p. 174.
3. Ivan Turgenev, Speech on Pushkin, June 1880, quoted in Richards and Cockrell, *Russian Views of Pushkin*, p. 71.
4. H. Gifford, *The Novel in Russia*, p. 15.

5. G.O Vinokur, *The Russian Language: a Brief History*, tr. M.A. Forsyth, ed. J. Forsyth (Cambridge University Press, Cambridge, 1971), p. 121.

6. Ibid., p. 125.

7. Ibid.

8. Troyat, *Pushkin*, p. 513.

9. Henri Troyat, *Tolstoy*, tr. N. Amphoux, 1968, p. 346.

10. Troyat, *Pushkin*, p. 515.

11. Lavrin, *Pushkin*, p. 190 and p. 193.

12. Quoted in N.L. Stepanov, 'Paths of the Novel' in Richards and Cockrell, *Russian Views of Pushkin*, p. 228.

13. Ibid., p. 226.

14. Anna H. Semeonoff, Introduction to *Kapitanskaya Dochka* (J.M. Dent, London, 1937, reprinted 1962), pp. viii-ix.

15. Nabokov, *Eugene Onegin*, vol. 2, p. 90, p. 354, p. 290; vol. 3, p. 471.

16. Mirsky, *A History of Russian Literature*, pp. 117-18.

17. Lavrin, *Pushkin*, p. 185.

18. Richard Hare, *Russian Literature from Pushkin to the Present Day* (Methuen, London, 1947), p. 38.

19. Slonim, *The Epic of Russian Literature*, p. 94.

20. Troyat, *Pushkin*, p. 417.

21. Lavrin, *A Panorama of Russian Literature*, p. 61.

22. Mirsky, *A History of Russian Literature*, p. 119.

23. Wolff, *Pushkin*, p. 198.

24. Simmons, *Pushkin*, p. 372.

25. Mirsky, *Pushkin*, p. 183 and p. 185.

26. V. Shklovsky, *Teoriya prozy and Pushkin i Stern*, no. 6, (Volya Rossii, Prague, 1922).

27. Bayley, *Pushkin*, p. 245.

28. Ibid., p. 309.

29. Troyat, *Pushkin*, p. 412.

30. Nabokov, *Eugene Onegin*, vol. 3, p. 180.

31. Quoted in Troyat, *Pushkin*, p. 417.

32. Mirsky, *Pushkin*, p. 179.

33. A. Kodjak, *Pushkin's I.P. Belkin* (Slavica, Columbus, Ohio, 1979).

34. Bayley, *Pushkin*, p. 318.

35. John Merserau Jr, 'Yes, Virginia, there Was a Russian Romantic Movement', *Russian Literature Triquarterly*, no. 3 (Spring 1972), p. 142.

36. Gifford, *The Novel in Russia*, p. 22.

37. One of Henry James's most successful stories, *The Aspern Papers*, appears to draw on Pushkin, and particularly *The Queen of Spades*. See A.D.P. Briggs, 'Alexander Pushkin: a Possible Influence on Henry James', *Forum for Modern Language Studies*, vol. VIII, no. 1 (January 1972), pp. 52-60.

38. Draft article on Prose, Wolff, *Pushkin*, p. 43.

39. Bayley, *Pushkin*, p. 334.

40. From 'Table Talk', *Sovremennik*, 8 (1837), quoted in Wolff, *Pushkin*, pp. 464-5.

41. Yarmolinsky, *The Poems, Prose and Plays of Alexander Pushkin*, p. 44.

42. Mirsky, *Pushkin*, p. 174.

Chapter 10: Reading Pushkin

1. Tertz (Sinyavsky), *Progulki s Pushkinym*, p. 121.

2. Ibid., p. 37.

3. Ezra Pound, *ABC of Reading* (New Directions Paperbook No. 89, New York, 1960), p. 191.

4. Nabokov, *Eugene Onegin*, vol. 1, p. 8.

5. Buckner B. Trawick, *World Literature*, vol. II (Barnes and Noble, New York, 1964), pp. 276-7.

6. Vickery, *Alexander Pushkin*, p. 192.

7. Richards and Cockrell, *Russian Views of Pushkin*, vi and viii.

8. Boris Pasternak, *Dr. Zhivago*, tr. Max Hayward and Manya Harari, (Collins and Harvill Press, London, 1958), p. 259.

9. Yevgeniy Yevtushenko, *Avtobiografiya* (Flegon Press, London, 1964), p. 103 and p. 46.

10. Lev Kopelev, 'Pushkin', *Russian Literature Triquarterly*, No. 10, (Autumn 1974), p. 192.

11. Nadezhda Mandelstam, *Hope Against Hope*, tr. Max Hayward (Penguin, Harmondsworth, 1970), p. 118.

12. Ibid., p. 76.

13. Tertz (Sinyavsky), *Progulki s Pushkinym*, p. 61.

14. Vladimir Solovyov, 'The Significance of Poetry in Pushkin's Verse' in Richards and Cockrell, *Russian Views of Pushkin*, pp. 104-5.

15. Lev Shestov, 'A.S. Pushkin', ibid., p. 119.

16. Ibid., pp. 110-11.

17. Amanda Haight, *Anna Akhmatova: a poetic pilgrimage* (Oxford University Press, New York and London, 1976), p. 90.

GENERAL INDEX

INDEX OF PUSHKIN'S WORKS: TITLE OR FIRST LINE IN ENGLISH

INDEX OF PUSHKIN'S WORKS: TITLE OR FIRST LINE IN RUSSIAN